MURDER

BEHIND THE BADGE

FOREWORD BY
PAT BROWN

STACY DITTRICH

MURDER

BEHIND THE BADGE

TRUE STORIES OF
COPS WHO KILL

Prometheus Books

59 John Glenn Drive
Amherst, New York 14228–2119

Published 2010 by Prometheus Books

Inquiries should be addressed to
Prometheus Books
59 John Glenn Drive
Amherst, New York 14228–2119
VOICE: 716–691–0133
FAX: 716–691–0137
WWW.PROMETHEUSBOOKS.COM

14 13 12 11 10   5 4 3 2 1

Library of Congress Cataloging-in-Publication Data

Dittrich, Stacy, 1973–
     Murder behind the badge : true stories of cops who kill / by Stacy Dittrich.
          p.   cm.
     Includes bibliographical references and index.
     ISBN 978–1–59102–759–1 (hardcover : alk. paper)
     1. Police misconduct—United States—Case studies. 2. Police corruption—United States—Case studies. 3. Murder—United States—Case studies. I. Title.

HV8138.D58 2009
364.152'30973—dc22

2009021869

Murder behind the Badge: True Stories of Cops Who Kill is a journalistic account of actual murders committed by police officers, and written with formulated opinions based on the author's experience as a law enforcement officer and investigator. The events of each story are true, although some names have been changed to safeguard the privacy of these individuals. The personalities, events, actions, and conversations portrayed in this book have been constructed using court documents, trial transcripts, personal interviews by the author, letters, books, personal papers, press accounts, and Web sites. Quoted testimony has been taken verbatim from trial and pretrial transcripts and other sworn statements.

Printed in the United States of America on acid-free paper

CONTENTS

CONTENTS

PART II: EQUAL RIGHTS APPLY

PART III: THE MOST UNUSUAL

When you think of the long and gloomy history of man, you will find more hideous crimes have been committed in the name of obedience than have ever been committed in the name of rebellion.

—C. P. Snow

For my honest and hardworking brothers and sisters in law enforcement who truly make a difference in society. Even though there are evils within our grasps on a daily basis, it's those of us who turn our backs with hands in pockets that are truly to be commended—and that number is many. All of you will forever be my heroes.

ACKNOWLEDGMENTS

This book couldn't have been written without some very special people. Yvonne Mason, author of *Silent Scream*, the story of Gerard Schaefer; and Chuck Hustmyre, author of *Killer with a Badge*, the story of Antoinette Frank, both helped me immensely in my research. Jamie Kinton and Dave Polcyn of the *Mansfield News Journal*, and Shelia Bradshaw of the Mansfield Police Department for your overwhelming help in the Oswalt case. Los Angeles Deputy District Attorney Robin Sax and violence expert Susan Murphy-Milano are two dear friends who listened to me scream while writing this book. My agent, Claire Gerus, who nudged me from the world of fiction over to true crime, and Donna Weaver as well. Criminal profiler Pat Brown and television crime show host Nancy Grace. There are so many others who I have likely forgotten, but saving the best for last, I want to thank my law enforcement family. My father, Joe; my uncles; John, Jan, Jim—the Wendlings; and my husband, Richard; the best police officers I've ever seen, who truly have my love and respect.

FOREWORD

Imagine that you a hardworking and caring police officer. You go out every day into the community and put your life on the line to get criminals off the street and protect the citizens from harm. You took your oath to be an honest and committed cop and you meant every word. Each morning or evening as you put on your uniform and holster your firearm, you know you are putting yourself in danger. By the end of the day you could be dead, your spouse widowed, your children without one parent. *Thank God*, you think, for my fellow officers; they have my back.

Each day you work with your squad, trusting them to look out for you as you look out for them. You work as a team, and when you finish your shift, your hang out with them at the police lodge, sharing stories, jokes, and supporting each other. They are your best friends, the ones who understand what you go through every day.

Then one day, you find out one of your own, someone you have spent more hours with than most of the people in your life, has done the unspeakable. He has broken the law, dishonored the badge, and betrayed your trust. He turns out to be worse than most of the criminals you have arrested. He is a lying, violent, murderous psychopath and you feel a fool that you had no idea. Sure, he may have been a braggart, or a bit chilly in his manner, or he may have told some tall tales that made your eyebrow go up, but how could you not have known he had such a severe personality disorder that he would cold-bloodedly kill his wife, his children, a fellow officer, or a member of the community you had sworn to protect?

Worse, the community now blames the police force for "sheltering" and "covering up" a bad cop. They become frightened of your uniform, suspicious that you too are nothing but a criminal in blue. Your department has to explain how such a rogue officer even got on the force in the first place. How did he pass the psych evaluation? Didn't anyone notice he was a power and control freak when he was at the academy? Did the department look the other way and let him commit smaller offenses and get away with unacceptable behavior? How could this happen? How could a cop be a psychopath? How?

Stacy Dittrich is one of those honorable police officers who knows what it is like to carry out her duty and expect the same of her co-workers. Her long career in law enforcement has given her an inside understanding of cops and the circumstances they work in: the best, the average, and, heaven forbid, the horific. *Murder behind the Badge: True Stories of Cops Who Kill* brings you the frightening accounts of these rare anomalies—police officers gone bad.

Police work is like any profession; it has its share of psychopaths who find the profession a useful tool for manipulating others and a cover for bad behavior. Furthermore, the very character requirements that draw men and women into this line of work, along with the desire for service—toughness, risk taking, being in control, having the respect of others through the badge and uniform, and the right to carry a gun—can draw in those who want to carry those traits to an extreme. Psychopathic police officers may find a way to abuse their authority in their work and they may also carry that failing into their personal lives. They may become angry at fellow officers, citizens, criminals, their girlfriends, and their wives and children if they don't get what they want. They may kill when they decide that murder is the solution to their problems. It is interesting that the number one choice of work for serial killers is law enforcement, and when they don't make it onto the police force they often take up private security work. Unfortunately, a few of these kinds of violence-oriented psychopaths slip in. You will find them here in this book, in these harrowing stories, psychopaths disguised as cops.

Stacy Dittrich has selected the best examples of these criminal cops, incredible and bizarre tales of murderous men and women with badges. You will learn much about these men and women, how they managed to stay in uniform so long, why they chose to commit their heinous crimes, how they attempted to get away with them. You will feel the pain of the other officers and experience what the families of these murderous cops went through. You will come to understand that these kinds of psychopaths can be anywhere in our society, even, on rare occasion, in your own police department.

Criminal Profiler Pat Brown
October 2009

INTRODUCTION

For centuries people have been fascinated, and disturbed, by the few of us who are chosen to protect and uphold the law. From the days of the unarmed constable, the town marshall, and the rogue sheriff, to our current state of policing, the appeal of the badge and the holstered gun has spawned an eclectic montage of dinner conversations, books, movies, and television series. What would many of us talk about if we weren't consumed with the latest high-profile crime? What would many of us watch on television if shows like *Adam-12*, *Dragnet*, and *NYPD Blue* never made it to the screen?

Society is not only fascinated with crime; it is fascinated with the crime fighters—even when they falter. It seems that we rarely hear the hero stories about those many officers who uphold their oath and go above and beyond their call of duty. We say to ourselves, "Well, that's their job." It's the stories included in this book that make us stop and pay attention. Since I've spent my life involved in law enforcement, these are the stories that truly fascinated me as well. These aren't your garden-variety "shake down of the local drug dealer," or "cocaine-induced" cops—these men and women committed murder (one allegedly).

As a police officer it's extremely difficult to wrap my brain around the actions of officers like Bobby Cutts Jr., Richard Wills, Roy Kipp, Ken DeKleine, and David Camm, who viciously murdered their loved ones and tried to cover it up. The murdering female officers like Antoinette Frank and Lawrencia Bembenek are simply mind-boggling to me. And when we break into the realm of officers like Craig Peyer and Gerard Schaefer, it's anyone's guess what drove them to the brink—they were no less than monsters. There are many cases out there of police officers who committed murder, many in the throes of divorce and financial ruin that ultimately led them to murder/suicide scenarios. The stories in this book are different; they are the crème de la crème of them all, the truly unique. You'll read how many of them used their training and expertise to make bold attempts to cover up their crimes, an opportunity most murderers don't have.

When close friends and family learned I was writing *Murder behind the Badge: True Stories of Cops Who Kill*, I was frequently asked the same question: How do your fellow police officers feel about your book portraying them in a bad light? The answer was simple.

The police officers I have been surrounded with throughout my career are honest, hardworking, men and women. To an extent, the thin blue line does exist, but there are many things— including murder—to which camaraderie doesn't apply. None of these men or women would lose a minute of sleep for turning their backs on someone who purposefully took the life of another human being outside the scope of their daily duties. Kent McGowen walked a fine line here, but it was his honorable co-workers who trusted their instincts. No police officers want bad apples within their department—a bad apple makes everyone's already difficult job more difficult.

There was a common element I noticed among many of the officers featured in this book. The way they conducted themselves in their personal lives undoubtedly filtered into their professional conduct. Arrogance, narcissism, and promiscuity were clearly a shared personality trait.

What I found most fascinating was that these men and women shouldn't have been hired in the first place. The day they filled out their job applications most had already been exhibiting unusual or irrational behavior. It was the law enforcement agencies that allowed them to slip through the cracks. In the agencies' defense, and having performed numerous background investigations myself, the background investigator is presented with a tedious and overwhelming job. When presented with twenty to thirty applications, it's very easy to make mistakes and overlook something very important. Police officers are also human. Unfortunately, there were many agencies in this book that had the problems brought to their attention and the applicant was hired anyway—shame on them. When I researched the story of Gerard Schaefer, my own jaw literally dropped.

When I hear the term "dirty cop," I ask the person to take a minute and think clearly. Let's use the New York City Police Department for an example. There are over thirty thousand men and women employed by the city. This number is actually the size of a small city in its own. If you look at a city with the population of thirty thousand people, there is going to be crime—period. Police officers are held to a higher standard, of course, but with a number this size it is a statistical fact that some "bad apples" are going to slide their way in. Don't blame the rest of the officers for it.

There were just a few stories included here in which I actually questioned the outcome: Charles Oswalt, Richard DiGuglielmo, and Steven Rios. I made it clear when writing these chapters what my own questions were. Granted, a true-crime book merely tells the story without an author's opinion, but since I was asked to write this based on my own law enforcement experience I felt compelled to raise those questions.

I took particular interest in Charles Oswalt. Why? Because I knew him and my family was involved with his case. In fact, my father and uncle were working with him the night of the murder. You'll read my uncle's (John Wendling's) take on the events of the night. When I sat down and spread the entire case file out before me, I found myself heading in another direction of a suspect. Based on my experience as an investigator, I felt that when a case has numerous agencies involved, key pieces of information have a way of getting lost. Of course, I could be wrong, I'm human, too.

Subsequently, I hope that you enjoy *Murder behind the Badge: True Stories of Cops Who Kill.* However, next time you see those red and blue lights flashing behind you after you rolled through a red light, don't assume you will fall prey to a murderous police officer. Assume you violated the law, and this honest, upstanding man or woman in uniform is simply doing his or her job.

PART I

'TIL DEATH (OR MONEY) DO US PART

CHAPTER 1

NO BODY NO CRIME

DREW PETERSON
POLICE SERGEANT, BOLINGBROOK, ILLINOIS

Unquestionably, the center of the most profiled alleged murder-by-cop mystery of this century, Drew Peterson is the only cop within these pages who hasn't been convicted of murder. Although he has been indicted, he is innocent until proven guilty.

Why has he been included?

It is doubtful that one could find anyone in a local coffee shop who hasn't heard of Peterson, especially one who doesn't think he is guilty of murder. His unceremonious mockery of the system that has, so far, allowed him to walk freely for almost two years before an indictment has compelled a majority of talk shows, news organizations, and radio stations worldwide to follow his story.

Drew Peterson, a fifty-three-year-old Bolingbrook, Illinois police sergeant, became the focus of media attention when his beautiful, twenty-three-year-old wife, Stacy, was reported missing by worried family members on October 29, 2007.

Stacy Peterson, formerly Stacy Ann Cales, grew up in a troubled family, plagued with traumatic events. Stacy, the third of five children born to Anthony and Christie Cales, lost two of her elder sisters—one to a fire and the other to sudden infant death syndrome. Both were under two years old when they died. Unable to cope with the loss of two children, Christie Cales abruptly left her family for parts unknown, leaving Anthony to start a new life somewhere else.

Anthony wasn't without his own troubles. He moved the family between twenty and thirty times according to Cassandra Cales, Stacy's younger sister. Anthony also fought alcoholism constantly, and often became verbally and physically abusive in his drunken rages. Stacy and Cassandra bonded even closer, as only two sisters who only had each other could, when their brother was convicted for aggravated sexual abuse of a minor. Finding herself back in Illinois from yet another move, Stacy took a job at a local hotel. It was there that she first met Drew Peterson.

Stopping in frequently during his shift while in uniform, suave Drew Peterson won the heart of troubled seventeen-year-old Stacy Cales. Capitalizing on Stacy's troubled life of financial instability and lack of parental love, Drew showered her with jewelry, expensive dinners, and compliments. There was a minor problem, however—Drew Peterson was married. Kathleen Savio, Peterson's wife, learned of his affair with Stacy, who was now pregnant with his child. Savio quickly filed for divorce, and Stacy and Drew married later that year. To Stacy, Drew was her knight in shining armor—her savior.

Now a mother to two young children, Stacy Peterson's dreams had come true—a beautiful home in a nice neighborhood, money, and the father figure she never had while growing up. She was happy, if only for a short while. Stacy's family and friends felt that her situation was entirely too good to be true. They felt Drew was too old for her and that his previous marriages suggested he could not commit. Stacy shrugged off the comments and advice until she began to see the darker side of Drew Peterson, a side she had never seen—one that frightened her. Recognizing the signs of abuse and feeling premonitions of disaster, Stacy planned to leave Drew once and for all. Unfortunately, on October 28, 2007, it was too late. Stacy, who was supposed to help her sister, Cassandra, with some paint work that day, never showed—and was never seen again.

Drew Peterson was not one of the family members who filed the report of Stacy's disappearance, merely insisting that she had "taken off," leaving their two young children behind. It was Cassandra Cales who actually reported her sister missing. With no physical evidence to suggest a crime, what was it that led investigators to believe Stacy had succumbed to foul play?

Kathleen Savio, Drew Peterson's third wife.

On March 1, 2004, months after her divorce from Drew Peterson was final, Kathleen Savio was found dead in the bathtub of her Bolingbrook, Illinois, home. She was discovered lying in a dry bathtub with a head laceration. Kathleen's death was ruled accidental by Will County coroner Patrick O'Neil. Prior to the ruling, an inquest convened into Kathleen's death under strong pressure from her family members. During the inquest, Kathleen's sister, Susan Savio, testified that Kathleen had predicted her own murder: "She just told me last week, and she was terrified of him [Peterson]. He always threatened her. He did many, many, things to her. He wished only for her to go away," she informed the coroner's jury. Many inquiries were also made into a series of domestic calls—nineteen in total—that involved Savio and Peterson and were handled by the Bolingbrook Police Department. Bolingbrook police chief Raymond McGury issued a statement that each incident was investigated fully, and there was no cover-up.

The Savio family, stunned at the ruling of their loved one's death, only learned after Stacy Peterson's disappearance that the jury—or the coroner—had no other option but to rule the death as accidental. One of the six members of the jury spoke out after Stacy's disappearance, stating that he would have ruled the death of Kathleen Savio "undetermined" but was not given the option. The coroner had to rule the death based on the jury's recommendation. Under extreme scrutiny for his ruling on the death, O'Neil passed the blame onto the law enforcement agency who "investigated" the death. "I asked them [Bolingbrook Police] if the suspicious death protocol should be followed—they said no," he claimed. "It's up to them to decide whether or not to use the protocol." O'Neil stood by his inquest and stated that the proper procedure was followed. Coroner candidate Charles Lyons said the Illinois State Police officer who testified at the inquest hadn't even been to the death scene, a fact he referred to as a "travesty of justice," and one that shouldn't have been overlooked by O'Neil.

Kathleen Savio's body was exhumed in order to search for more clues surrounding her—and Stacy Cales's—mysterious death.

Dr. Larry W. Blum performed the autopsy on Savio's body after it had been exhumed, on November 16, 2007, and in the subsequent report delivered to the Will County Coroner's office on February 21, 2008, declared it undeniably as a homicide. The family of Kathleen Savio took the exhumation a step further when they hired famed forensic pathologist Dr. Michael Baden to perform an independent autopsy. Baden stated there were "indications then of multiple blunt force traumas, of being beaten up. Those bruises were still there and could be seen from the naked eye. They were still fresh."

One wonders how such a flagrant display of evidential violence was missed by a coroner who boasted in presiding over forty thousand death investigations.

With each new revelation of erred justice and allegation of a cover-up, the public's perception of Drew Peterson became considerably darker and more disturbed. A man who for over twenty years possessed the ability to take away one's driving privileges, order a common citizen into submission, take one's freedom, and legally kill if need be is now the suspect in two murders—and may very well be found innocent. In the public's eyes, Drew Peterson is a monster. In the eyes of police officers across the country, he is an embarrassment to their careers in law enforcement. With no support from the community, and no backing from his brothers in blue, Drew Peterson is now isolated and alone.

In regard to Savio's murder, numerous questions began to arise, specifically what the motive was behind the killing. According to investigators, Drew Peterson and Kathleen Savio were engaged in an intense battle over the proceeds from the sale of a local tavern they owned. Kathleen was angry that Drew kept all of the money from the sale, and she took legal action to recover her half.

Did Drew confess his part in Savio's death to Stacy Peterson? Could this possibly have played a key role in Stacy's own disappearance? According to her local pastor and friend—definitely.

Approximately two months before Stacy Peterson disappeared, she requested a "face to face" chat with her pastor. Pastor Neil Schori of Westbrook Christian Church testified he met with Stacy and that she "feared for her life." Drew Peterson also took note of Stacy's meetings with the clergyman, publicly stating, "She'd get all dolled up every time she went to see him." Allegations that Stacy implicated Drew in the murder while in private talks with the pastor spread. As to why the church failed to report the threat to law enforcement, Pastor Rob Daniels was quoted as saying, "The church's clergy are only legally mandated to alert authorities of allegations of child abuse or if someone threatens to harm themselves or others."

According to Drew Peterson's attorney, Joel Brodsky, Schori testified before the grand jury that Stacy Peterson frantically tried to contact Drew via her cell phone the night of Kathleen Savio's death. Brodsky also indicated that the pastor testified that Stacy told Schori she saw Drew in a black ninja outfit the night before Savio's body was found. Brodsky cited these as "leaks," when the pastor's testimony was later discussed on the nationwide media circuit.

Throughout the ever-growing media circus, Drew Peterson continued to portray himself as a clown. Images of him parading in front of the numerous cameras and wearing a bandana across his face while cursing the media and his arrogant and incessant mockery of the lack of evidence against him further fueled the public's opinion of Peterson as a coldhearted monster. Upon exiting the room of the grand jury that had convened to indict him for the murder of Kathleen Savio, Peterson heckled the cameras about the influx of ex-wives and girlfriends who were brought in to testify. "Let's have a party! I didn't know it was going to be a reunion!" he joked.

Furthermore, the focus became narrowed on the fact that Drew still had custody of the four children he fathered with Kathleen Savio and Stacy Peterson. In a heartless and grotesque move, Peterson taped Stacy's "missing" poster to his backyard barbeque grill, telling his children that she went on vacation. In a contradictory defense, Brodsky toured the talk show circuit with the claim that Stacy was hiding out in the Philippines, having left with a secret lover and not wanting to be found.

Peterson's narcissistic attitude, even after the new ruling on Savio's death, promotes a growing discomfort that he is confident that he will beat any, and all, murder raps. The evidence, if there was any collected at all, in Savio's death is four years old, and the body of Stacy Peterson has yet to be found. So what do investigators hold to solidify the notion that Drew Peterson murdered both wives? Since the investigation is still ongoing, the testimony from a friend of Drew's stepbrother, the financial transactions Drew Peterson made days after Stacy's disappearance, and the testimony of family and friends that painted a horrific picture of Peterson certainly help, but will they be enough to bring forth a conviction?

On October 28, 2007, Walter Martineck claimed he received a phone call from Peterson's stepbrother, Thomas Morphey. According to Martineck, an acquaintance of Morphey, Morphey called in a "panic" and needed to talk. Meeting with Morphey, Martineck stated that Morphey told him a disturbing account of what allegedly transpired at the Peterson home just hours earlier. According to Martineck, Morphey took him by the shoulders and told him he could never tell anyone, but alleged that he believed that he had just helped Drew Peterson dispose of Stacy's body. He had been at Peterson's home assisting Drew move a large blue container from the couple's bedroom into the back of Drew's SUV. Morphey never looked inside the container, but it was warm to the touch and he had a "terrible feeling."

Peterson denies this claim. On the night of Stacy's disappearance, he stated that she phoned him around 9:00 PM to inform him she was leaving; she had allegedly fallen in love with someone else. This disputes Peterson's earlier timeline. At 2:30 PM that day, Peterson phoned in to the police department, advising he couldn't work his 5:00 PM to 5:30AM shift because his wife was gone and he had no babysitter.

Furthermore, Stacy Peterson's sister, Cassandra Cales, had been kept informed about the Petersons' volatile marriage by Stacy. Cales stated she received a frantic phone call from Stacy in August—a phone call in which Stacy declared she was terrified of Drew and was thinking of taking the kids and leaving the state. This would correlate with the testimony of Stacy's conversation with her pastor, which also took place in August. The key focus of Cales's testimony is the "children." Stacy would never leave them. Nonetheless, in the early afternoon hours of October 28, 2007, Cales repeatedly tried to reach Stacy, to no avail. Frustrated, Cales went to the Peterson home and found Drew gone and the kids alone. The kids told her that their parents had fought and that Stacy had gone to Grandpa's house. Cales knew this to be false. At 11:26 PM, while sitting around the corner from the Peterson house, Cales called Drew Peterson on his cell phone. He claimed he was at home and told her that her sister had left him. Stacy had called him around 9:00 PM and said she was leaving and going on a vacation. "She left her car somewhere in Bolingbrook," he further added. "She took $25,000 from the safe, her bikini is missing, and her passport is missing. . . . She disappeared just like your mom." Drew referred to the disappearance of the Cales sisters' mother when Stacy was a teenager.

Confident that Stacy would never leave her children, and confirming that Drew was lying about being at home, Cassandra drove to the Bolingbrook Police Department at 1:36 AM and then to the Illinois State Police to file a report that Stacy Peterson was missing. Two days later, Drew Peterson transferred $200,000 into his older son's bank account. According to Brodsky, Drew was confident his wife was with another man and he didn't want her "cleaning him out."

By November 9, 2007, the Illinois State Police declared Stacy Peterson's disappearance as a potential homicide and

Drew Peterson as the only suspect. On November 16, 2007, Kathleen Savio's body was exhumed.

Now armed with a high-powered media publicist, and with no sign of Stacy Peterson, Drew Peterson continues to evade the system in which he spent almost thirty years of his life.

His neighbors paint a disturbing account of a man crumbling, and have taken to posting signs emblazoned with slogans such as "Where's Stacy?" across the street from the home that he and Stacy shared. Drew's next-door neighbor, Sharon Bychowski, has launched a community-wide action against Peterson, posting signs in the town, on the Internet, and calling for a boycott of the tavern that Peterson frequented. Bychowski recently accused Peterson of reprogramming his garage door opener so that he can open and shut her garage door repeatedly in an attempt to harass her. Peterson maintains he cannot move because Stacy's name is on the title to their home and counterclaims that he is the one being harassed.

In March 2008, a grand jury officially convened to hear testimony regarding the death of Kathleen Savio. Ex-girlfriends, ex-wives, friends, and family members of Drew Peterson and the deceased were called in to paint a dark, monstrous portrait of Peterson for the jurors. In the meantime, the search for Stacy Peterson's body resumed. A criminal charge filed against Drew Peterson for possessing an illegal weapon was thrown out. He is currently engaged to be married to a twenty-three year-old woman. Drew filed for divorce from Stacy in the latter part of 2008, claiming abandonment.

On May 7, 2009, the grand jury officially indicted Drew Peterson for the murder of Kathleen Savio. In his trademark class clown demeanor, Peterson smiled and joked for the cameras as he was being led into the jail. He continues to maintain his innocence and no trial date has been set. Is Drew Peterson an innocent man wrongly convicted by the press and the public? Or, is he a cold-blooded killer who believes he is getting away with murder?

At this point, only time will tell.

CHAPTER 2

MOMMY'S IN THE RUG!

BOBBY CUTTS JR.
POLICE OFFICER, CANTON, OHIO

Friday, June 15, 2007—7:56 AM

"911. What's your emergency?"

"We need help at [private] *Essex Avenue!"* the female voice shrieked over the phone. *"My daughter was nine months pregnant and she's gone!"*

[Unfortunately, due to unknown errors, the 911 call was cut off. The female, Patricia Porter, frantically called back.]

"Please! The two-year-old is home alone—the house is trashed!"

"Ma'am," the 911 operator did her best to keep the woman calm, *"I need you to go outside, not touch anything, and wait for the officers to arrive."*

Patricia Porter began sobbing. *"Okay, can you please call Officer Bobby Cutts? He's a Canton police officer, his . . . his son is here alone!"*

Doing her best to keep from unraveling, Patricia Porter, along with her daughter Audrey and two-year-old grandson, Blake, went outside to wait for the arrival of someone from the Stark County, Ohio, Sheriff's Office. Patricia's other daughter—Blake's mother—twenty-six-year-old Jessie Davis, was nowhere to be found. Jessie would have found it unconscionable to leave Blake alone.

Patricia knew that Jessie, an attractive woman with a magnetic smile, sparkling blue eyes, and strawberry blonde hair, was overwhelmed by her single mother status and desperate financial situation. But she would never leave Blake by himself. Being a mother, and seeing the inside of Jessie's house, Patricia knew that something was wrong—very wrong. Blake's father, Officer Bobby Cutts, arrived within minutes.

Bobby Cutts Jr., a thirty-year-old Canton police officer, did little in terms of providing Jessie with the basic necessities that she required. Born in Canton, Ohio, Bobby was an honor roll student who aspired to become a police officer. Tall and muscular, he also had an obsession with women that usually resulted in him fathering a child or a breakup of his current relationship. Jessie fell into both categories. Even the disturbing fact that he was married rarely kept him from looking elsewhere.

Blake was the spitting image of his father; his dark skin, curly black hair, and deep brown eyes made everyone instantly fall in love with him. Jessie suspected that Blake would grow up to be as handsome as Bobby was.

However, on this morning, Blake began immediately crying at the sight of his father instead of running to him for affection as he usually did. Audrey Davis, Jessie's sister, expressed her disdain at Bobby's arrival.

"Why are you here?" she questioned, angrily.

"Don't you want me here?" he fired back.

"No, I don't!"

Audrey held nothing back that morning.

As panicked and frightened as Patricia was, she felt a slight sense of relief when the first sheriff's cruiser arrived. Margaret Midkiff, Jessie's neighbor, came outside to inquire if everything was okay.

Deputy Darin Baad, already suspecting a long morning ahead, asked Margaret if she would be willing to take care of Blake for a while. The boy was in dire need of a diaper change and some food. Margaret agreed. She took Blake into her house, she cleaned him up, changed his diaper, and made some breakfast for him. Afterward, she put out some coloring books and crayons and turned on cartoons for him. All the while, the intensity of the events next door grew stronger.

While other deputies continued to arrive, Deputy Baad and Sergeant Eric Weisburn went inside the home of Jessie Davis— a modest, two-story duplex in Lake Township, Stark County, Ohio, just outside the city of Canton—where the officers noticed a black leather purse lying on the floor by the kitchen table. Its contents were strewn all over the floor. In the upstairs bedroom, officers found a stripped bed that had been pushed somewhat off of its frame and a large bleach stain on the blue carpeting. A bottle of Clorox sat on the floor approximately three feet away from the stain.

With a heightened sense of concern, Sergeant Weisburn went outside to speak to Bobby Cutts, turning his tape recorder on in the process. The other deputies were still interviewing Patricia and Audrey when Weisburn noticed a cut on Bobby's hand.

Cutts stated, "I was working on my patio and cut it."

Sergeant Weisburn questioned Bobby regarding his relationship with Jessie Davis. Although he acknowledged that he was Blake's father, Bobby questioned the paternity of the baby Jessie was currently carrying. He claimed that Jessie had sex with another man around the time she became pregnant. As far as the depth of their relationship was concerned, Bobby downplayed it as much as he could. "It was mostly sex," he informed the sergeant. "I'm married, and I've been trying to work things out with my wife."

Bobby claimed the last time he spoke with Jessie was on Wednesday, June 13, 2007. She was supposed to drop Blake off at his house the following morning, but never showed up.

Across the lawn, Patricia Porter was hysterically telling the deputies that she also last spoke with Jessie on the evening of June 13. Blake was to stay with Bobby on the fourteenth, and Jessie would drop him off at Patricia's the morning of the fifteenth—today. It wasn't unusual for Patricia to not talk to Jessie on days Blake was with Bobby, but it was Audrey's claims that caused her concern. Audrey stated that she had tried to call Jessie more than five times on the fourteenth, but could not reach her—highly unusual of Jessie.

When Jessie failed to show with Blake that morning, Patricia tried to call her and received no answer—only voice mail. That was when she and Audrey grew increasingly concerned and drove to Jessie's residence to check on her.

What Patricia found inside Jessie's home made every nerve in her body come alive. Running through each room, Patricia acknowledged screaming, "Where's my daughter?" a scream that Margaret Midkiff later testified to hearing. It was after seeing the contents of Jessie's bedroom that Patricia called 911.

After his conversation with Bobby Cutts, Sergeant Weisburn decided to make an attempt to interview the only known witness to the disappearance of Jessie Davis—her two-year-old son, Blake.

Entering the home of Margaret Midkiff, Sergeant Weisburn found Blake sitting on the floor, coloring intently in one
of the coloring books that Margaret had given him. Sitting
next to Blake, Sergeant Weisburn picked up a crayon and
began coloring with him. A direct attempt at establishing trust,
coloring with a child is a key tactic prior to interviewing him.
After creating several colorful masterpieces, Sergeant Weisburn felt that Blake had warmed up to him enough. It was time
to start asking him questions. It was the most obvious that he
decided to ask first: Where was Jessie? Blake continued to
color while answering him, not looking up or making eye contact. "She's at work," he said cheerfully.

Sergeant Weisburn decided to ask Blake the question again,
in hopes of garnering his full attention. This time, Blake put
his crayon down and looked at him with his large brown eyes,
full of concern. "Mommy's crying. Mommy broke table!
Mommy's in the rug!"

At that moment, Sergeant Eric Weisburn doubted that
Jessie Davis would ever be found alive.

Most police officers reserve a bit of skepticism when
responding to the type of call that mirrors the one dispatching
officers to Jessie Davis's residence: an adult woman, gone from
her home, leaving her two-year-old son home alone. In law
enforcement, cases of child neglect occur daily and don't necessarily point to murder. However, with each passing minute
the level of intensity grew, the investigators' instincts buzzed,
and they knew more and more that this was not a typical child
endangerment call.

With a sense of urgency, investigators began to retrace the
activities of Jessie Davis over the past several days. It was further learned that she was last seen inside the Acme Fresh
Market, a local grocery store, on June 13, 2007. After
arranging with her mother and sister to drop Blake off at their

house on Friday morning, June 15, no one spoke to Jessie again—except for Bobby Cutts Jr.

For the most part, Bobby cooperated fully with the investigation, even partaking in the search on the day Patricia reported her missing. Later, records showed that Bobby tried to call Jessie's cell phone twice on the fifteenth, as did numerous other family members. Cool and calm, with seemingly no concern over the fact that his two-year-old son was left alone for almost thirty hours, Bobby gave his own whereabouts over the last several days to investigators.

After playing a game of softball on June 13, Bobby and several friends went to the local Champs Bar and Restaurant for several beers. While there, Bobby was met by Denise Haidet, one of his numerous lovers. Staying until midnight, Bobby left the bar and went to the home of another woman, Stephanie Hawthorne. Coincidentally, Stephanie was also pregnant with Cutts's child and had an abortion the same day Jessie was reported missing. Neither Hawthorne nor Haidet knew about the other, nor were they aware of Jessie Davis. Bobby stayed at Stephanie's house until approximately 2:00 AM.

According to Bobby, Jessie never dropped Blake off the following morning like she was supposed to, subsequently costing him an "inconvenience" fee to the babysitter he'd hired, Myisha Ferrell. Bobby had a scheduled 9:00 AM interview for a freshman football coach position at GlenOak High School and needed Myisha to watch Blake while he was gone. He told investigators it was not unusual for Jessie to back out of a visit, so he wasn't worried. Bobby arrived for the 9:00 interview at 10:15.

Regardless, while Bobby was out searching for the mother of his son and unborn child, investigators were delving deep into Bobby's financial situation—a situation that painted a grim picture for the upstanding police officer. They learned that had Jessie given birth to her daughter (who she had already named Chloe), Bobby would be paying upward of $1,300 per month in child support to various women. Recently separated from his wife, Kelly Schaub, Bobby was ordered to pay her $496 per month for their six-year-old daughter, Breonna. He also owed former girlfriend Nikki Giavasis $300 per month for their nine-year-old daughter, Taylor, and Jessie Davis was receiving $411 per month for Blake. Investigators further learned that Bobby owed $2,810 per month for various debts and earned only $48,438 per year.

Bobby was clearly feeling the crushing pressure as his biweekly paychecks continued to shrink. However, what Bobby Cutts evidently didn't prepare for is what most likely led to his ultimate confession: the extraordinary response by the American media to find his missing former girlfriend.

Within hours of Jessie's disappearance, news stations and various media outlets converged on Canton, Ohio, displaying pictures of an attractive Jessie Davis and spreading information on mainstream cable networks, local stations, in print, and on the radio. Across the country, people were glued to the story in hopes of finding the pregnant Ohio woman. This, of course, also led to increased pressure on law enforcement to find Jessie. The Canton Police Department refused to call Bobby a suspect, while the FBI and Stark County Sheriff's Department remained tight-lipped.

Bobby made an unusual phone call to Patricia Porter on Saturday, June 16, inquiring about Blake. He didn't ask about Blake's mental or physical well-being, as any parent would think, but he wanted to know if Blake saw anything the day Jessie disappeared, and what he said.

"He saw mommy in the carpet—and you mad!" Patricia fired back.

No longer trusting of Bobby, family members launched a

daylong flyer distribution of Jessie's picture. At the end of the day, over twelve hundred flyers were handed out or posted on utility poles in the area of Jessie's home.

After a press conference was held on Sunday and no suspects were officially announced, Bobby ignored the rumors and suspicious stares as he, again, helped the growing crowd search for Jessie.

By Monday, June 18, the FBI's evidence response team was searching Jessie's home, Bobby's Chevy Silverado pickup, and Kelly Schaub-Cutts's Saturn Ion. Since the only information on Bobby at the time from either law enforcement agency was that "he is being cooperative," rumors began to run rampant through the media that Kelly Cutts was being eyed as a serious suspect. Several members of both families had anonymously given the media accounts where Jessie and Kelly had "run-ins," including an incident where Jessie purposely left her underwear in Kelly's makeup drawer. Heated phone calls were also exchanged between the two. Investigators continued to deny that Bobby was a suspect.

Each day that passed during the massive search for Jessie Davis brought a unique twist in the case or a possible sighting, but always hopes of finding Jessie and her baby alive. On Tuesday, June 19, as Bobby was giving an interview to the *Canton Repository* newspaper, a newborn infant was found on the doorstep of a home in nearby Wooster, Ohio. Members of Jessie's family held their breaths as it was learned the baby did not belong to Jessie—an astonishing coincidence.

During this time, the number of volunteers searching for Jessie Davis grew into the thousands, including members of Texas Equusearch—a group of handlers and trained cadaver dogs. Since Jessie's car, purse, and other personal items were still inside her residence, searchers logically combed the area in a large radius from her home. However, on the same day the

FBI was searching Bobby's truck, searchers held their breaths as a volunteer found a shallow grave with a sheet sticking out; flies and maggots covered the mound. It turned out to be the grave of a German Shepherd and everyone gave a sigh of relief. But Jessie still had yet to be found.

By June 20, investigators were searching Bobby Cutts's home in Plain Township, still maintaining that Bobby wasn't even a "person of interest." However, they recovered clothes, cell phones, and several pieces of carpet from Bobby's bedroom. The FBI deemed these items as suspicious but declined to comment further. The two items missing from Jessie Davis's apartment—her bed comforter and cell phone—still couldn't be found; however, these items were also not found in Bobby's house. Included in the warrant was an order to obtain fingerprints and a DNA sample from Bobby. Contradicting their daily statements to the media, it appeared that law enforcement was honing in on Bobby Cutts Jr.

It was clear that Bobby was unraveling under the watchful eye of his fellow law enforcement officers. On Saturday, June 23, 2007, one hour after logging off of a sex site on the Internet, Bobby Cutts phoned the FBI and said he would lead them to the body of Jessie Davis.

Skeptical, but hopeful, investigators escorted Bobby as he led them to an area in Hampton Hills Metro Park in Summit County. The past week had been unusually hot for June and they could only imagine the state that the body would be in after such exposure to the elements. Their fears were confirmed when Bobby pointed to an area of tall, thick grass that was situated directly in the sunlight. Finding Jessie's body almost skeletonized owing to the advanced state of decomposition, she was now unrecognizable. However, the fact that she was still wrapped in the missing bed comforter confirmed the notion that the body was that of Jessie Davis.

After investigators made the dreaded phone call to the awaiting Porter family, Bobby Cutts Jr. was arrested and charged with the murder of Jessie Davis and her unborn daughter, Chloe.

Bobby immediately assumed the role of the innocent victim, initially telling investigators that Jessie was already dying when he arrived at her home. He explained that she was on the floor, reached up, and grabbed his pants as her eyes rolled into the back of her head, and then she died. Fearing no one would believe his story, he disposed of the body. Unfortunately, the presence of another party in the murder shredded his story into oblivion: Myisha Ferrell.

The missing link in the events on that fateful day of June 14 Myisha proved Bobby's story as an outright lie, something investigators were already aware of, and admittedly helped Bobby get rid of Jessie's body. Myisha, a longtime friend of Bobby's, frequently babysat Blake. However, when investigators executed a search warrant at Myisha's apartment the day after Jessie's body was found, people across America were wondering who this woman was and where she came from. Until that day, after it was announced she had been arrested and charged with obstructing justice—a felony—Myisha's name had never been mentioned in front of the media. Nonetheless, like Bobby, Myisha claimed her own degree of innocence, saying she had only helped him out of fear. "This is a police officer, so what am I supposed to do? It's a friend, yes, but he's a police officer first, for real," she declared.

Weaving a thick web of lies in her initial interviews to investigators, Myisha maintained Bobby's version of events, claiming she was supposed to babysit. She showed up, but Jessie never dropped off Blake.

What Myisha failed to add was that as she was only working part-time at a local Denny's restaurant and was to be evicted from her apartment. Bobby frequently gave her money. In fact, the day she drove with Bobby to the Hampton Hills Metro Park with Jessie's body in the back, Bobby gave her one hundred dollars—not an "inconvenienced babysitter fee" as Bobby had previously claimed. While giving investigators a detailed statement of what transpired immediately following Jessie's murder, Myisha continued to interject that she was fearful of Bobby and felt she had no other choice but to help him.

Bobby had asked Myisha in advance to babysit on Thursday, June 14. Regardless, Myisha said she stayed up the night before drinking and smoking marijuana. In fact, her friends were just leaving when Bobby pulled in to pick her up at around 6:00 AM. As soon as she got into the passenger side of Bobby's truck, she knew something was wrong. According to Myisha, Bobby appeared nervous, disoriented, and "out of sorts," prompting her to ask him what was wrong.

"Something's wrong with my baby's mother. . . . She's in the back of the truck," he mumbled.

Myisha said that she didn't understand what he meant at first, and asked him to explain. Not responding to her question, Bobby made a strange gesture with his arm. At that point, Myisha was nervous and realized they were driving northbound on the interstate, away from Bobby's house. Having to use the restroom, Myisha asked Bobby to stop at a truck stop that was nearby.

Within minutes, they were back on the interstate, exiting shortly after, and then driving around an isolated area before stopping near a field. Both got out of the truck and walked to the rear, where Jessie's feet were sticking out from underneath the comforter. Myisha claimed she told Bobby that she didn't want to see any more and got back inside the truck. It took Bobby only a few minutes to dump Jessie's body before they were back on the interstate heading home. Myisha admitted to throwing Jessie's pink cell phone out the window as they drove. She also later testified at Bobby's murder trial that Bobby immediately called Jessie's phone and left a voice mail saying, "If you weren't going to drop off Blake, you should have called."

Perhaps one of the most damaging statements from Myisha, albeit devastating to the Porter family, was of Bobby repeating Jessie's last words over and over while dumping the body: "And he drove and he just kept saying—he was like, 'Man, all I remember is her last words—*I'll leave!*' he kept saying it," Myisha told investigators.

After dumping the body, Bobby stopped at a car wash to spray out the bed of his truck, before buying a load of mulch and putting it there. After paying Myisha one hundred dollars, Bobby pulled his shirt up and asked her if she could see the faint scratches on his chest—scratches from Jessie. Myisha told him they were vague, but he then immediately showed her his finger, claiming that Jessie also bit him.

Myisha further claimed that after being taken home, she didn't talk to Bobby again until the following day when he called her. He told her his baby's mother was missing and he was upset. "I thought Bobby had gone crazy at that point," she recalled.

Myisha Ferrell accepted a plea arrangement with the state in exchange for her "honest" testimony during Bobby's murder trial. Myisha pled guilty to obstructing justice and complicity to gross abuse of a corpse and was sentenced to serve two years in prison.

After Bobby Cutts was formally charged with aggravated murder, the state began to build its case against him with a vengeance. With the prosecution seeking the death penalty, the trial began on February 4, 2008. Listening to the various testimonies of former lovers, current lovers, friends, and family members of Bobby Cutts, the most shocking testimony came from Bobby, who, in an unusual move, took the stand in his own defense. His detailed, never-before-heard testimony of Jessie's death horrified the courtroom and devastated the Porter family. He maintained that the murder was only an accident.

As Bobby Cutts began to testify, the courtroom settled with an uneasy quiet; jurors fidgeted in their seats, the media held their breaths, and the Porter family closed their eyes, preparing to hear the unimaginable.

Talking softly, Bobby began by stating that he last talked to Jessie at 8:00 PM on June 13, 2007. There was no argument, their relationship was at a status quo, and they spoke only about arrangements for Blake. In fact, just the prior Monday, Bobby had gone over to Jessie's house when she called him because she thought that she was going into labor. Realizing it was a false alarm, Bobby left. Everything was just fine between him and Jessie.

After leaving Champs bar the night of June 13, Bobby drove to Stephanie Hawthorne's—his lover's—house. He fell asleep there, ultimately waking around 2:00 AM and making the ten-minute drive to his home. Bobby even claimed that Stephanie called him while he was on his way home.

Since Bobby was scheduled to pick Blake up before 6:00 AM, he set his alarm for 5:30, because Jessie's house was only ten minutes away. Waking up early, at 5:20, Bobby went to Jessie's house, only to find that she didn't have Blake awake and ready to go. He claimed that when he walked into her bedroom, she was sitting on the floor.

"I kept telling her to hurry up, but she wouldn't listen. She kept saying she was too tired to do anything," he recalled. "I told her I could be back in my bed asleep by now."

Jessie responded by telling Bobby that if he wasn't out drinking all hours of the night, he wouldn't be so tired. After continuing to verbally battle with Jessie, Bobby stated that he'd had enough and said he was leaving. He told Jessie he would pick Blake up for the weekend and she could make other arrangements for him that morning. Angry, Jessie stood in front of Bobby to prevent him from leaving the bedroom.

Sniffling and wiping his eyes while on the witness stand, Bobby continued his testimony. He said that he gently pushed Jessie to the side and started toward the bedroom door, but she immediately stepped in front of him again. Putting his finger to his nose, he stuck his finger in her face in a gesture of wiping imaginary "snot" on her. Instead of her moving, he claimed Jessie bit his finger. "I didn't expect for her to do that," he admitted.

Pushing her to the side more forcefully this time, Jessie grabbed Bobby's arm tightly in an attempt to pull him back into the room. Bobby claimed he jerked his arm forward and then back, feeling his elbow strike Jessie, who immediately let go. He thought that would be the end of it until he heard Jessie fall—hard. Turning around to see her on the floor, it was then that Bobby realized he had struck her in the throat.

Bobby immediately went over to her and asked her if she was all right. Receiving no response, he began to shake her repeatedly before attempting CPR. Not finding a pulse, Bobby remembered that ammonia sometimes brought someone to who had been knocked unconscious. Not finding any ammonia, Bobby grabbed a bottle of bleach from the closet and filled up the bleach cap. Sticking it under her nose, Bobby became extremely panicked when she didn't respond and wound up knocking the bottle of bleach over. Not knowing how to turn Jessie's phone on to call for help, Bobby claims he fell on her bed crying.

"I didn't mean to hurt her!" Bobby sobbed on the witness stand.

Realizing no one would possibly believe his story, Bobby thought of Myisha. He would get her to watch Blake while he figured something out. Wrapping Jessie's body in her comforter, Bobby claimed that Blake was still asleep and he didn't want to wake him. Placing Jessie's body in the back of the truck, Bobby headed for Myisha's house, where he arrived at around 6:00 AM. He claimed that after they stopped at a truck stop for Myisha to use the restroom, he saw a state trooper and became further panicked. That was when he decided to get rid of Jessie's body.

Bobby claimed he even called Jessie's phone later that day, in hopes that she would answer, proving the entire ordeal nothing but a nightmare.

After dumping the body like a bag of garbage, Bobby admitted that he sprayed out his truck. He said he bought the mulch afterward because he was supposed to mulch his yard that day. When he arrived home, he showered and "washed and washed and washed" everything away. He said he tried to make it all go away and wanted everything to be normal—so normal, in fact, that he went to a job interview, picked up his daughter, Brionna; bought her a sno-cone maker; and then mulched his yard before going to work as a police officer on the night shift.

As Bobby finished his testimony, wiping his nose and eyes, the prosecution fiercely attacked his credibility—and his show of emotion. Stark County Assistant Prosecutor Dennis Barr was the first to lash out at Bobby:

"Mr. Cutts, do you have a cold?" Barr asked calmly.

"No," Bobby sniffed.

"Because I don't see any tears. . . . Did you cry this much when you dumped Jessie Davis's body in the woods?"

Bobby claimed that he cried a lot. However, Barr dismissed the testimony as pure show. He explained to the jury how not to be swayed by Bobby's lies, including his claim that he went to Stephanie Hawthorne's house after being at Champs bar—a fact that Stephanie Hawthorne disputed. She claimed she only talked to Bobby at around 2:00 AM, on the phone. Since she heard him open his car door, she assumed he was at home.

Barr explained that, angry over the upcoming birth of another child he would surely have to pay child support for, Bobby drove to Jessie's house—not to Stephanie's house. While there, a heated argument ensued that resulted in Bobby strangling the life out of Jessie Davis while their son, Blake, watched. There was even prior testimony from one of Bobby's good friends, who claimed that Bobby told him, "I'm gonna kill that bitch and throw her in the woods," only a month prior to the murder.

What was seemingly missed during the trial was Bobby's claim of not being able to turn on Jessie's cell phone. Bobby admittedly used his own cell phone to call Jessie's phone after dumping her body, therefore proving he had it with him at the time of the murder. Jessie also lived in a duplex. The possibility of knocking on the neighbor's door to seek help or to use their phone was also obsolete to Bobby. Bobby's calls to Jessie the day after the murder were shown on cell phone records. However, as the prosecution pointed out, they were made to cover his tracks—not, as Bobby claimed, in the hope that Jessie would answer.

Barr reminded the jury that here was a man who just murdered the mother of his child, washed out his truck, bought mulch, played with his daughter, landscaped his yard, and then went to work after dumping a body. Bobby's claim that the death was accidental was incredible. His actions, after the fact, paint the portrait of the true coldhearted monster that he really is.

Tragically, Jessie's obstetrician testified that, had Bobby sought help the night of the murder, the unborn baby would have most likely survived. Bobby unquestionably knew that by taking Jessie's life, he would also take the life of his unborn daughter. As for the well-being of Blake, who had stayed alone and in fear for over twenty-four hours, Bobby admitted that his son was not his top priority at the time. Finally, Barr summed up the horrors of the crime to the jury in a simple sentence: "For nine days, Bobby Cutts lived a normal life while Jessie Davis and her unborn child were left rotting in the woods."

However, Jessie's body was so badly decomposed that the coroner couldn't determine a cause of death other than "homicidal violence." This was something the defense used to back up Bobby's story. Fortunately, the jury didn't buy it.

On February 15, 2008, Bobby L. Cutts Jr. was convicted of the murder of Jessie Davis and the aggravated murder of her unborn daughter. He was also found guilty on lesser charges of aggravated burglary, gross abuse of a corpse, and child endangering. Waiving the death penalty, jurors sentenced Bobby Cutts to life imprisonment without the possibility of parole for fifty-seven years—a sentence that shocked and angered much of the public and the family of Jessie Davis.

Patricia Porter and the rest of Jessie's family still continue to pick up the pieces after the tragic events that changed their lives in June 2007. Now raising Blake, Patricia has him in continuous counseling. She says that Blake still talks about "Mommy being in the rug." Regardless, Patricia has taken Blake to visit Bobby in prison on several occasions—an act that has some eyebrows raising.

Kelly Cutts filed for divorce from Bobby exactly four days after Jessie's body was found. Throughout the search for Jessie, Kelly had publicly supported Bobby and maintained his innocence.

As for the whereabouts of his parents, Patricia tells Blake that "Mommy is in Heaven, and Daddy is in a long time-out for doing something bad."

CHAPTER 3

WHO'S YOUR DADDY?

CHARLES OSWALT
POLICE LIEUTENANT, MANSFIELD, OHIO

Charles Oswalt continues to maintain his innocence. He is out of prison now and back in the community where he served as a police officer for so many years. He lives with his wife, who stood by his side after he was convicted of murdering a local prostitute who had sued him for paternity. Perhaps the murder trial surrounding Oswalt will best be remembered for the breakthrough forensic analysis of carpet fibers that led to his conviction—a conviction that was a black eye on the city of Mansfield, Ohio, and the officers who served under Oswalt's stern night watch.

The city had already had two sheriffs who ended their careers in prison, and another was soon to come. A book about the city and its law enforcement corruption, *Rotten to the Core*, was later published, furthering the dismal reputation of Johnny Appleseed's hometown.

In June 1988, Mansfield Police Lieutenant Charles Oswalt,

forty-three, was found guilty of murdering thirty-two-year-old Marjorie "Margie" Coffey. Her strangled body had been found by a Boy Scout troop in a river in the remote and heavily forested region of southern Richland County, Ohio—the Appalachian foothills. It was sheer luck that the Boy Scouts happened upon the body, for it could have been months before she would have been found, if it all.

However, not much care was taken to conceal the body, as if the murderer was mocking the investigative skills of law enforcement. The old adage "it takes one to know one" seemed to ring true in this particular case, and the arrest of one of Mansfield's finest sent shock waves throughout the city. The fact that Oswalt murdered Coffey inside his own police cruiser while on duty made the case even more horrific.

Before O. J. Simpson, the notion of watching a murder trial unfold on television was a fairly new form of entertainment. However, the local television station allowed the city to literally watch a play by play of the dark and disturbing details of the grisly murder. It would be years before movies like *The Shawshank Redemption* and *Air Force One* would be filmed in Mansfield at the old Ohio State Reformatory, so this was as close to Hollywood as the residents could get. They talked about it in coffee shops, libraries, offices, banks, and on the street corners. The city was fixated on what was to become of Charles Oswalt.

To an outsider, his complex personality may have foretold the grim events that occurred that winter night. To those who worked for him, he was simply "Charlie." Certainly not a favorite among the ranks of the police department, Oswalt kept to himself other than to parlay duties to his subordinates. To those who knew him, Oswalt had a face that looked like it was cut directly from stone—a hard, cold look that was anything but friendly. Oswalt meant business twenty-four hours a day.

Some felt that his tour of duty in Vietnam played an integral part in his hardened persona, and others said that was simply the way he was. As one of his subordinates it would be a mistake to cross or upset him. If his treatment toward the patrolmen was bad, his treatment of his own sergeants who worked directly under him was considerably even more brutal.

On one particular occasion, Oswalt was in his office questioning a sergeant about a report. According to witnesses in the room, another of Oswalt's sergeants rudely interrupted him. Instead of saying, "Excuse me, Sergeant, can you wait until I'm finished?" Oswalt simply grabbed a book from the table in front of him, stood up, and threw it with a vengeance—hitting the sergeant square in the face. Without missing a beat, he immediately sat back down and continued his conversation.

In another incident recalled by one of his former subordinates, a second sergeant of Oswalt's noticed that one of his headlights wasn't working as he was getting into his cruiser at the beginning of the shift. Alerting Oswalt to this fact, Oswalt told his sergeant to "punch the headlight, it'll come on." Apparently, the sergeant hit the headlight a little too hard and broke the glass, cutting his hand in the process. As Howard approached Oswalt, he informed him of the injury.

"Sir, I've cut my hand."

"No shit, stupid! Take your fucking dumb ass up to the hospital," was Oswalt's only response.

Most of those who knew Oswalt feared him. However, a choice few looked at him differently.

"He had a reputation for being an asshole . . . If you stood your ground with him, he was okay. . . . We had a mutual respect," said John Wendling, a patrolman who worked for Oswalt and later became a pivotal witness in his murder trial.

Oswalt's wife, Linda, undoubtedly respected him. She

stood by him during his murder trial and, subsequently, his prison term—alone raising the three children that they shared. She mirrored her husband's sentiments in proclaiming his innocence, even though she was kept in the dark about his relationship—and illegitimate child—with former prostitute Margie Coffey.

Those close to Margie maintained that she was trying to get her life back together, and she was doing a damn good job. Although she was only thirty-two, her past had been dark and sordid. No one could blame her upbringing; she was raised by Clarence and Marjorie Remy on a large farm in the small village of Butler, approximately fifteen miles south of the city of Mansfield. Although it was only a twenty-minute drive to the city, the difference between it and the small village was night and day.

Those who lived in the small towns and villages in Richland County looked upon the crime-ridden and drug-infested county seat as "the big city." The city lived up to its reputation when, in 1994, it was honored with having the highest crime rate per capita in the country. *Money* magazine also listed it as one of the top ten worst cities to live in during the 1990s. Most never ventured there, completely content with their villages and local grocery stores, and no one could have possibly predicted that Margie Coffey would sell her soul to the streets of Mansfield.

She grew up milking cows and running around the rural areas of the Clearfork Valley, the prelude to the large foothills that would later be her final resting place. She graduated from rural Clearfork High School, and found herself working the streets less than a year later. The fifth of six children, Margie was close with her youngest brother, Tim Remy. He recalled Margie's troubles right out of high school: "When she started getting into trouble, it just never stopped. It was a terrible time," he recalled to a news reporter. "By the time she was out of high school, she was over her head."

Margie's mother believes she fell in with the wrong crowd in the latter years of high school—a crowd who introduced her to the nightlife of the city. In 1975, at the age of nineteen, she was charging twenty dollars per man and living at a house known for prostitution on the city's notorious West Fourth Street. She was arrested in 1974 and 1975 for soliciting prostitution. During those years, she had become pregnant by a man who later beat her so badly that she was hospitalized. After he was sent to prison for dealing heroin, Margie decided it was time to get out of "the life," if only for her newborn daughter's sake.

Taking on a few odd jobs, Margie met Stephen Coffey, whom she married in 1978. Realizing they were both too young, the couple divorced in 1981. They had been separated for ten months prior to the divorce, at which time Margie had been seeing another man, Mansfield police lieutenant Charles Oswalt. Not necessarily what one would deem a relationship, the two mainly met up for sex, and Margie happily obliged. At the time of her divorce from Stephen Coffey, Margie learned she was pregnant with a child, Brandon—Oswalt's son.

Of course, she didn't divulge this information to Oswalt—at least not right away. In fact, he found out about Margie's pregnancy from another officer, Stephen Crose, who was now seeing the troubled woman. When the baby was just several months old, Oswalt halfheartedly asked Crose, "How's Margie?" Crose replied, "She's fine, and so is the baby." According to Crose, Oswalt asked, "What baby?" Crose informed Oswalt that the infant was two months old. As Oswalt walked away, he counted his fingers. ". . . eight, nine, ten . . . oh, shit," he mumbled.

Crose, a shady character in his own right, had resigned before Coffey's murder and had taken a job as a private investigator. His downward spiral would continue with later and frequent run-ins with law enforcement, and he was sent to federal prison for drug trafficking in 2004.

Crose was also obsessed with Margie, even though he, like Oswalt, was married. He admitted to investigators that he had followed her frequently, but claimed she was aware of it. "I followed her several times . . . and we used to joke around and do that. I would follow her like someplace and wave and honk, then leave, you know . . . never followed her to check on her or anything," Crose claimed.

Of course, his statement would contradict his actions on the day of Margie's disappearance.

Regardless, Margie would keep the illegitimate child out of Oswalt's life for several years. At the time she didn't want to involve him or disrupt his marriage. That all changed the day she became a Jehovah's Witness.

The church, compelling her to tell the truth—coupled with the urging of the county welfare department who was paying her child support benefits—convinced Margie to file a paternity suit against Oswalt. This was a claim he vehemently denied.

At this time, Margie moved back to the quiet, peaceful village of Butler; a place free from the crime-ridden streets where she could safely raise her children. She began taking Bible classes and even enrolled in college courses at the state college in Mansfield. At this time she became a frequent customer at Mr. T's Coffee Shop—a police officer's haven. According to her friends, Margie couldn't deny that she loved the men in uniform.

On the two nights a week that Margie had classes, she would sit in the coffee shop with her books spread out and consume anywhere from three to five cups of coffee while watching the parade of police officers coming in and out, refueling for the night. It was during this time that the paternity suit was beginning to heat up.

On November 20, 1987, exactly two months before her

murder, Margie and Oswalt were seated across from each other giving their depositions in the paternity case. His wife still was unaware of the suit—or the child. At one point, it became clear that Oswalt was weaving a story that completely infuriated Margie.

"Then she goes and relates a story that a couple weeks prior she had been at the Continental Lounge on Walnut Street and had offered a ride to three individuals to [the village of] Shiloh," he testified. "And, while en route to Shiloh, apparently, they stopped and all three of these men had sexual relations with her."

"You are lying!" Margie interrupted.

"Margie!" her attorney chastised. "You are not allowed to say anything, just listen!"

"But, he's lying!" Margie continued. "I don't want to stay for this! I don't want to stay here!"

Since her client was clearly upset, Margie's attorney called a brief recess to calm her down. Margie felt that she was up against a brick wall in battling the respected police officer, and the depositions were no different.

When it came to Margie's relationship with Stephen Crose, Oswalt took advantage of the opportunity to add to the picture of her that he was painting. "She called me. . . . She just had a fight with Mr. Crose; they had set a date for him to leave his wife and take up residency with her and the date had come—that date. He reneged on some promise he made and as a result she was out imbibing in some alcohol," he testified. "As an afterthought, she stated, 'Oh, by the way, what would you say if I told you that you had a son you didn't know about?' And I started laughing at her. . . . I said, 'Well, I don't have one so we don't have to worry about it.' . . . She called later that night and said, 'Charlie, I want you to know that Brandon is not your son, I don't know why I told you that, I was drinking."

However, blood tests taken in June 1987 confirmed to 99.66 percent accuracy that Charles Oswalt was indeed the father of Margie's child, Brandon. In mid-October 1987, Margie began to relay threats made by Oswalt to those who knew her. In a meeting with her drug and alcohol counselor, Margie began to backtrack on the suit, unsure of how it would affect Oswalt's family—and she was afraid of what he might do to her. In a tearful phone call to her counselor the day after the meeting, Margie spoke of one of these threats: "He said he'd rather see me dead than go through with it."

Margie began the last day of her life, January 20, 1988, with an appointment at her attorney's office. The attorney, Bambi Couch, was handling Margie's paternity suit against Oswalt. On that particular morning, Margie came to the appointment armed with a settlement from Oswalt's attorney. She was also wearing the same clothes that would be found on her body almost two weeks later. Oswalt offered to pay her five thousand dollars to drop the suit, not legally name him on the child's birth certificate, and simply go away. Margie seemed somewhat excited about this deal until Couch reached for her calculator and explained to Margie, in detail, exactly what she would be giving up. The five thousand dollars would equal approximately five dollars per week until Brandon was eighteen years old. But that wasn't the worst of it. "I explained to her that if she accepted any sort of large cash amount of money, she would probably be immediately terminated from the welfare rolls. That's the policy," Couch testified. "When you receive that amount of money, they assume you can live on that money for some period of time. She would then lose not only her children's welfare benefits, but also her medical benefits. . . . She would probably have to drop out of college and find a job."

When Margie realized the deal included an agreement to

not publicly or legally name Oswalt as the father, she refused the offer and the deal was off the table. Since she had become a Jehovah's Witness, she was adamant that her son know the truth.

Nonetheless, Couch provided Margie with information that would set the tone for the events to follow. Information had come in from Planned Parenthood that corroborated Margie's claims that Oswalt was Brandon's father. Coupled with the paternity test results, Couch was confident that Margie would win the suit in a trial and collect a substantial amount of money per month for her son. Margie was elated.

After leaving her attorney's office, Margie went directly to her counselor and relayed the news. "She had good news and bad news," the counselor recalled. "The bad news was she didn't know how Oswalt was going to react."

From there, Margie headed out to the campus for her regularly scheduled classes. She was pursuing an associate's degree in secretarial science in addition to being enrolled in juvenile delinquency and typing classes. During a break in classes, Margie told her good friend Mari Lynn Smith of the news. Smith remembered how happy Margie had been and how excited she was at the prospect of putting the paternity suit behind her and moving on with her life. "I'll remember her like the last day, vibrant, proud of herself. She had a look on her the last day, I've never seen this in a person, and it was like two beams of light came out of her eyes. She had the most loving, strong vibration as she sat across from me," Smith recalled.

After her classes, Margie met a friend, Harold Marshall, at a local Denny's restaurant to discuss Margie's brother getting Harold's wife a job. Margie also gave Harold some Jehovah's Witness literature before she headed off to Mr. T's. At that time, she had less than three hours to live.

She wasn't in the coffee shop for long. According to the owner, Tom Bunfill, "Mr. T," she didn't drink her usual five-or-so cups of coffee. It could possibly be because shortly after she arrived so did Mansfield police officers James Reid and John Wendling, and Lieutenant Charles Oswalt. According to witnesses, Margie and Oswalt didn't even make eye contact. Oswalt acted as if she weren't even there—an unusual talent considering the events that had taken place earlier in the day. Margie was seated in her usual booth with her headphones on, listening to music and quietly sipping her coffee while pretending to look at her books.

At approximately 11:30 PM, Margie Coffey gathered up her belongings and walked out of the coffee shop. It was the last time she was ever seen alive.

Shortly after Margie left, the officers grabbed coffees to go and began their nightly tours of duty. This was when things began to unravel.

According to those who worked for Oswalt, to hear him on the radio was a rare occurrence. Essentially, he would disappear for the night unless someone needed a breathalyzer test for a DUI arrest. Oswalt insisted on doing every breathalyzer test so he would earn an automatic four hours of overtime for testifying in court about each test. He was also known for conducting secret investigations on other officers. One investigation in particular that was common knowledge focused on an officer who was allegedly having sexual relations with his girlfriend at her house while he remained on duty.

At 11:53 PM, Oswalt's voice came over the radio with an order that made the rest of the officers' jaws drop. An officer with a DUI arrest needed a breathalyzer test. The dispatchers called Oswalt on the radio, to which he responded, "Have 090 [the shift sergeant] handle the test!"

Everyone was shocked. However, after Oswalt was convicted of murder, locker room talk focused on his radio com-

Mr. T's Coffee Shop, the last place Margie Coffey was seen alive. Photo by author.

munication that night and how it sounded like it came from his handheld portable radio instead of the one inside his car. "We all talked about it later, since it never came out during the trial," Officer John Wendling recalled. "That night, when he had Billy Howard take the DUI test, his radio traffic was all broken up and you could tell he was out on his portable radio somewhere. I thought to myself, 'Where the hell is *he* at?'"

Around 1:15 AM Officer Wendling took a brief opportunity to go through a fast-food drive-through for something to eat. Wendling was eating in his cruiser in an empty parking lot when he saw something extremely unusual.

His lieutenant, Charles Oswalt, was walking west on Park Avenue wearing a dark leather jacket instead of his uniform coat. He was walking toward the police station, his police cruiser nowhere in sight. At the time, Wendling assumed Oswalt had been watching the home of the girlfriend with whom the officer he was investigating lived, which was nearby. Wendling even told his brother, Joseph, also a police officer on night shift, about the incident. "I told him, 'Damn, Oswalt's getting slick!'" he recalled, referring to Oswalt's investigation into other officers.

Wendling recalled another unusual incident involving Oswalt that night. At 2:17 AM Oswalt contacted him via radio and asked to meet. When Wendling arrived, Oswalt immediately asked him about his son, who had recently been admitted into the hospital. "I was shocked," Wendling said, "I thought to myself 'since when do you give a shit about my son?' I mean, here's this guy that rarely says a word to anybody and he was an absolute motormouth that night. I honestly think he had just got done disposing of the body at that point. After it all came out, I realize he was going around establishing alibis."

Wendling dismissed the events of that night until days later.

Oswalt left the shift that morning two hours early, which wasn't very unusual. Night shift officers frequently did this if they had a lengthy trial or court appearance the next day so they could go home and get some sleep.

On January 21, 1988, Stephen Crose contacted the Mansfield police and advised them that Margie's family had filed a missing persons report with the small Butler Police Department earlier that day. Crose felt that Margie was last seen at the college campus in the city of Mansfield and that Mansfield Police should investigate it. Crose claimed that he had been asked by Margie's family to try to find her. Margie's car had been entered into the National Crime Information Center (NCIC) and an "attempt to locate" teletype had been sent out to area police agencies. Crose told the investigating officer at that time that Margie's mother suspected foul play because of a paternity suit Margie had against a Mansfield police officer—but Crose refused to name that officer.

Over the next twenty-four hours, the question of who would investigate the disappearance came into play. The Butler police force was simply too small and did not have the proper resources, so it was down to either the Mansfield police or the Richland County Sheriff's Department. Margie's family had contacted the sheriff's department to investigate the disappearance, because they were afraid of a cover-up by the Mansfield police.

On January 22, 1988, Margie's car was found by her family. It was parked along a city side street, a few hundred feet away from where John Wendling had seen Oswalt walking on the night of Margie's disappearance. The family contacted the sheriff's department, who in turn contacted the city police. It was determined that the city police would investigate the disappearance, and the car was subsequently towed to the station for evidentiary purposes. Word of Oswalt's involvement quickly made its way to the upper echelons of the department. The department was taking no chances at being accused of a cover-up. The family was enraged.

Mansfield police lieutenant David Messmore, who was in charge of the major crimes unit, was contacted at his residence regarding the vehicle. He gave the order for the vehicle to be thoroughly searched and processed. A short time later, Messmore was contacted by Richland County prosecutor John Allen. He had received information from the Coffey family that Margie had a letter at home that implicated Charles Oswalt if she were ever to disappear. In fact, Margie had even called a part-time Butler police officer to her home to look at and verify the letter. The officer stated Margie was determined that if she were ever to go missing, Oswalt was to be held responsible. It seems that she had predicted her own death.

The following day, Messmore made an extensive series of phone calls in an attempt to construct a timeline leading up to Margie's disappearance. He spoke with her friends, members of her church, attorney Bambi Couch, and members of Margie's family. All of them pointed to Charles Oswalt as the primary suspect in Margie's disappearance. Later, Messmore had Margie's brother, Tim, come to the Mansfield station. As predicted, Tim expressed his lack of confidence at the Mansfield Police Department's ability to fully investigate one of its own without showing favoritism. Tim also asked an interesting question: Why was Stephen Crose investigating the case? The family never asked Crose to investigate it. Messmore assured Tim that all would be done to find his sister and prosecute a suspect.

The reaction to Margie's disappearance was a little unusual. Missing persons reports are taken daily, and usually not much investigation is done—if any at all. Drug users, prostitutes, and unruly teenagers typically take off and then return a short while later. However, numerous fingers were now pointing at one of the Mansfield department's own officers. The department was now under a microscope. There was zero room for error.

Not much from an evidentiary standpoint was found in Margie's car: just schoolbooks, unopened groceries, gloves, and half a cup of coffee from Mr. T's. The area surrounding where Margie's car was found was also checked extensively, including some nearby abandoned drug houses and Dumpsters—all to no avail.

As Lieutenant Messmore was going home that evening, Saturday, January 23, he received a phone call from Officer Stephen Crose. Crose stated that he felt further investigation was necessary and proceeded to tell the veteran lieutenant exactly what needed to be done. Messmore cut him off instantly. "I told him that he had lied to the family, and he had lied to me, and that he is to have no further involvement in this investigation. I further advised Stephen Crose that we would not be needing any information from him and that the family had indicated to us that he was a frequent visitor to Margie over a period of several years; and, as far as I was concerned he could be a suspect as well as anybody else," Messmore wrote in his report.

Crose was later brought in to give a statement to specifically explain how he knew Margie's exact whereabouts on the day that she disappeared. This seemed to contradict his assertion that he had never followed her. Crose claimed to have found out the information in the course of his own investigation.

On January 25, 1988, a picture of Margie with a small article relating to her disappearance appeared in the *Mansfield News Journal*. Upon seeing the article that day, John Wendling then realized that the events of January 21 weren't as insignificant as he had previously thought. "I saw her picture in the paper and thought, 'Oh my God, he actually killed her,'" the "he" referring to Oswalt.

Wendling was aware of the ongoing paternity suit betwen Oswalt and Margie. He had even suggested to Oswalt weeks earlier that he should offer her a lump sum of money to drop the suit. For several days, Wendling kept quiet about what he had witnessed. However, when talking with private investigator William Spognardi later at Mr. T's, he mentioned that "I may have seen something that night, but I'm not sure."

Spognardi went directly to the investigator for the prosecutor's office and told him about his conversation with Wendling. In the taped conversation recorded by the investigator, Spognardi recounts the conversation word for word.

"I'm gonna go get him right now for a statement," the investigator said.

"No, no!" Spognardi urged. "Wait a couple of days or he'll know I'm the one who told you!"

Wendling was confronted by several of the investigators, at which point he told them of the unusual events he witnessed on January 20.

On January 29, 1988, Charles Oswalt was brought in for questioning. His explanation was a simple one. He had seen Margie in the coffee shop and that was it—period. Investigators kept the interview short, allowing for more evidence to be gathered and Margie Coffey to be found—dead or alive.

The wait wouldn't be long—less than twenty-four hours. On Saturday, January 30, 1988, a group of Boy Scouts was out in the forest collecting trash and aluminum cans. Walking along the edge of a small frozen river called Possum Run, the boys came upon what they thought was a mannequin with a hand protruding out of the nearly frozen water. The hand did not belong to a mannequin; the Scouts had, in fact, discovered the body of Margie Coffey.

The site of Coffey's body was situated in the Richland County Sheriff's Department's jurisdiction. Richland officers responded to the scene, along with crime lab technicians and the bureau of criminal investigations. Margie's body was found with a scarf wound tightly around the neck. After the scene was processed, the body was taken to Cincinnati for an autopsy where it would be determined that Margie had been strangled. Now the investigation into Margie's disappearance had turned into an investigation into her homicide.

Stephen Crose and Charles Oswalt agreed to give hair and DNA samples. Their vehicles were searched extensively, including Oswalt's police cruiser. It was the trunk of Oswalt's cruiser that contained some of the most damning evidence; several hairs that appeared to be consistent with Margie's were found there. FBI special agent Sam Adkins was called in. A hair and fiber specialist, Agent Adkins was credited with the evidence found in the case of the Atlanta child murders, and

The icy waters of Possum Run Creek, Margie Coffey's final resting place. Photos by author.

he had also helped put a known serial killer in Florida behind bars. In addition to hair and fiber samples, the clothing taken from Margie's body was also sent to the FBI laboratory for processing.

After all the potential suspects were ruled out, whether by polygraph examinations or alibis, one suspect stood alone: Charles Oswalt.

On February 24, 1988, Mansfield police chief Matthew Benick and Captain Wayne Cairns arrived at Oswalt's home. They were there for two reasons. The first was to inform Oswalt that he was being placed on administrative leave from the police department. The second was that he had just been indicted for the murder of Margie Coffey and would be taken to jail.

The lab results had returned from the FBI. Two fibers that matched the trunk of Oswalt's cruiser were found on pieces of Margie's clothing. Since Oswalt's cruiser was the only make and model of its kind in the entire fleet of cruisers, the evidence was compelling.

While Charles Oswalt was in jail, a document was placed inside a file in his former office. This document was a secret drug investigation that Oswalt was allegedly focused on. The document specifically described Oswalt watching houses between 1:00 AM and 2:30 AM on the night of the twentieth—the times he was unaccounted for. Oswalt's friend and co-worker James Reid's name was raised as to who allegedly placed the document in the file. Two supervisors, in official statements, documented finding Reid in the supervisor's office going through files. The prosecution claimed that the mysterious paperwork was nothing but a bogus attempt at an alibi.

The Oswalt murder trial began before a standing-room-only crowd in June 1988. Observers brought in packed lunches for fear of losing their seats, and a closed-circuit television streamed the proceedings to those outside of the courtroom

Charles Oswalt listens to Carol Eckart's testimony. Photo courtesy of the *Mansfield News Journal*.

who wanted to watch the play-by-play. Some wore T-shirts that read: "Oswalt's Defense: I just wanted some Coffey!" a sick attempt at humor surrounding the events that took place at the coffee shop before the murder.

Throughout the course of the trial, Oswalt continued to maintain his innocence and further denied that he was the father of Margie's child. However, on June 18, a surprise witness provided explosive testimony for the prosecution. Her name was Carol Eckart and she was a former girlfriend of Oswalt. Eckart's name first came up when she phoned the police department and attempted to provide an alibi for Oswalt the night of the murder. She had initially stated that he was in a motel room with her. But she now testified that she was overwhelmed with guilt and fear, apprehensive to tell anyone what she really knew. According to her testimony, Oswalt confessed that he had murdered Margie Coffey and that James Reid had dumped the body.

Eckart's testimony shocked police officials. They now realized that they had another officer to investigate. Reid was called to the stand and vehemently denied Eckart's accusations. Shortly thereafter, Reid was put on leave and an investigation began that failed to result in any evidence that substantiated her claims. John Wendling never believed that Reid had anything to do with the case. "That was impossible, he was with me all night handling calls," Wendling recalled.

Halfway through the trial, the judge dismissed the charge of aggravated murder against Oswalt, stating that no one had proven any "prior calculation or design" in the murder of Margie Coffey. However, the jury could still find him guilty of murder or voluntary manslaughter.

During the closing arguments, prosecutors stated their case powerfully. They painted a clear picture for the jury, stating that after Margie Coffey left the coffee shop, she waited outside for Oswalt so that they could talk. Once inside Oswalt's cruiser, he and Margie continued their conversation while he drove, until the talk began to get heated, at which point Oswalt pulled over. Once parked, he strangled her to death and put her lifeless body in the trunk of his cruiser. Parking his cruiser at the police station, with the body still in the trunk, Oswalt then retrieved Margie's car and drove it several blocks away, parking it on a side street. Oswalt then walked back to the police department, which was when Officer John Wendling spotted him on foot—and out of uniform. Upon arriving at the station, Oswalt got back into his cruiser and drove out of the city to the remote area where he dumped Margie's body.

The jury hung onto every word. Regardless of whether the statement that Eckart gave about Reid proved false or not, the jury clearly believed her testimony about Oswalt's confession. The confession, along with the two fiber samples found on Margie's remains, was enough to sway the jury.

Charles Oswalt was found guilty of voluntary manslaughter and gross abuse of a corpse. He was sentenced to a term of ten to twenty-five years. The family of Margie Coffey felt vindicated.

The case involving Charles Oswalt continued to be portrayed on radio and television. It was later featured on shows such as *Forensic Files* and on televsion networks such as the Discovery Channel.

The two key pieces of evidence came under fire in the late 1990s when Carol Eckart allegedly told an appeals attorney that she had lied on the stand about Oswalt. Now she claimed that Oswalt told her he absolutely didn't commit the crime. The expertise of Special Agent Sam Adkins was called into question by the Department of Justice as well. There were accusations that he had embellished testimony and lied about fiber and hair results in hundreds of cases. This news convinced some of Oswalt's innocence—but not the family of Margie Coffey.

The questions regarding the evidence against Oswalt could certainly play upon any prudent person's mind. Was it really possible for Oswalt to murder Margie Coffey, move her car, and make the twenty-minute drive to the river and back in an hour and a half? In that hour and a half, he was seen by two police aides, an officer, and he emitted radio traffic. Could this have been done to establish an alibi on Oswalt's part? Is it possible that Stephen Crose, a former police officer turned convicted criminal, urged Margie to write the letter incriminating Oswalt in case of her disappearance in an attempt to lay the groundwork for her murder? Crose was admittedly obsessed with Margie and had been following her on the day she disappeared. Crose also admitted in his statement that Margie had recently said that she was done with him. Her newly found religion prohibited her from engaging in relations with a married man like Stephen Crose. Crose alerted the Mansfield Police Department to Margie's disappearance, lied about being hired by her family, and immediately gave a motive fingering Oswalt as the suspect. Coincidentaly, Crose's first wife had died under suspicious circumstances.

If Margie had sat in Oswalt's cruiser that night discussing the paternity suit, would she have the fibers on her even if she got out alive? Were they being watched by Stephen Crose? John Wendling assumed that Oswalt was watching another officer on the night he was observed walking. Wendling thought for sure that this information would be used as an alibi by Oswalt, but he was wrong in his assumption. Perhaps Oswalt was telling the truth about watching drug houses; perhaps he wasn't. Was the judge presiding over the trial in error when he allowed hearsay testimony from the deceased?

Perhaps it isn't so complicated. After being hit with a paternity suit, Oswalt murdered Margie Coffey out of fear of being exposed to his wife and the community he worked in. It sounds simple enough, but is there truth in this simplicity?

During the mid-1990s, the city of Mansfield and the Richland County Sheriff's Department undoubtedly cleaned up their act. With a newly elected sheriff and a new police chief, the area's law enforcement now consisted of honest, hardworking men and women looking to make a difference. However, they will never forget the past.

The Remy family's vindication was short lived—Oswalt came up for parole in 2004. As hard as the family fought to keep him incarcerated, their efforts proved fruitless.

"How can you be rehabilitated if you have not admitted your wrongs?" Margie's now grown daughter, Angie, pleaded with the parole board. With the family's pleas falling on deaf ears, Oswalt was released from prison in March 2004 after serving almost sixteen years. He continues to claim his innocence and states that he will not stop fighting to prove it. In the meantime, he said that he will take comfort in the time spent

Charles Oswalt in prison just before he was granted release. Photo courtesy of the *Mansfield News Journal*.

with his wife, who stood by his side all these years. "She is as assured of my innocence as I am. A lot of women would have packed their bags and been gone," he claimed.

Margie's daughter, Angie, will never be convinced: "There is no doubt in our minds that when he gets out, he's going to be a menace to society. He's going to put fear into countless people."

CHAPTER 4

IT WAS SUICIDE!

KEN DeKLEINE
POLICE OFFICER, HOLLAND, MICHIGAN

After a day of tiptoeing through the tulips of Holland, Michigan (six million of them to be exact), feel free to stop and get a chocolate milkshake. However, it's probably best to skip the milkshake if you took a pass on the tulips and instead hanged your wife in a basement—posing it to look like a suicide.

Visitors to Holland, Michigan, a city quite reminescent of the Netherlands, would find it hard to believe that such a crime could occur in a city where the streets are lined with colorful flowers. Situated near the east shore of Lake Michigan on the Ottawa-Allegan county line, the city of Holland proudly boasts the largest municipality and metro area in the region. With a population of roughly thirty-five thousand people, the city was founded by Dutch Americans and was earlier known as "The City of Churches." Though the city draws tourists with its floral beauty, it is also home to the world's largest pickle factory. H. J. Heinz and Company settled in Holland in 1897 and currently processes over one million pounds of pickles per day.

Regardless, the city's main focus is the alluring splendor of the tulips. Holland's tulip festival is the third-largest festival in the country. And if you remember how Dorothy, Toto, and her counterparts skipped through the field of Tulips toward the Emerald City, it would make sense that the idea had to come from somewhere. That somewhere was Holland, Michigan. L. Frank Baum was so inspired by the millions of tulips there that he wrote *The Wonderful Wizard of Oz* while in town.

As wonderful and picture perfect as the city appears, it found itself locked within the doom and gloom of the Wicked Witch's castle on January 10, 2008. That evening, forty-three-year-old Lori DeKleine was found dead in her basement—a rope around her neck. She was found by her own sixteen-year-old son, Christopher. It was clear that the scene was arranged to look like Lori had taken her own life, but police officers and investigators who responded to the scene quickly realized she had actually died at the hands of someone else. That someone else happened to be her estranged husband and a member of the Holland Police Department, Ken DeKleine.

Ken, forty-four, was a thirteen-year veteran of the Holland Police Department at the time of Lori's death. He was well respected and liked, and the residents of the city looked upon Ken and Lori as a loving, churchgoing couple. A few who were close to the couple knew there were problems in their marriage, but no one ever imagined the problems would end as gruesomely as they did on January 10.

It had been only a few years prior that the city held a parade honoring Officer DeKleine. He had taken a year off from the department to train police officers in Iraq. Lori and their two children, Christopher and Breanne, proudly rode along the parade route on a float while Ken was halfway around the world. Mayor Al McGeehan thought that the Tulip Time Parade would be a perfect setting to pay homage to one of the city's own police officers who chose to sacrifice his family life to make the lives of the Iraqi people better.

A 1987 graduate of Calvin College, DeKleine joined the police department in 1995. He was known by many citizens because of his position as a community police officer within the Holland Police Department. As a proud father, he coached his son's lacrosse team and would frequently change his work schedule to travel with his daughter's high school drama team. DeKleine was also active within his church, the Holland Heights Christian Reformed Church, where Lori was employed as publications editor. Ken would frequently lead the congregation on trips.

Although there were problems in the DeKleine marriage before Ken left for Iraq, some believe that the escalation and disturbing nature of the relationship truly began when he returned.

By Christmas 2006, Lori finally had enough of the marriage and quietly asked Ken to move out. It was shortly after that when he returned to the home they once shared and broke into Lori's locked bedroom, leaving a bloody trail and papers scattered everywhere. Becoming increasingly frightened by her husband's behavior, Lori contacted the Holland Police Department. She was told that because there was no protection order or divorce papers granting her exclusive use of the residence, there was nothing the police department could do. Kenneth had as much right to the home as she did.

Realizing what needed to be done, Lori filed a personal protection order against Ken in January 2007. By his own admission, this was the first time he began to contemplate murdering his wife. Nonetheless, he quickly disputed the protection order. Lori had been diagnosed with bipolar disorder and was battling bouts of depression from the problems in her marriage. Ken went so far as to claim that Lori made several suicide attempts and wasn't stable enough to properly care for the children, a point he tried to get across in an e-mail: "This is a very poignant reminder to me that both Breanne and Christopher are very aware of Lori's several suicide attempts (once by overdose) and of her struggle with severe depression when she is under stress," he claimed. "Most people have become wise to her manipulation, but the children have grown up with this and do not recognize it for what it is. . . . I have 'complete support' from police commanders who have full knowledge of all of Lori's mental health issues and have discussed her suicidal behavior."

The next year proved incredibly difficult for Lori. Ken DeKleine was stalking her, harassing her, and continuously violating the protection order—violations he was never charged with. He was also intrusively curious about Lori's relationship with her therapist. DeKleine found creative ways of keeping tabs on his estranged wife. He was able to reroute Lori's e-mails to his computer, he read her diary, and he even hid a tape recorder in her backpack, all with the hope of catching her and the therapist together.

Unbelievably, when it came to the protection order, the judge added a provision to the order that still allowed Ken DeKleine to carry a gun so he could keep his job. Not that it really mattered; it appeared that the police department had no problem with DeKleine's marital problems. His fellow officers continuously turned a blind eye. After the murder, Holland police chief John Kruithoff defended his actions to the local newspaper: "If there would have been alarm signs, we would have done something," he claimed, apparently oblivious to the numerous calls to the department from Lori. "I didn't see there was a significant event that went on in his life that would have triggered this. Ken was a very talkative person, everyone's friend. He didn't suppress the fact he was having marital troubles. But, obviously, he suppressed something enough where he committed this."

Regardless of the boundless fear that Ken instilled in his wife, it was he who ultimately filed for divorce.

His daughter, Breanne, who was eighteen at the time of the murder, blasted her father in a letter shortly after the divorce was announced. "This shattered my world and my heart. . . . You would not cry in front of the family, for this family, that you created, invested in, laughed with, got angry at, and loved deeply for the past twenty years. Sitting at that table was like a business meeting. You were the CEO, telling your board of directors that the company had just gone under," Breanne wrote. "You were just that cold. . . . My mother put up with more than she should have, and more than most people would have. We've, I've, put up with your bull . . . for a long time, but this goes too far. . . . I love you, Daddy, with all my heart, and that will never go away. I am, however, more pissed off than I've ever been."

His children could clearly see that the man who was beginning to emerge after the divorce was not the man they knew to be their father. At this point, DeKleine was quickly unraveling from the pressures of the divorce and protection order. For this, there was no one else to blame but Lori, and she was all too aware. "You know, if I come up dead, if something happens to me, make sure Ken's investigated," she told a close friend.

It was apparent that Lori felt she had hit a brick wall and had nowhere to turn for help. She couldn't count on the police, the judge, her church, or the system to protect her. She had seemingly given up. A close friend of Lori's literally lashed out at everyone after Lori was found murdered—the system had failed: "DeKleine violated the PPO [personal protection order] three times! . . . Lori stood in front of Judge Van Allsburg sobbing, terrified that her husband has so much power, that the harassment from other officers is scaring her. . . . She was told by the judge that he had more power than Ken DeKleine, obviously that is proven false, Ken demonstrated greater power than Judge Van Allsburg now didn't he?" the friend scathed. "Lori was NOT supported by her church, although she spoke out about her fears. . . . The church officials reprimanded her, telling her that the PPO she had against Ken was interfering with their ministry. . . . Well I guess that interference is finally resolved now isn't it? . . . The church she continued to attend and the criminal justice system dedicated to serve her, hung her as much as her estranged husband did."

These are emotionally and powerfully charged words, but they are well deserved. After all, a woman who repeatedly begged for help from those who were supposed to protect her now lays dead. Her death was foretold numerous times by her own voice, but no one listened.

It had only been a few days earlier that Lori predicted her death to a friend. It was less than a month before Ken and Lori's final divorce hearing and battle over child custody that was set for February. On the afternoon of January 10 Christopher was home from school for several hours before walking downstairs and into the laundry room. There, lying on the floor with a rope around her neck, was his mother. He tried to move her and repeatedly yelled at her—to no avail. It was Christopher who made the emotional 911 call.

"I was in shock," he testified at his father's trial.

As officers arrived in droves, well aware that the home they were in was a fellow police officer's, it soon became startlingly clear that Lori was the victim of a homicide. It was obvious she had been strangled. Knowing the marital problems the couple faced, officers could look nowhere else other than at Ken De-Kleine. As investigators began to process the scene, an Ottawa County Sheriff's detective found a hiking boot print on the roof of Lori's car, which was parked in the garage. Noticing that the car was directly under an attic door, investigators searched the attic and found a bloody shirt belonging to Lori, a nylon strap, and a pair of black plastic medical gloves—the same kind as used by the Holland Police Department.

Less than twenty-four hours after Lori DeKleine's body was found, investigators arrived at the Holland Police Department to arrest Ken DeKleine and charge him with her murder. Ironically, at the time of his arrest, he was teaching a self-defense class and explaining how to put someone in a chokehold. Investigators from the Ottawa County Sheriff's Department noticed that the veteran officer had a prominent lip injury. When asked about it, DeKleine told them he had been trying to get a dutch oven from atop a high shelf when it supposedly fell, striking him in the lip. The injury required six stitches.

During the first two interviews, DeKleine vehemently denied having anything to do with Lori's death. Investigators asked him to explain the bloody shirt and nylon strap found in the attic. At that time, they omitted the fact they had found the black plastic gloves. DeKleine stated that he had been working on an air vent in 2006 and accidentally cut himself. He used the shirt to stop the bleeding. His explanation was simple enough, but DeKleine kept talking, and in the process he offered a key piece of evidence that was never brought to his attention in the first place. He added that the black gloves in the attic were from his son, who was there "playing with them." Investigators knew they now had DeKleine.

Shortly before his third interview with investigators, Ken DeKleine made a shocking confession to his brother, Keith, and sister-in-law, Jan. "I did this to Lori. I will be going to jail

Mugshot of Ken DeKleine.
Courtesy of Michigan Department of Corrections.

for a long time. . . . Do what you do best and love my children," he admitted.

Ken DeKleine attempted to justify the murder to his brother by telling him that he was tired of having to call people repeatedly to go over to Lori's and check on the children to make sure they were okay; he had to do this for his family. He went further and said that he would rather suffer in prison than see his children suffer with their mother, referring to Lori's alleged emotional problems.

Going into his third interview with investigators less than a day after the murder, Ken DeKleine confessed. Investigators listened intently as DeKleine gave them every detail of the murder. They were shocked at his coldhearted demeanor and utter lack of remorse.

DeKleine explained that in the very early morning hours of January 10 he went over to Lori's and gained entry to the garage by pulling up the main garage door. Stepping on top of Lori's car to hoist himself into the attic, DeKleine stayed there for almost seven hours in the frigid winter temperatures, waiting for his children to leave for school. At approximately 7:45 AM, after Christopher and Breanne had left the house, DeKleine came down from the attic and assaulted Lori in the kitchen.

DeKleine wrapped the nylon strap around Lori's neck and began to strangle her. And by his own admission, she fought desperately for her life—at one point biting his lip and causing it to bleed profusely all over him and Lori. According to Ken, Lori died on the kitchen floor. He stoically repeated Lori's last words before she died: "Please, think of the kids," she said. "I am thinking of the kids," he responded—as he brutally murdered their mother.

DeKleine then dragged Lori's body down to the laundry room before placing a rope around her neck to make it look like a suicide. He knew that there would be problems. His lip was bleeding heavily and blood had dropped onto the carpet. This evidence would later be tested and used to confirm his DNA. Taking Lori's bloody shirt, the nylon strap, and the black plastic gloves, he made his way back to the attic and hid the evidence under the insulation there.

Driving away from the house, he threw his blood-soaked sweatshirt out the window on the way to the hospital. There, he gave the dutch oven story to medical personnel when they questioned him about his lip injury. After leaving the hospital, DeKleine went through the McDonald's drive-through and treated himself to a chocolate milkshake before going to work at the Holland Police Department.

As the murder trial of Ken DeKleine began on July 8, 2008, no one could possibly predict what his defense would be after such a horrific and damning confession. The prosecution planned to call forty witnesses to testify against DeKleine. The prosecution presented a series of motives, one of those being Lori's alleged affair with her therapist.

Witnesses were presented who testified that DeKleine knew every aspect of Lori's life by secretly going through her diary and e-mails. A few days before the murder, DeKleine found an e-mail that Lori was scheduled to speak at a stalking and domestic abuse conference and tell her story—something that would further humiliate her husband within the community.

Lori's affair with her therapist was finally substantiated. He testified to being romantically involved with Lori and later had his license suspended for six months. If this was DeKleine's defense to the murder charge, it was quickly discarded when the prosecution presented a surprise witness—Richelle VanderWal.

VanderWal provided testimony, along with cell phone records, that she had been involved in a lengthy affair with DeKleine, starting as far back as to when he was still living with Lori. Even more damaging, a close friend of DeKleine's, Holland police reserve officer Brian Ehler, testified to a conversation he had with DeKleine almost two years prior.

During the conversation, Ehler claimed that DeKleine was somewhat obsessed with forensic science. Ehler commented to DeKleine that he didn't know why anyone would try and get away with murder considering how technically advanced forensic science is today. He then claimed that DeKleine matter-of-factly told him, "Strangling someone would be difficult to investigate." Furthermore, when Ehler visited DeKleine in jail and asked if there was anything he could've done to prevent the murder, DeKleine simply replied, "You can't beat yourself up about this. I knew what I was doing."

When the Ottawa County medical examiner testified regarding Lori's death, he explained that she certainly didn't die without pain. She had broken bones in her face, broken cartilage and bones in her neck, scrape marks on her feet from being dragged, and a head injury.

Perhaps the most powerful testimony came from DeKleine himself. Although he never actually testified on the witness stand, jurors were able to hear him coldly describe the horrific details of Lori's death—a complete lack of emotion in his voice—during the taped confession. He had written three disturbing letters to family members while in jail all claiming that he committed the murder to save the emotional well-being of the children. His own admission of guilt was utterly disturbing. "Yes, it was selfish in a lot of ways. I even feel guilty about how free I feel in so many ways," he wrote.

Ken DeKleine had absolutely no remorse.

Not surprisingly, his attorney didn't call a single witness. He only asked that the jury find DeKleine guilty of second-degree murder, as opposed to first. "You have before you on trial a man, I think, who was between a rock and a hard place. He was totally frustrated by what was going on and made a choice," DeKleine's attorney, Floyd Farmer, contended.

The jury wouldn't budge. After deliberating for only seventy-five minutes, Ken DeKleine was found guilty of first-degree murder and automatically sentenced to life in prison. He showed absolutely no emotion during the verdict and just smiled at his family members.

For those left behind in the DeKleine family, including Christopher and Breanne, it's difficult for a prudent person to understand the rationale behind Ken DeKleine's actions. The man who prosecuted him, Ottawa County prosecutor Ron Frantz, certainly didn't understand: "How in the world would it ever be under any circumstances in your children's best interest to murder their mother?"

CHAPTER 5

HE KILLED ONE OF HIS OWN

ROY KIPP
FORMER SHERIFF'S LIEUTENANT, COLLIER COUNTY, FLORIDA

The city played host to some of the most rich and famous in history. Harvey Firestone, Greta Garbo, and Hedy Lamarr were just a few of the celebrities who strolled along the beautiful, white sandy beaches of Naples, Florida. Tucked away in Florida's most southwest point in Collier County, the city boasts its weather to be "perfect." Known as Florida's Last Frontier, Collier County spreads over 1,276,160 acres of land and includes most of the everglades. But for several members of the Collier County Sheriff's Department, the events that stunned the community in the year 2000 opened their eyes to the dark side of this paradise.

These events were the ones surrounding the murder of their own sergeant, Jeffrey Klein, at the hands of their former lieutenant, Royal "Roy" Kipp, as well as the brutal murder of Kipp's wife, Sandra.

Roy Kipp proudly joined the ranks of the Collier County Sheriff's Department in 1981 when he was just twenty-three years old. Working diligently to rise through the chain of command, Kipp eventually made lieutenant. However, continuous problems seemed to follow him throughout his career, especially toward the end. While he was married to his first wife, Nancy, with whom he had two sons, Kipp's temper would almost always maintain a strong presence within the relationship. An amateur bodybuilder at one point, Roy Kipp first came under the scope of an internal investigation for allegations of steroid use.

His troubles were exacerbated in 1989 when Nancy came forward with allegations of severe verbal abuse and threats from Kipp. Describing her husband as jealous and verbally abusive, Nancy Kipp filed a complaint with the Collier County Sherriff's Department and obtained an order of protection prior to filing for divorce. The complaint merely resulted in the sheriff issuing Kipp a stern warning. Nancy and Roy Kipp's divorce was final in 1990.

If Kipp was distraught over the end of his marriage, he certainly didn't show it. He immediately resumed his womanizing lifestyle, eventually honing in on a petite twenty-six-year-old blonde named Sandra Baxley.

Sandra, "Sandy," worked as a customer service representative at North Collier Hospital in North Naples. Described by friends as friendly but somewhat naive, Sandra fell prey to Roy Kipp's charm and good looks and eventually married the seasoned police officer in 1991.

But what appeared to Sandra as a bright and stable future wasn't exactly the case. Less than a year after Roy and Sandy's wedding, Nancy Kipp filed another complaint against her ex-husband. In 1992, Nancy alleged that Roy had been threatening her and her new boyfriend. Regardless, Sandy ignored the complaint and continued in her marriage to Kipp, even giving birth to a daughter, Danielle. When Roy's problems at work began to escalate, the problems within his second marriage did as well.

Drinking excessively and becoming increasingly critical of Sandy, Kipp would frequently tell friends, "I got her from a trailer park—she'd be nothing without me." Kipp even tried to cut Sandy off from her own family. Her parents were never allowed to stay at the house but could visit for only short periods at a time.

The constant degrading from Kipp seemed to put, and keep, Sandy down. Years of verbal abuse can make the most confident women question their self-respect and perception. For Sandy, who wore braces and already had insecurity issues, the abuse from Kipp was overwhelming. During the last five years of their marriage, his verbal abuse escalated—as did his drinking.

By 1998, Kipp was supervising a police substation, but continuing his downward spiral. Several officers at the station, including a young sergeant named Jeffrey Klein, tried numerous times to help Kipp with his drinking problem. Their efforts proved fruitless. After a random drug test, Kipp tested positive for marijuana and was given the option to either resign or be fired. This disgraceful end to a prominent career did nothing to help Kipp's already crumbing marriage to Sandy.

At the end of his career, Sandy had decidedly had enough of her husband's tirades and substance abuse. Emerging from the shell that kept her hidden for years, Sandy had her braces taken off and enrolled in college courses to ensure her and Danielle's future would be solid. Sandy began to feel better about her appearance and ultimately began a relationship with Collier County Sheriff's Sergeant Jeffrey Klein.

Klein, age thirty-five, was an air force veteran who joined

the sheriff's department in 1993. A hard worker who was respected by his co-workers, Klein quickly attained the rank of sergeant and had hopes of commanding the marine patrol. He was described as a rising star within the department.

Roy immediately suspected his wife was having an affair. After his law enforcement certificate was revoked by the state, Kipp obtained a job at an elevator company in Sarasota. Having to live there part-time in an apartment with other employees, Kipp began to sense something wrong in his marriage. In late April 2000, Kipp called Sandy's sister, Wendy Poston, and demanded that she tell him whom Sandy was seeing. "If I ever catch her with another man, I'll kill her," Kipp informed Wendy.

Wendy denied having any knowledge of an affair but later told detectives that Sandy frequently stated how Kipp was "obsessed" with her. He even went so far as to put mirrors up around the bathroom so he could watch her shower.

Seemingly undaunted by Kipp's threats, Sandy secretly rented an apartment in May 2000. Sandy's doctor, Robert Tober, told Sandy about a few Transient Nursing Apartments she could apply for. He was aware of the situation between Sandy and Kipp, later testifying that Sandy confided in him about a shoving match that she and Kipp had gotten in, along with accounts of his alcoholism and verbal abuse. Sandy was convinced that she would never be able to obtain her degree while still living with Kipp.

Sandy was leaving Roy Kipp for good and he was now convinced—without a doubt—that she was cheating on him. When she informed Roy that she was leaving on May 19, he was furious, specifically because Sandy refused to tell Kipp where her new apartment was. As angry as he was, Kipp begged and pleaded for Sandy to stay. She refused.

The thought of Kipp finding her plagued Sandy's mind, a

thought she relayed to her sister. "If he shows up, I just won't let him in," Sandy told her sibling.

Unfortunately, Sandy Kipp never had the choice. On Saturday, May 20, 2000, Sandy stopped by her former home to visit her daughter. Sandy had left Danielle with Kipp while she moved and got settled in. That night, Jeff Klein visited Sandy in her new apartment while Kipp seethed at home. At approximately 10:11 PM, Kipp called Sandy's apartment and received no answer. As his daughter slept in her bedroom, Kipp got into his truck and made the six-minute drive to Sandy's new apartment. How Kipp found the address remains unknown.

Enraged at his wife's newfound freedom and lover, Kipp cut the phone lines to the apartment when he first arrived. Kipp then went to the rear lanai and saw Sandy and Klein on the couch. He later testified that Sandy was in her underwear and Klein was pulling his pants up. Cutting the screen to gain entry, Kipp entered the apartment and shot Klein seven times as he stood in the master bedroom doorway. He then shot Sandy once in the back. It was Roy Kipp's defense that Klein first pulled a gun on him and that he shot back in self-defense. Sandy lay on the front stoop of her new home, apparently trying to get away. Her cordless phone was mere inches from her hand.

Neighbors in the complex heard a loud commotion of voices and what they thought were fireworks. No one bothered to call the police.

After committing the brutal and senseless murders, Kipp drove back to his home and woke up his daughter. Just before 11:30 PM, Kipp drove his daughter to his brother's home and asked him to babysit. While there, Kipp called an aunt and asked to borrow her car, stating, "The deputies will recognize my truck."

Back at the scene of the crime, the Collier County sheriff's deputies who first arrived at the scene were thinking of nothing but the gruesome massacre that lay before them. It took some time to find the bodies. After receiving the 911 call from Pete Lewkowicz, a neighbor, the deputies checked several addresses first in an attempt to find Sandy and Jeff.

Sandy's new white townhouse had two sets of stairs in front: one leading to the landing of the upstairs unit, and the other, consisting of only three steps, leading to the landing of Sandy's unit. This was where the deputies found Sandy, wearing a two-piece negligee and jewelry, sprawled out and facedown. Rigor and livor mortis were already present, indicating that she had been dead for at least two hours. Her head, farthest from the door, was turned to the left. Her right knee was bent, and her left knee was tucked under her torso. Her face and right hand were covered in dried blood. The deputies noted the portable phone inches from her hand, but they took exceptional notice of the 9 mm cartridge shell that was found on the welcome mat a few feet away—an eerie foreshadowing of what waited for them inside.

As they entered through the front doorway, they noted another 9 mm shell just inside on the floor. Looking around the quaint and modern townhouse, deputies saw that a lamp was knocked from a coffee table and lay broken on the floor. Walking toward the sliding-glass doors that led to the lanai, the place that Kipp had clearly made entry, they noted another shell behind the loveseat where the dead couple had sat just hours before. The back of the loveseat faced the sliding-glass doors. Next to the couch was a small staircase, consisting of six steps, which led to a hallway where the bedrooms were. Three more shell casings were found at the base of the steps.

As the deputies entered the hallway, they were heartsick to see one of their own sergeants lying in the entrance of the spare bedroom, riddled with bullets. Wearing only a hospital scrub shirt and shorts, Klein unquestionably took the brunt of Kipp's rage. Klein's legs extended into the bedroom and his face rested on the door jamb. He had numerous gunshot wounds including one in the back and one to the head. Paint chips, wood, and other debris were scattered around the area of Klein's body and throughout his hair. A visible bullet hole was noted just above his head, in the doorframe. This particular bullet traveled through the bed and toward the farthest wall, taking a clump of Klein's hair with it. Three shell casings were in plain view next to Klein's head.

Deputies entered the master bedroom and found Klein's Collier County deputy shirt hanging in the closet and a caller ID box next to the bed. This was when they realized that Roy Kipp had been one of the last callers to the residence. After obtaining a description of Roy's truck from Pete Lewkowicz, Roy was found outside his apartment in Sarasota and arrested at approximately 5:15 AM—the morning after the murders. After a warrant was issued for Kipp in connection with the murders, detectives from Collier County eventually brought him in for questioning at around noon. Kipp's own underlying admissions would make for a nightmarish defense. "I was going to make it easy and turn myself in," he told detectives. "I should not have stopped. I should have just kept going; the only reason I'm here is because I stopped."

Some detectives interpreted Kipp's statements as a suicide threat, a wish that he would have finished himself off immediately following the murders. Others thought it was an intricate plan to flee the state. Kipp further requested that detectives not "tear his house apart," because "you won't find anything in there."

By 8:45 PM, on May 21, 2000, Roy Kipp was officially served his arrest warrants charging him with two counts of aggravated murder. He now faced the death penalty if convicted.

The following day, a search warrant was executed on

Kipp's truck. A pair of boat shoes, whose treads matched those found at the murder scene, were found behind the driver's seat, along with a hair fiber on the sole of the right shoe.

However, what would seem like an airtight murder case wasn't. Kipp's defense attorneys, public defenders Robert Jacobs II and Michael Orlando, made a strong attempt to prove that he committed the murder during the "heat of passion," a defense that would drop the charge to involuntary manslaughter. They also argued police misconduct, stating that responding officers tainted evidence at the scene in an attempt to protect Jeff Klein who, in their opinion, fired the first shots at Kipp. Klein shot at Kipp first, the defense maintained, and the officers placed Klein's gun back inside his truck to protect him. Since the murder weapon was never found, and Klein also carried a 9 mm handgun, they argued that the shots could have come from either gun—proving their theory correct. The responding deputies even turned over another gun found in Jeff Klein's truck, a .40-caliber pistol, to Klein's family—instead of logging it into evidence. Furthermore, the deputy who found Klein's gun inside the truck didn't document it until almost eleven months after the murders.

Kipp's defense even tried the insanity card briefly, claiming that Kipp suffered post-traumatic stress disorder immediately following the murders and was being watched for signs of suicide. Kipp's own psychiatrist testified that Kipp was unfit to stand trial; however, the judge disagreed and the proceedings commenced.

The case brought such overwhelming publicity that it became one of the first murder trials to succeed in a venue change in years. The trial was held in Charlotte County.

Despite the defense's statements, the prosecution presented some compelling evidence against Kipp. On the list of witnesses the prosecution planned to call were Kipp's own brothers, Billy and Scott. During the investigation it was learned that after Kipp went to his parents' home and called his aunt, his brothers were seen by Scott's girlfriend, Lisa Patner, taking something from behind the dryer in the garage. They placed the item, wrapped in a cloth, inside her backpack. The three of them drove to the Gulf of Mexico near Ft. Myers. Lisa testified that she stayed inside the car and watched as the two men walked with the unidentified object to a bridge over the water. When they returned, they had nothing in their hands but an empty cloth. The prosecution maintained that both men disposed of the murder weapon that night to aid their troubled brother. The area under the bridge was searched extensively by law enforcement dive teams, but no weapon was ever found.

Collier County Deputy Chief Medical Examiner Dr. Manfred Borges Jr. refuted the defense's claim of police misconduct. He maintained that Jeffrey Klein's body was already suffering from rigor mortis by the time responding officers arrived. Had they taken the gun from him and gotten rid of it, the outline of the gun would have surely shown on his hand. It did not.

Although Danielle Kipp did not testify, she was questioned by investigating officers about her account of the night of the murders. She maintained she never showed her father where Sandy lived and had no idea how he found the apartment.

Perhaps some of the most damaging testimony came from twelve-year-old Shannon Hagenbuch, one of Sandy's neighbors. She claimed that on the night of the murders she was watching television in her bedroom. After hearing what she thought was two gunshots, she looked out her bedroom window and saw a man fitting Kipp's description running across the parking lot. Hagenbuch watched as the man, who was wearing a white shirt and blue jeans, got inside a white truck and sped off. She told her mother about the incident; however, the police were never called.

The defense continued to fire back at witnesses, refuting their claims, and even telling the jury that the telephone company had been at the complex and had inadvertently cut the phone wires—not Kipp.

Historically, in most murder cases the defendant doesn't take the witness stand. But, when it comes to police officers, their arrogance supersedes anything else. Like some other officers in this book, Kipp took the stand in his own defense. Appearing tearful and apologetic, Kipp maintained that Sandy told him she was being followed recently, and he was worried. When he couldn't get ahold of her, he decided it best to go see if she was okay. He also maintained that he and Sandy's separation wasn't permanent; they were going to get back together when she finished school. He further added that when he went to the apartment and saw her on the couch with Klein, he became enraged and confronted the couple. Klein shot at him first. In self-defense, Kipp shot back at Klein, but Sandy ran in front of him, getting caught in the cross fire.

The defense then continued to present witnesses who were close with the Kipps who testified to the fact that they were a loving couple with normal problems. These witnesses claimed that they never sensed the possibility of violence between the two.

However, the medical examiner testified that Sandy Kipp had not only a gunshot wound to her upper back but also blunt force injury to her forehead, left buttock, and knee. Klein had gunshot wounds to his lower extremities, abdomen, chest, back, and head. The medical examiner maintained that Klein was first shot in the back, which completely shredded Kipp's self-defense claim.

Not only was Kipp incensed over the fact that his wife would have an affair, but some believe that the fact it was with one of his own law enforcement "brothers" is what sent him completely over the edge. Nonetheless, without a murder weapon, and with a strong case by the defense, the jury simply didn't buy it. Although they spared his life, Roy Kipp was ultimately found guilty of two counts of aggravated murder and sentenced to life in prison.

With her mother dead and her father in prison, it is Danielle Kipp who is surely paying the price for the horrific events that occurred that fateful night.

CHAPTER 6

I WAS PLAYING BASKETBALL

DAVID CAMM
STATE TROOPER, INDIANA STATE POLICE

He was as arrogant and pompous as anyone could be. This was a frequent description of former Indiana State Trooper David Camm. Only in his later years, after becoming a trooper, would he be forever branded with that reputation—a well-deserved reputation. Regardless, no one could have possibly predicted that labeling David as a self-righteous "ladies man" would also include with that his potential to commit murder. However, the David Camm who was ultimately charged and convicted of viciously murdering his entire family was not the man who most people knew.

Growing up, David Camm was described as a typical midwestern boy. God fearing, with a love of fixing cars, David was no different than most of the teenagers in the small town of New Albany, Indiana. One of four children born to Don and Susie Camm, David was undeniably "the quietest." Despite his insecurities, David Camm proved to be a formidable athlete in high school, excelling mainly in basketball. Suffering from debilitating migraines that plagued the Camm family, David fought and pulled through high school, earning average grades and involving himself with a nice young local girl who would soon become his girlfriend—Tammy Zimmerman.

Life was good for David Camm—he had his hopes set on becoming a minister in his family's church. Unfortunately, those hopes were shattered soon after graduation when he learned that Tammy was pregnant. Working at the time as a car mechanic, David had no other option but to marry Tammy. Their daughter, Whitney, was born in February 1983.

Tammy and David Camm remained in New Albany near his large family—several of whom were former police officers. Realizing that he would be unable to support his new family working on cars, David began expressing an interest in becoming a law enforcement officer.

Joining the New Albany Police Department as an auxiliary police officer, David soon set his sights on becoming part of the Indiana State Police. It would take several years for David to attend the requisite college courses while continuing to work as a mechanic and auxiliary officer until he would finally be accepted as a state trooper. Unfortunately for David and Tammy, it was already too late. Like many other young couples, they found that they were much too young to make the marriage work and ultimately separated. They shared custody of Whitney for a while until Tammy could get on her feet. The couple planned to eventually remarry. However, it was David's mother, Susie, who found herself watching Whitney the most. David was too busy trying to achieve his goal of becoming a state police officer. David and Tammy Camm's divorce became final in April 1986.

For the next two years, David applied diligently to various police departments as a full-time officer while he waited to hear from the Indiana State Police. It was in 1988 that he met a woman who he described as "the love of my life," Kimberly Renn.

Set up on a blind date, David and Kim were amused to find out they had attended the same high school, New Albany— Kim was a year younger than David, but they never met each other until their first date.

Like David, Kim Renn was a shy, quiet person. However, unlike David, Kim excelled in school. She earned excellent grades, was a cheerleader, and was well liked among her friends and teachers. Kim and David even attended the same college together, unbeknownst to them. As David slowly worked his way through police administration courses, Kim plowed through various accounting courses.

After graduating, Kim moved quickly through the corporate world, having no problem landing well-paying jobs at top insurance companies. In the meantime, her relationship with David Camm continued to blossom. Both families welcomed each other, and it was only a matter of time before David proposed. However, there was to be a slight string attached: Catholic-raised Kim would have to convert to become a Protestant, like David. Ignoring the mild protest of her family, Kim did this without giving it a second thought. She wanted nothing more than to marry David Camm.

Welcoming Whitney with open arms, Kim's life was a fairytale made even better in 1989 when David received an interview with the state police the week of their wedding. The wedding was as close to perfect as anyone could describe. The ceremony was performed by David's uncle, Reverend Leland Lockhart, and was followed by a weeklong vacation in Florida with David's older brother, Donnie.

After they moved into their first apartment in New Albany, David was officially offered a job with the Indiana State

Police—all of his dreams had come true and his hard work had finally paid off. He was now a full-time state trooper.

"He wanted to reach out. He looked for a way to help, he stepped up to the plate," David's sister, Julie, explained.

Even though Kim was making substantially more money than David, he was proud of his job and uniform. He consistently impressed his superiors with his dedication and hard work on the job. During his rookie years, he proved to be an accomplished marksman and expert with guns, earning him a coveted spot on the state's SWAT team. These were the years when that Trooper David Camm began to emerge slowly from the shell that kept the quiet, likable, Christian man hidden for the majority of his life. What emerged, to some, could only be described as Satan himself.

It's no secret throughout the inner sanctums of law enforcement that a powerful distraction lurks on every street corner, in every coffee shop, convenience store, domestic call, and dispatch center. The distraction poses itself in the form of a young, attractive female—also known as a cop groupie. Also referred to as "badge bunnies," "cop chasers," and other raunchy police jargon, these particular women are determined and defiant. Some will even go as far as speeding on purpose in front of a particular officer with the hopes he will pull her over and acquire her phone number. Most groupies pay no mind to the fact that an officer is married, or has children, or whether he's on duty. It is their sole purpose to walk among the cops and, hopefully, to marry one. It's all about the uniform. Some may find this type of lifestyle odd; however, most police officers, on any given day (no matter what they look like), could easily acquire two to three phone numbers from females in one eight-hour shift. In fact, police officers often find themselves keeping score among each other, determining which officer rises to the rank of the ultimate "stud" among the groupies. It's an ongoing game.

David Camm quickly learned that when it came to finding women, putting his trooper uniform on was like Christmas morning. His good looks only magnified this. They were everywhere, ready and willing, and David was only too eager to accommodate. The shy, quiet kid from New Albany was becoming a distant memory to his family, friends, co-workers, and most important, his wife.

"He was very flirty," explained Andrea Craig, a police dispatcher who worked with David. "He was always trying to rub my feet underneath the radio console. He would ask me several times if I wanted to get together, hook up."

After only two years on the job, David was promoted to the position of field training officer (FTO). A sought-after position in most law enforcement agencies, an FTO trains new rookies at an overtime rate. It was one of David's first trainees, Trooper Shelley Romero, who landed him in the throes of a full-blown extramarital affair. Unlike the previous random acts of sex he had had in the backseat of his cruiser, Shelley Romero was different. According to her testimony during David Camm's murder trial, their relationship lasted for almost two years, even surpassing the birth of David and Kim's first child, Bradley.

"He was very trusting, very loyal, extremely honest," Romero explained in a CBS News documentary for the show *48 Hours*. "He could be trusted with anything, just one of the most upstanding people you would ever fathom in your life."

But, unknown to Shelley Romero, she wasn't the only woman David had his eye on. There were countless other indiscretions on his part, but it was the women with whom David had distinct emotional and sexual relationships who brought his former paramours into the thick of his murder trial, ultimately leading to his conviction.

"It was given he was going to hit on you," Romero

explained further. "He was going to propose an innocent kind of liaison or something like that."

Stephanie McCarty led those women with what was, undoubtedly, the most powerful testimony regarding David's character and his loyalty to his wife and family. McCarty was a personal trainer at the gym where David exercised frequently. They met and became "friends" in 1991 while David was working out at the gym. At the time, Stephanie was deeply involved with someone else. However, David's relationship with her turned in 1994 when Stephanie and her boyfriend broke up. Stephanie knew that David was married, but she described him as being very unhappy and frequently speaking of divorce.

David fell hard for Stephanie. They began an intense relationship that David had no intention of hiding. He paraded Stephanie around town, in front of friends and co-workers, flagrantly showing the ultimate disrespect toward his wife and toddler son. Things came to an abrupt halt when Kim almost caught Stephanie inside the Camm home. Whether sensing something awry or giving into a woman's strong sense of intuition regarding her marriage, Kim Camm informed David that night that she was five weeks pregnant. Feeling trapped and miserable, David called Stephanie with the news. Now faced with the notion that any type of relationship with David was unattainable, Stephanie called it quits.

It didn't last. Stephanie eventually went back to David, and when Kim, almost five months pregnant and suspecting something wrong with the marriage, confronted David, he confessed to the relationship. "I no longer want to be married to you. I'm in love with someone else," David later testified that he told Kim.

Reacting as any woman would, Kim left David and went to her mother's, giving strict orders for David to find somewhere else to live. This was the first time that local law enforcement and David's co-workers got a view of his temper.

Shortly after Kim left, David phoned his mother, explained the situation, and asked to stay with her for a while. Susie Camm refused, still angry at David's infidelity. While on the phone with his mother, David flew into a vicious rage—tearing up his kitchen, breaking things, and putting holes in the walls. Terrified, Susie called David's co-workers to settle him down.

Eventually, Kim and David sold their home and moved into separate apartments—David's happened to be next door to Stephanie McCarty. Throughout their short relationship, David kept his distance from his own family, who was helping Kim on a daily basis. David never even stayed at the hospital the day his daughter, Jill, was born—February 28, 1995. Now a single mother to a newborn baby and a two-year-old toddler, Kim was feeling emotionally and physically exhausted, receiving seemingly no help from David. His family began to pressure him to leave Stephanie and go back to Kim—he vehemently refused.

However, after meeting with an ex-boyfriend one night, Stephanie found David waiting for her outside their apartment building. Angry that she went to see her ex, David produced a handgun and put it to his chest, telling her he could kill himself if he wanted. Already ill at ease with the birth of Jill, Stephanie decidedly had enough of David Camm and ended their relationship.

Within hours of the breakup, David was on the phone with Kim, asking her to take him back. To the family's astonishment, Kim agreed.

Rebuilding their tattered lives as a family, David and Kim built a new home on Lockhart Road, named after David's relatives; no one but family lived on the road. Kim was looking forward to putting the past behind them, while raising their two children around the people who had always supported her the most. David promised his family, Kim, and God that he was a changed man, acknowledging that he'd made a horrible mistake and vowing never to let it happen again.

His promise was short-lived. His indiscretions quickly resumed, soon including a young woman who he had pulled over for speeding—Michelle Voyles. After exchanging phone numbers, Michelle met David a few days later while he was on duty. After engaging in sexual intercourse inside his cruiser, Michelle and David began a six-month relationship that consisted of sex two to three times a week.

A key piece of testimony during David's trial came when Michelle admitted that she shaved off her pubic hair—at David's request. As they were beginning to have sex again, she testified that David made a strange comment: "Now, if I think I can do this without thinking I'm fucking a six-year-old . . . " he said to her.

Incredibly, Michelle maintained that throughout their relationship she never knew that David Camm was married. Only after being told this by a friend did Michelle finally break up with David. According to the women who knew him and the friends who worked with him daily, David never wore his wedding ring, nor did he speak much about his wife.

During his relationship with Michelle, David also was involved with a local real estate agent, Lisa Korfhage. But, unlike with Michelle, David got Lisa's attention in a way that portrayed him as a maniacal, manipulative, and terrorizing man. After he pulled her over for expired license plates and they exchanged numbers, Lisa testified that she received a series of disturbing anonymous phone calls later that night. She became so terrified that she contacted the state police. It was David Camm who responded to her home, playing the role of the "white knight," helping her feel safe. At the suggestion of her fiancé, Lisa tape-recorded another phone call that came in the following morning. The mysterious caller apologized for making her so upset the night before but, again, didn't identify himself. The only person who could have known how upset she was would be David Camm—something Lisa didn't consider at the time. Furthermore, it was David Camm who returned to Lisa's home to take the tape as evidence.

Adding a layer of oddity to the situation, Lisa's fiancé, a fireman, was home when David arrived, and they quickly formed a friendship. Lisa was introduced to Kim, and the four adults frequently did things together. However, neither Lisa's fiancé nor Kim Camm was aware of the sexual relationship going on between Lisa and David. Lisa ended her relationship with David when she was married.

With his extracurricular activities and full-time job, David was rarely around to assume his role as father and husband. During the rare times he was at home, the attention was usually focused on him. Kim carried the weight of the world on her shoulders—she cared for the kids, shuffling them between school and activities; she cared for their home; and she worked a full-time job making twice as much as David did. Her salary seemed to be a touchy issue for David. According to Kim's family members, Kim never mentioned the salary situation, as it didn't seem to bother her. David, however, was very bothered.

During a conversation with Beth Minnicus, a police dispatcher, he repeatedly complained about Kim. Beth testified, "He would call her names like, 'bitch.'"

Throughout the later years of his career, David became increasingly bitter toward the Indiana State Police. After an incident where excessive use of force was claimed, David felt he was being offered up as the sacrificial lamb by his superiors. Finally, in May 2000, David Camm officially resigned as a trooper, taking a job at the company owned by his uncle, Sam Lockhart—United Dynamics.

Making more money, and with normal hours, David proved himself to be a top employee in his uncle's eyes. However, things in the Camm home were becoming increasingly tense. With David still involved in sexual trysts with numerous women, a new concern for Kim Camm slowly made its way to the surface.

The same month David began his new job, Kim noticed a growing rash on her five-year-old daughter's, Jill's, vaginal area. Jill was also complaining of soreness. According to Helen Schroeder, a friend of Kim's, Jill was crying and holding her vaginal area one night at dance class. The little girl was clearly in a great amount of pain, and Helen offered to take Jill to the bathroom, but Jill refused. Kim had left to pick up her son, Brad, and Helen informed Kim upon her return.

Just a few weeks prior to the incident at dance class, Janice Renn, Kim's mother, testified to seeing a bad case of "diaper rash" on Jill's vaginal area. Janice told Kim at that time if the rash didn't clear up in a few days she should take Jill to the doctor. Nonetheless, Kim Camm was seemingly too exhausted to pay attention. Or was she?

Even though David was working normal hours, he rarely helped Kim with anything. Her day started in the early morning hours and ended late. In the late evenings she would return home after picking the children up from their sport activities or dance class, and David would merely be sitting at his computer, relaxing—a term completely foreign to Kim Camm. After putting the children to bed, Kim would then prepare her husband's work clothes for the next day, washing and ironing them. Several times a week, Kim didn't go to bed until 11:00 PM.

All the while, David continued to bask in his newfound career and string of girlfriends.

During the summer of 2000, David and Kim significantly increased their life insurance policies. David's brother Daniel, an employee of Nationwide in Florida, put together the policies for the couple, which named David Camm a primary beneficiary for Kim and the children.

It was in the first few weeks of September 2000 that Kim's friend Marcy McLeod received a strange phone call from her. Marcy lived in Florida, and Kim was asking if she and the kids could come for a visit. Kim was not acting like herself. "She was very preoccupied and depressed," Marcy testified.

Kim told Marcy, "History is repeating itself," but declined to elaborate. Marcy assumed that meant David was having another affair. Unfortunately, she never had the chance to speak to Kim Camm again to find out.

September 28, 2000, started out like most days in the Camm family. However, no one could have ever predicted how badly it would end. Kim did her usual running around after work, shuffling the kids to their sporting events, while David had—what he later described as—an unusually busy day at United Dynamics. Since David had begun playing in a basketball league, he would be home later that night.

At 7:00 PM, David left his house to attend a basketball game two miles away. At the same time, Kim and the children were just leaving swimming practice to come home. At 7:35, a neighbor witnessed Kim's black Ford Bronco pulling into the driveway of the Camm residence. What occurred from that point on is highly debated by David Camm and his family.

According to statements given by David to detectives, he was at the gym playing his usual basketball games. At one point, David claimed his muscles were sore so he sat out for a while. This was at approximately 8:10. Eleven people testified that David was, in fact, at the game. At 8:45, the group took another break and Sam Lockhart held a sideline meeting for his United Dynamic employees, which included David. The group called it a night at 9:15.

As David arrived home, he saw the garage door open, a door Kim usually shut. Walking into the garage, David saw a body lying on the floor and immediately mistook it for his daughter, Jill.

"She'd had pants or a skirt on. They'd been ripped off," David claimed. "But I first saw her there with that black, whatever she had on—it looked like Jill's dancing outfit."

After realizing it was Kim, and seeing a large pool of blood trailing out of the garage, he thought that maybe Kim had slipped and hit her head. With his thoughts racing to Jill and Brad, David looked inside the vehicle and saw his children. While providing this statement, David added an extremely odd observation: "Because of where they were positioned in the car I knew that they were trying to get away," he claimed. "I know they were trying to hide because they were both ducked down in corners."

He went further, "And then I saw them I checked Jill and she was gone. And then Brad was still kind of warm and somewhat limber, and I thought, 'maybe he's got a chance.' And I pulled his butt out of there and tried to do CPR on him. I take that back. In between, before I pulled Brad out—you know, the funny thing about it is, guys, I was thinking so clear. I didn't get rattled, I didn't go nuts. I was thinking so definite 'cause I knew I needed to call somebody."

At that point, David went inside his residence and made the following call to the Indiana State Police: a call that came in at approximately 9:30 PM. For a reason he cited as "being professional," David didn't call 911—a call that would have rang into the New Albany Police Department, a department that was more than three times closer than the state police was.

    Dispatcher: Indiana State Police radio control. This is Patrice, may I help you?

Camm: Patrice, this is Dave Camm, let me talk to post command right now.

Dispatcher: OK, he's on the other line.

Camm: Right now! Let me talk to him right now.

Dispatcher: OK, hold on.

Post Commander (Andrew Lee): Dave?

Camm: Get everybody out here to my house now!

Post Commander: OK. All right.

Camm: My wife and my kids are dead! Get everybody out here to my house!

Dispatcher: (Go to Dave Camm's house. Now.) OK, David, we've got people on the way, OK?

Camm: Get everybody out here!

Post Commander: Calm down. Everything's going to be OK, all right. We're going to get . . .

Camm: Everything's not OK, get everybody out here!

Post Commander: They're coming. (Go to Dave Camm's house now!)

Camm: [unintelligible]

Post Commander: Do you know what happened, David?

Camm: No! God—I just got home from playing basketball. Oh my God, what am I gonna do? [unintelligible]

Post Commander: Listen, I'm going to let you talk to Patrice, while I get people coming.

Camm: I've got to go across the street, I've got to get some help!

Post Commander: OK, David, do you need an ambulance?

Camm: I've got to go across the street to my parents' house!

Post Commander: Do you need an ambulance?

Camm: Get everybody out here!

Post Commander: I am. Do you need an ambulance?
Camm: I've got to go!
Dispatcher: Dave? [ringing sound] He hung up.

The first two state troopers pulled up to the Camm residence at 9:45 PM. When later asked about why he called the state police, David responded with another odd statement: "I ran, picked up the phone, thought about dialing 911, didn't want to call the sheriff's department, figured I'd get some stupid ding-y dispatcher."

Kim Camm had been shot in the head and died on the garage floor. Brad Camm had been shot in the left shoulder, and Jill Camm had been shot in the forehead—both children had died in the backseat. By initial observations, it appeared that Brad Camm was trying to escape to the backseat when he was shot.

After making the emergency call, David claims he went back out into the garage and pulled Brad out of the car, thinking he could save his son with several attempts at CPR. It was too late—Brad Camm was already dead. David then ran screaming to his grandfather's home, screaming that someone had killed his wife and kids. David's uncle, Nelson Lockhart, accompanied David back to the horrific crime scene to wait for the troopers to arrive. By then, David was completely inconsolable—or so he appeared.

The detectives and prosecutors in the case painted a completely different picture regarding the events of September 28, 2000. They maintained that sometime during the day Jill Camm confessed to Kim that she was being sexually molested by David. At approximately 7:30 PM, David left the basketball game, unnoticed, making the two-mile drive home and arriving shortly after Kim and the children. Not expecting David, and in the throes of emotional turmoil, they contend

Kim confronted David with the molestation allegation. At that point, David completely snapped. Grabbing a gun, he shot Kim in the head before walking over to the passenger side of the Bronco. Seeing a monster in the image of his father, Brad Camm desperately tried to climb into the backseat before being shot. Doctors believe Brad would have lived had his wounds been treated immediately following the shooting. They also theorize that he would have been awake to see David walk to the other side of the car and shoot Jill Camm in the head.

No weapon was found at the scene, but another crucial piece of evidence confiscated was a sweatshirt with the word "backbone" written on it. The deciding factor to arrest David Camm for the murders of his family came in the form of DNA found on his T-shirt—Jill Camm's DNA. Not only was it DNA, but there was a high-velocity blood spatter that could have only come from the shooter or someone standing close by when the shooting occurred. David Camm was officially arrested and charged for the murder of his wife and children.

During the trial, the prosecution paraded in the numerous lovers of David Camm, presenting them in front of the jury, in hopes of creating an unlikable character. They presented experts who testified that the high-velocity blood spatter could only come from someone present at the scene of the crime. However, the defense put forth a compelling case, citing the fact that the DNA found on the "backbone" sweatshirt was found to be unknown. This same unknown DNA was also found on Kim and Brad Camm's pants. The defense claimed this was hardened factual evidence that someone else committed this brutal, violent act.

Evidently, the jurors didn't buy it. But their decision didn't come easy. There were several instances when the jurors didn't believe they'd be able to reach a unanimous decision and even contemplated leaving it as a "hung jury." Subsequently, the last juror holding out finally gave, and David Camm was convicted of three counts of murder and sentenced to 195 years in prison.

His family was astonished. They had provided evidence to the defense that shot holes all through the prosecution's theory—specifically, the prosecution's presentation of the Camms' phone records. In the phone records, a phone call was made from the Camm home at approximately 7:19 PM, a time that David and his eleven witnesses say he was playing basketball. The prosecution affirmed that this proved David had snuck out of the game and was at home. The eleven witnesses' testimony was scattered and contradictory. No one could really say for sure they noticed if David was gone or not.

However, David's uncle, Sam Lockhart, investigated further and found the phone company had made a mistake with the time zone—the call had really been made at 6:19 PM. This was acknowledged by the phone company but remained inconsequential to the jurors. They still felt he was guilty.

The Renn family felt that justice had been served. They had long disassociated themselves from the Camm and Lockhart families, believing in David's guilt. During the sentencing phase, Kim's mother, Janice Renn, didn't mince words while addressing David: "Since the night of September 28, 2000, I have felt mostly emptiness and pain. My pain came when I think about the brutal way they died, how scared they must have been."

But what the Renn family thought was closure and a time to grieve was only the beginning. On August 10, 2004, the Indiana Court of Appeals overturned David Camm's conviction, claiming the testimony of David's various lovers should not have been admitted into the trial. "The trial court abused its discretion in allowing the State to introduce evidence of Camm's adulterous conduct. There was no evidence that David Camm was having an affair at the time the murders occurred," the court claimed.

After denying various appeals by the state, who refiled murder charges against David, the court released him on a $20,000 cash bond in January 2005. After almost five years in prison, he was now a free man. At that time, his retrial was scheduled for August 2005, a date that would certainly change.

In March 2005, the DNA found on the "backbone" sweat-shirt and on Kim and Brad Camm finally came back with a match—a former New Albany resident and convicted crim-inal, Charles Boney.

The Camm family was ecstatic believing all charges against David would be dropped. They learned that Boney worked at the same church Kim did and had a history of attacking women.

Brought in by investigators for intense questioning, Boney eventually admitted to being paid by David Camm to provide the gun that was used in the murders. In fact, fibers from the carpet in David's bedroom were found on the sweatshirt, indi-cating the gun had been wrapped in the sweatshirt and hidden in David's bedroom for several days prior to the murders.

According to Boney, David pulled the trigger, believing that Kim was going to leave him. Boney admitted to being present at the murders and claimed that he had taken Kim's shoes and placed them on the top of the Bronco afterward, but he denied taking part in the actual killings. David claimed Boney's con-fession "outrageous," referring to him as a child molester and murderer. David maintains he never knew Charles Boney.

However, the prosecution claimed that there were too many consistencies in both Camm's and Boney's stories. Murder charges were refiled against both men, with additional charges of conspiracy tacked on as well. David Camm was picked up and put back into jail on the new charges.

On March 4, 2006, David Camm was again found guilty of the murders of his wife and children. Charles Boney was convicted in January 2006 and sentenced to life in prison.

Unfortunately, for the Renn family, the case may never truly be over. David Camm's attorneys have filed another appeal and are waiting on a decision from the court.

CHAPTER 7

NO ONE WOULD LISTEN

KENT McGOWEN
DEPUTY SHERIFF, HARRIS COUNTY (TEXAS) SHERIFF'S DEPARTMENT

"**W**henever there was a personnel problem, a 'problem child' as we called them, I would say, 'How did this moron get into the system?'"

A damning statement made to the Houston press by a close associate of the Harris County (Texas) Sheriff's Department. He was refering to sheriff's deputy, and convicted murderer, Joseph Kent McGowen. Certainly a justifiable observation, the thoughts of those wondering how McGowen skirted through so many law enforcement agencies echo similar characters within the pages of this book. To ask the question "Exactly, how does a man go through three law enforcement agencies, getting fired from two, leaving on a bad note from the third, and ultimately get rehired at a fourth?" may very well be a common denominator of police officers who chose to use their badge as a means to commit murder. Kent McGowen was no different. He displayed the same type of narcissistic arrogance that is frequently seen in these rogue officers.

A former desk sergeant at the Houston Police Department clearly wasn't blind to McGowen's undesirable traits. "He was always a problem—the guy was an asshole. If there was a problem with a patrol car, he'd tear the mirror off so he wouldn't have to drive it. I couldn't prove it. But every time he got a car with no air conditioning, something would turn up wrong with it. He was a malingering malcontent with crusader arrogance."

Considering several violent and irrational incidents in his youth, it's startling that McGown was ever hired as a police officer to begin with. His first agency, the Houston Police Department, no doubt wishes it had delved a little deeper in researching his past.

Born April 3, 1965, in Midland, Texas Joseph Kent McGowen was the firstborn to his parents, Bill and Carolyn. He also had a younger sister and two half brothers. When McGowen was in the fifth grade, the family moved to Conroe, just north of Houston. Born-again Christians, the family is still well liked by many, including a retired Waller county deputy, Howard Lester. "It was really a religious family," Lester told the Houston Press. "He [Kent McGowen] was married and had kids. They lived on his dad's place there and worked on the ranch. I had a boy who got cancer, and then I had had a boy who got murdered, and the family [McGowen's parents], they'd come over and talk with us. They were really religious-type people."

Bill McGowen was in the oil business and was quite successful, a fact his prized son had no qualms about sharing with others. The father and son were as close as two could be. Bill repeatedly defended his son's future downfalls. Regardless, what Bill failed to see was a son in trouble. In school,

McGowen was described as a loner who loved guns, repeatedly lied, and treated women like garbage. More than anything, McGowen would brag to those who would listen about how rich he was. Most would simply turn their backs and smirk while a choice few were actually drawn into his continuous deceptions. One of these few was Michelle Morgan.

Michelle was McGowen's first serious girlfriend and the one Bill later blamed for most of his problems. Considering some of the earlier accounts of their relationship, anyone would be hard pressed to blame Michelle. It was McGowen that displayed the controlling, manipulative, and violent behavior early on in the relationship.

He first threatened suicide when they were both sixteen years old. Showing up at Michelle's sister's house with a knife, he put it to his throat. He was angry that Michelle had done the unimaginable and gone out with her friends. In later incidents, it wasn't uncommon for McGowen to put a knife to his throat or a gun to his head during one of their arguments. He was so obsessive about Michelle that he actually dropped out of high school during his junior year because she had already graduated. He saw no point to school and certainly couldn't waste his time there when he needed to be keeping track of Michelle's whereabouts. Moreover, McGowen had always had his sights set on becoming a police officer and knew he didn't need college for it. In the early 1980s, most police departments hired strictly by civil service tests and no college degree was required. If one scored high enough on the test, training was paid for by that respective police department.

It was shortly after dropping out of high school that McGowen joined the air force. Michelle's family was ecstatic, believing his six-week basic training was far enough away to put a permanent wedge in the teens relationship. Their joy was short-lived when Michelle married McGowen in April 1983, when both were just eighteen years old. McGowen further distressed Michelle's family when he moved her to a Montana air force base where he could work as a security specialist. Now that he had her all to himself, his control and violence quickly escalated. Only a few months after their wedding, Michelle flew home and filed for divorce. Of course, not to be undone, McGowen flew to his wife and begged for her forgiveness and a second chance. She conceded and ultimately returned to Montana where she soon became pregnant.

The couple returned to Texas in 1984, where McGowen could pursue his dream of becoming a police officer. His first choice was undoubtedly the city of Houston Police Department. He quickly began the hiring process, which included a series of interviews, background checks, and a polygraph examination. During the polygraph, McGowen proudly admitted his prejudice against blacks, Hispanics, Asians and women. Astoundingly, it wasn't this admission that caused his application to be rejected. The problem was the fact that he had smoked marijuana within the previous year—a violation of Houston's hiring policy. Defeated, McGowen had to wait a full year before reapplying. During that time, he enrolled at the local Community College and obtained his state peace officers certificate on his own dime. After he finished his training, he and Michelle moved to his father's sprawling ranch in the country. McGowen obtained a position as a reserve deputy at the Waller County Sheriff's Department and worked on the ranch during the day.

McGowen almost saw an immediate end to his brief law enforcement career while jogging with his cousin one day on a desolate country road. A car came barreling down on them, breaking McGowen's collar bone and killing his cousin. He ultimately recovered just in time to resubmit his application to the Houston Police Department—it had been exactly one year.

This time, McGowen was quickly accepted and started the department's academy in October 1985. Kent McGowen's dream of being a police officer had finally started to become a reality.

One would think someone as driven as McGowen would know the formal and informal rules of wearing a badge, but he didn't. In his first few years at the Houston police department, he quickly garnered an unsavory reputation. As in high school, he was viewed as arrogant, a liar, untrustworthy, and a cowboy who liked to do things his way. These could possibly be the most unwelcomed traits in a police officer at any department across the nation. Policing is about trust, brotherhood, and having each others' backs—McGowen shunned all of these necessities. In his normal fashion, he frequently bragged about his family's wealth and that his career in law enforcement would be short, as he would be inheriting a substantial amount of money in the years to come. Possibly the most damaging thing to his relationships with other officers was the fact that he continuously took credit for their achievements—a colossal taboo.

If his behavior on duty wasn't under scrutiny, his personal life was. McGowen was on the afternoon shift, ending his tour at 10:00 PM. Like most departments, officers would get together after work for a couple of drinks and McGowen frequented these get-togethers so often that there were many of his co-workers who weren't even aware he was married because McGowen would frequently crash at officers' apartments after a night of drinking. For the most part, he acted like a spoiled child, flirting with and degrading women, and talking himself up. Behind closed doors, McGowen's marriage to Michelle was just as volatile as ever.

A brief affair with a female officer led to McGowen's ultimate demise in the Houston Police Department. After breaking off their relationship, the female officer alleged that McGowen made several threatening remarks to her. "He told me I was going to regret breaking off with him. He said he'd ruin my life," she told investigators.

A heated argument between the two brought on the involvement of Houston Police Department's internal affairs division (IAD), and McGowen followed through with his threats. He filed a formal complaint alleging that the female officer had expressed suicidal thoughts to him and held a gun to her head—an allegation she vehemently denied. Regardless, she was suspended for forty five days and ordered to undergo a psychological evaluation. Needless to say, the fact that McGowen filed such a blatant complaint against a fellow officer didn't bode well for the rest of the department. Investigators also began looking into his role in the relationship with the female officer. His fellow officers ignored him for months, and McGowen's last straw came when he refused an order from a sergeant while investigating a traffic accident. Sensing a larger battle ahead, McGowen turned in his resignation in January 1989. He claimed that he "had enough financial resources to further his education."

However, the same sergeant who referred to him at the beginning of this chapter as "a malingering malcontent," and the same one whose order he refused, pulled no punches when writing McGowen's exit report:

> Performance poor with a lack of maturity. A general bad attitude toward the department. . . . I did not observe any significant strengths worth noting. . . . He has poor relationships with supervisors, brought on by his lack of orientation to authority. . . . He asks for special favors and threatened bogus IAD complaints about supervisor that would become part of his permanent record. . . . When he gave notice, his actions turned from disrespectful to mutinous. . . . He was a disruptive influence among peers. . . .

When fellow officers and other supervisors were asked to describe their experiences with McGowen, statements such as "a chronic complainer," "immature and conceited," and "dangerous" were written. The lieutenant who put all of the exit reports together summed up the opinion of Kent McGowen:

> Negative information was received from all levels of supervisors and from co-workers associated with Mr. McGowen during his tenure as a police officer with this department.

It was further recommended that McGowen not be rehired should he reapply. Unfortunately, all of these damaging statements were placed inside his IAD file, not his personnel file. The IAD file was not open to the public or other agencies—a crucial mistake.

Taking a few brief months to pursue a career as a veterinarian at a local college, McGowen again felt his itch to be a police officer growing. He missed the job, began to chastise himself for leaving the Houston PD, and reapplied. In May 1989, McGowen applied as a reserve officer in the small town of Tomball while waiting for his Houston PD application to be processed. He had the standard background check performed, one that didn't discover the negative responses in his IAD file, and he was sworn in. The police chief at the time Leroy Michna admitted to receiving a phone call from a Houston police officer who had heard that McGowen was applying. The officer told Michna it would be a grave mistake to hire McGowen. The chief chalked the call up to a personality conflict and thought that an officer with Houston PD training would be a great asset to the department.

History continued to repeat itself when McGowen's personality reared its ugly head. The regular officers thought him to be incredibly arrogant, and questioned his personal priorities when he continuously showed up at bars with his current girlfriend—not his wife.

Michelle McGowen had decidedly had enough and, now with three children, officially divorced him in August 1989. She ended up reconciling with McGowen off and on, but they never remarried. In fact, the violence between them continued to worsen—Michelle appeared with several bruises on her face and the police were repeatedly called to their home.

Still under the scope of a reserve officer, a nonpaid position, McGowen took an assignment with the county drug task force. The veteran investigators within the task force thought McGowen to be somewhat of a joke. He made bogus drug buys and tried to make himself more important than all of the other men put together. He claimed to be chasing after big Columbian drug lords in a town where one was lucky to find a marijuana roach in an ashtray. It was almost humorous—almost. McGowen's demise from the Tomball Police Department came the day he cried wolf.

After calling the department and informing other officers that he had received a threat against his family from a drug informant the department ran around frantically trying to track the threat down. It was Chief Michna who discovered the call actually came from one of Bill McGowen's (Kent's father) offices. Cornering one of Bill McGowen's employees, he learned that Bill asked the employee to phone the threat in because Bill didn't like his son being a cop. Since the chief already had been receiving complaints from the task force about McGowen forging his mileage (the officers actually received money for gas), he felt that McGowen was nothing more than a liability and promptly terminated his commission with the department.

After he was rejected for rehire by the Houston PD, McGowen launched into a series of harassing phone calls to chief Michna, accusing Michna of bad-mouthing him to area

law enforcement agencies and keeping him from being hired.
The calls escalated to the point where the chief had to inform
McGowen that if he kept it up, he would have him criminally
charged and a restraining order would be issued.

"I told him that I was without influence, but that his daddy
might be doing this to him," Michna told the Houston press.
"Then I said, 'Don't ever call me again at my home. If you ever
call me at home again, I'll try to file charges. You're crazy and
I don't want to talk to you.'"

Later, Michna testified to the grand jury that indicted
McGowen about the true scope of his fears when dealing with
the young unstable police officer. "This is the first time I ever
had fear of reprisal for my testimony," he told them. "I think
the boy's crazy. He's very much capable of retaliating against
witnesses . . . go out there and look at the poor woman who's
dead and tell me you don't think he's dangerous to witnesses. If
he'd kill her, he'd kill me."

Following his stint at the Tomball department, McGowen
made a mind-boggling move and was hired as a reserve officer
at the Precinct 4 constable's office. The office never gave an
official statement as to what type of background check was
performed on McGowen. Nonetheless, McGowen only lasted
two months before he was fired. He had taken a position as a
courtesy officer in an apartment complex, a rent free position
allotted for only full-time officers. McGowen chased down a
speeding vehicle in the complex parking lot and, without
reason, stuck his gun in the driver's face. After the driver
reported the incident and the precinct discovered McGowen
had taken a position as a courtesy officer, he was out.

Out, but not to be deterred, McGowen literally went next
door from the precinct's office and applied as a reserve deputy
with the Harris County Sheriff's Department. At the time of
his application, a new jail was being built, and thousands of

employment applications were being processed by a minimal number of background investigators. Quite a few unwanted people slipped through the cracks of the background checks. When McGowen sensed his application would be approved, he quickly changed his application to a full-time, paid deputy position remarkably, he was hired.

Like most sheriffs' departments, McGowen had to start out working in the jail, transporting prisoners. Still unable to focus on anywhere but Houston, he reapplied yet again at the Houston PD and was quickly rejected. This time, McGowen threatened to sue. Cowering in the face of the impending threat of civil litigation, the Houston PD informed McGowen that it would consider him if he passed a psychological test. But, should he fail, the department could send the results to the state, and he could lose his state certification completely. McGowen decided to take his chances. Not surprisingly, McGowen failed, not only one—but two—psychological exams. Unfortunately, the Houston PD never made good on its threat to send the results to the state, nor was the Harris County Sheriff's Department made aware of the results.

In fact, McGowen was promoted to road patrol in April, 1992. Once again, he would be on his own to patrol the citizens. Word began to spread through his past agencies that he'd obtained another job as a police officer, and most knew that there would soon be trouble.

During this time in his career, the excitement level dropped to an all time low. McGowen was assigned as a contract deputy, or community police officer, to strictly patrol an upscale neighborhood known as Olde Oaks. To make matters worse, he was assigned to the night shift, 10:00 PM to 6:00 AM. To an aggressive, young officer, an assignment like this is not only boring but simply hell. McGowen didn't seem to mind, because he was in control again, and that was all that mattered.

Not only did his fellow officers and supervisors grow to despise him quickly, but the residents that McGowen patrolled downright loathed him. Essentially, he bullied everyone he could get his hands on. When the newspaper delivery boy was the only car out at 3:00 AM three nights in a row, McGowen pulled him over—three nights in a row. He stopped people for ridiculous reasons, what other officers referred to as "chicken-shit stops," and repeatedly harassed the neighborhood teens. One of these teens happened to be Jason Aguillard.

Known for his reputation as the punk of the neighborhood, Jason had been a troubled boy from an early age. His mother Susan White was of no help. Susan had her own issues, and neighbors knew they couldn't count on her if they had a problem with Jason. In Susan's eyes, Jason was perfect. Unfortunately, she wasn't able to look at herself in a quite so positive light. For the last few years, Susan had been living the life she had always dreamed of, but it was fading fast. Her younger years hadn't been very pleasant, and the memory of those years continued to haunt her.

Susan Diane Harrison grew up extremely poor in Louisiana. Born on October 8, 1949, she was the fourth of five children to O. L. and William Harrison. Her poor upbringing always brought forth the longing for more. Tall, blonde, and attractive, Susan broke out of the dismal lifestyle in 1967 when she joined the navy. Out of high school for only six months, this was her way of seeing what the world had to offer. After only one year, she decided she had made the wrong choice and was granted a discharge. She enrolled in Louisiana State University in Baton Rouge to study psychology and business. It wasn't long before she met her first husband L. J. Aguillard a six year marine veteran who was a heavy equipment operator. His family wasn't exactly rich, but they had a lot more than Susan was used to. Like Bill McGowen when referring to Michelle, Susan's family blamed L. J. for the bulk of her problems. They charged it was L. J. who introduced Susan to drugs and alcohol. During their violent relationship, Susan began a lifelong battle with prescription drugs. The violence, caused by both sides, didn't help the addiction. In one incident, after she smashed L. J.'s stereo in a fit of rage, he broke her jaw in three places. But, like Kent and Michelle McGowen, they continuously reconciled and ultimately married in November 1972 in a small backyard ceremony at Susan's sister's home.

In 1975, Susan gave birth to Jason, but even that wasn't enough to overcome her battle with pills or the violence in the relationship. At one point, L. J. admitted her into a nearby psychiatric ward where she was released an hour later. Nevertheless, the marriage endured for seven years before L. J. filed for divorce. He had fallen in love with someone else, and Susan was devastated. She ferociously fought the divorce until she realized there was nothing more she could do to stop it. What followed was a vicious custody battle that went on for years. At the time of the divorce, Jason was only six years old and was bounced between households while custody was being determined. Doing her best to acquire a stable life for her son, Susan began nursing school in the early 1980s, believing this would help her obtain full custody. In the meantime, the divorce was taking its toll on the young boy. He was suffering from severe behavioral and emotional problems at home and at school. Even after L. J. had him officially diagnosed, Susan refused to believe it. In fact, she never disciplined him at all.

L. J. was awarded permanent custody of Jason in 1982. The decision left Susan so irrational that she resorted to kidnapping her son from L. J.'s mother while grocery shopping at a local market. L. J. had to call the sheriff's department to retrieve the boy and no charges were filed against Susan. Needless to say, the custody decision caused Susan's drug abuse to skyrocket. Only after her sister, Gloria, insisted that she enter rehab did Susan finally get clean—briefly.

Susan remarried, but ended the marriage amicably less than a year later. Intent on finding someone to love and take care of her, she found the man of her dreams in the mid-1980s when she met Ron White. A wealthy engineer who drove a Porsche and lived in Houston, White was going through his second divorce as well. The couple quickly fell in love and White insisted that Susan move to Houston with him. What looked like a break in the clouds for Susan almost didn't happen when she was arrested for forging a prescription right before the move to Houston. Ultimately, the judge took pity on her after she completed another stint in rehab and was stripped of her nursing license. The road was cleared for Susan and Ron to begin their lives together in the big city.

It was a life that she could only dream about as a child— trips to Europe and country club memberships. Only, the other members of the country club quickly realized an outsider was among them. Susan was loud, brash, and low class in their eyes. Times spent on the golf course proved to be a powerful tool when White's divorce was finalized. It was there that Susan surprised him with a justice of the peace to marry the two. Some say White wasn't looking to get married so quickly but had been cornered.

Two months later, White made Susan sign a legal agreement that gave her nothing but what she brought to the marriage should they divorce. At the time, Susan gave it little thought. They were happy and continued to flourish in their relationship until Jason came to live with them. L. J. and his new wife simply couldn't handle the twelve-year-old problem child any more. Susan was thrilled, and her life, which now included her son, was nearly perfect. Buying a large, impressive home in the upscale neighborhood of Olde Oaks, Susan—just like at the country club—didn't garner a high opinion from her neighbors. And they absolutely despised Jason.

In the beginning, they felt sorry for Jason. Susan had obtained her Realtor's license and was always working, so Jason was constantly alone. The neighbors would invite him over for dinner and such until Jason's true colors became known—bullying the smaller children of the neighborhood, he even stole a necklace from a house down the street. When the neighbor confronted Jason, wearing the necklace, Susan defended him, claiming it must be a "mistake." The problems grew when Jason found friends who consisted of nothing more than juvenile delinquents who delighted in terrorizing the neighborhood. Inside the White household, the fragile relationship between Ron and Jason continued to unravel. They absolutely couldn't get along. A pivotal point in their battle came when Jason put antifreeze in White's coffee. He didn't drink it but chased after Jason in a fury.

Jason's problems escalated until he was eventually transferred to the city's school for troubled youth. Police were a common sight at the White home.

In 1989, after he had just returned from a business trip, Susan discovered a photograph of another woman in White's clothing. Susan fell apart. In an attempt to reconcile, he threw out their agreement and drew up a new will leaving everything to Susan and Jason. This seemed to satisfy her for a while. It was later that year when White took a job transfer to Korea and the family moved, leaving the neighborhood to rejoice. Unfortunately, Susan hated Korea and became ill, so they moved back after only a few months.

Sometime in 1991, about the time Susan obtained a job as a mortgage broker, Jason began hanging around a nineteen year old troublemaker named Michael Shaffer. Michael stayed off and on at the White home. Like before, Susan and Ron were gone much of the time, so Michael and Jason caused trouble. Calls to the sheriff's department became more frequent, but Michael moved in permanently.

In 1992, Susan received an anonymous letter, accompanied by photos, saying that White was having another affair and would soon be leaving her. White initially denied the affair, but it was apparent their marriage was over. Susan even took to tracking the other woman down and physically attacking her at the woman's office. The marital problems took their toll on Susan, and she fell into a deep depression that included a renewed addiction to prescription drugs. She lost control of her home to Michael and Jason, and the White home was soon the continuous focus of the sheriff's department—mainly, Kent McGown.

The White home in Olde Oaks.
Photo by Vanessa Leggett

As much as they were at her home on official business, Susan befriended several of the deputies, frequently bragging about it to her friends. She told her friends how one of the new deputies on night shift, McGowen, had even stopped her to ask her out. At first, she thought it was flattering.

It was the summer of 1992, and Susan's friends began to notice a significant change in her demeanor, specifically her attitude toward deputy McGowen. Now dating a local businessman, Ray Valentine, Susan would tell anyone who would listen that McGowen was threatening and stalking her. In fact, Susan spoke to Ray about her fear of McGowen so often that he initially didn't believe her. She told anyone who would listen. Friends, family, members of the sheriff's department, coworkers, and she even made a phone call to the local newspaper to no avail. No one seemed to think that a prestigious law enforcement officer could be so threatening. Susan told one friend that McGowen would stop at her home every night when he knew she was alone and she constantly made the statement that "I don't want to make him mad, I'm scared of what he'll do to me or Jason."

McGowen frequently watched the White house. It was during one of the many times that he stopped Michael Shaffer leaving that he begin to put his horrific plan in motion. McGowen insisted that Michael become an informant. Michael was terrified of the deputy and agreed. McGowen wanted a "big bust" in the neighborhood and heard rumors of stolen guns. Essentially, he ordered Michael to set up a buy for a stolen gun. Whether McGowen had a premonition of who Michael's choice would be is anybody's guess, but it was his good friend, Jason, whom Michael approached. Unaware Michael was a snitch for McGowen, Jason was lead to someone who would sell him a stolen gun. During the sting operation, McGowen closed in and promptly arrested Michael, Jason, and the gun provider. Susan was enraged, and, for the first time, Ray Valentine actually believed her that McGowen was out to get her and her family.

To McGowen's outrage, the District Attorney refused to approve charges against Jason for possessing or selling stolen guns. His plan wasn't working out like he'd thought. However, he was pleasantly relieved when Michael Shaffer called to say that Susan had found out he was the snitch. Susan allegedly told Michael and his mother, "You know, snitches get killed in Houston."

It was all McGowen needed. He called the district attorney and gave a false account of the incident, claiming he was with a task force working with the Bureau of Alcohol, Tabacco, and Firearms on gunrunners. He further claimed that an informant had been threatened and his life was in immediate danger. McGowen expressed the urgency of an arrest warrant for Susan. Going on his word, the search warrant was approved. Now, Susan White would forever regret rebuffing and humiliating Kent McGowen.

Armed with a search warrant and two back-up officers who believed McGowen's web of lies, McGowen knocked on Susan White's door just after midnight on August 25, 1992. He identified himself and announced he had a warrant for her arrest. Susan became terrified and called 911.

911 Operator: What's your emergency?

Susan White: There's a [unintelligible] here at my door. I've filed several complaints with him for sexual harassment and I need some help immediately. . . . So you can but get McGowen away from my house. Get McGowen away from my house!

[White hangs up before calling back a few seconds later.]

911 Operator: Do you need a deputy out to your house?

Susan White: They are trying to break into my house, please!

911 Operator: What's your address?

Susan White: 3407 Amber Forest.

911 Operator: Who's breaking into your home?

Susan White (crying): I don't know. They say they are detectives, but I have been threatened by one of them.

911 Operator: How many are there?

Susan White [her voice more frantic, and the burglar alarm ringing in the background]: I don't know, but puleeze! They just broke in!

911 Operator: What are they doing?

Susan White: Okay . . .

911 Operator: Ma'am?

Three shots were fired, and Susan White was dead. After kicking in the front door, McGowen ran straight to Susan's bedroom where she sat on her bed speaking to the 911 operator. He shot her first in the face and then twice in the torso. The other deputies couldn't keep up with him and weren't in the room when the shooting occurred.

McGowen's version of events quickly unraveled when investigators began looking into the shooting. First, he was ecstatic at the scene, braging in his usual manner and feeling proud of the fact that he had just shot someone. McGowen claimed that when he entered the bedroom, Susan pulled a gun on him. Her small .25-caliber handgun that she kept for protection lay on the floor. However, there were several problems with this theory. McGowen claimed Susan had been holding the gun with her right hand, when she was left-handed. Also, Susan's fingerprints weren't even on the gun. Investigators determined that McGowen entered the room before his backup arrived and blatantly shot Susan White as she sat on her bed clutching the telephone. During the investigation that followed, detectives were astonished to find out that McGowen had been inquiring how to obtain one of the bullets from the shooting to put on a plaque, as a type of trophy. When they learned the wealth of lies he had told to obtain the search warrant, they felt they had enough to move forward with the grand jury.

Kent McGowen's reign of terror was over when he was indicted for the murder of Susan White on October 28, 1992. To the dismay of White's family, McGowen's trial didn't *start* until March 1994. The jury learned of McGowen's obsession with Susan, and how her constant rejections caused his blood to boil until he finally erupted.

The jury found him guilty of murder on March 9, 1994, and sentenced him to fifteen years in prison.

In an event that was as bizarre as his career, McGowen's attorneys filed an immediate appeal the day the verdict was announced. Under Texas law, if someone is sentenced to fifteen years or less, he is able to await his appeal out of jail—walking freely among the public. Susan White's family was shocked. Furthermore, it wasn't until almost a decade later that McGowen faced a retrial. On March 19, 2002, he was again found guilty of Susan White's murder and instead sentenced to twenty years in prison. This time he went directly to jail.

Susan White's family filed a civil suit against the Harris County Sheriff's Department for failing to provide an adequate background check on Kent McGowen. They were awarded more than $5.3 million. However, the award was overturned and the appeals are expected to take years.

Nonetheless, the failure of the law enforcement system to adequately prevent a criminal like McGowen from entering their ranks has no doubt revamped numerous hiring policies.

PART II

EQUAL RIGHTS APPLY

CHAPTER 8

BAMBI IN THE HEADLIGHTS

LAWRENCIA BEMBENEK
FORMER POLICE OFFICER, MILWAUKEE, WISCONSIN

You've probably heard the story, or at the very least remember the frenzy that followed the case of convicted murderer Lawrencia "Bambi" Bembenek. Known to her family and friends as Laurie, she was a former Milwaukee police officer and a security officer for Marquette University at the time of her arrest. Two books and two made-for-television movies later, the controversy surrounding the case continues. Laurie is one of two female police officers convicted of murder featured in this book.

What began as a seemingly quiet and beautiful spring day ended with a decadelong battle involving murder accusations, cover-ups, and police corruption.

It was May 27, 1981, and thirty-year-old Christine Schultz, an attractive brunette, was working diligently in the garden of her Milwaukee, Wisconsin, home. Formerly married to Milwaukee police detective Elfred "Fred" O. Schultz, Christine was adapting to life as a single mother to the two sons they shared—eleven-year old Sean and seven-year-old Shannon. With her divorce from Fred final in November 1980, Christine had even begun to casually date again. This proved to be a difficult task since Christine was forever under the watchful eye of her ex-husband.

Their relationship of ten years was tempestuous from the very beginning. Fred, a tall, handsome man of thirty-two years, was known as a womanizer who made no attempt to hide his adulterous nature. By his own admission, Fred had slept with half of the female police officers at the Milwaukee Police Department. In addition, Christine made numerous claims to friends and family regarding Fred's verbal, and sometimes physical, abuse. By the time their divorce was final, Christine had a court order preventing Fred from coming to the home that they formerly shared on West Ramsey Road. Despite the order, as a seasoned detective, Fred usually ignored the decree and felt compelled to be involved in every aspect of Christine's life when it came to their sons.

Shortly before her death, Christine Schultz told even her attorney, Eugene Kershek, that she feared Fred might kill her. In fact, she told Kershek, "He told me he wants to blow my fucking head off!"

Nonetheless, on May 27, Christine put these thoughts aside as she waited for the arrival of her current boyfriend, George Stewart Honeck Jr., known to friends as "Stu." He was also a police officer with the Milwaukee Police Department, a fact that didn't sit well with Fred. It was unconscionable that an officer would date a fellow officer's ex-wife. For the most part, the two kept their distance from one another.

After he helped her in the garden for a while, Stu accompanied Christine into the home, where she made dinner for him and her sons. After dinner Christine put the boys to bed before she and Stu cleaned up the kitchen. Sean and Shannon heard their mother tell Stu to "lock the door behind you" when he left. As they fell asleep, they heard their mother's usual sounds throughout the house as she wound down and fell asleep watching television.

It was sometime before 2:00 AM when Sean woke up to a large gloved hand covering his face and a rope being tightened around his neck. While Sean writhed and struggled, Shannon woke up and began to kick at the large figure that was attacking his older brother. For these two young boys what was happening inside their bedroom was unimaginably terrifying. However, their nightmare was only beginning. After a struggle, both boys watched as the large man, wearing a green army jacket—and with a reddish blonde ponytail—ran from their room and into their mother's. The boys listened in shock as they heard her scream, "God! Please don't do that!" followed by what sounded like a firecracker going off. Running to aid their mother, the boys were passed in the hallway by the attacker who proceeded to run down the stairs, his jacket flapping behind him.

Concerned for their mother, Sean and Shannon ran into her bedroom and found Christine on her bed. She had a large hole in her back that was bleeding profusely, her hands had a cord wrapped around them, and she had been gagged. Determined to help their mother, the boys quickly took gauze from the nearby medicine cabinet and tried to stop the bleeding. It was too late. They made the first phone call to Stu Honeck around 2:30 AM. Shannon, waking Stu out of deep sleep, explained to him the severity of the situation in his young mind: "Stu! Someone put a firecracker in Mom's back and she's bleeding! . . . She's not talking, just gurgling!" the young boy exclaimed.

Interpreting Shannon's claims more realistically, Stu realized what had happened and called the police department to report that someone had been shot. He and his roommate, Ken

Retkowski, quickly drove down the street to Christine's home. By that time, Christine Schultz was dead.

What followed could only be described as a barrage—a circus—of officers (including Fred Schultz) that paraded and trampled through the home, tainting evidence and gawking at the body of Christine Schultz. It wasn't until 5:30 AM that the first ambulance was called to take her body away.

Thus began the tedious process of trying to locate a suspect—or suspects. Investigators combed through the quiet neighborhood, a neighborhood that had never experienced such a violent crime or could even grasp the notion that there could be a killer among them. The residents were rightfully stricken with panic, and local gossip circles were on fire as to whom the killer may be.

At least twelve neighborhood residents pointed investigators to a jogger who had been spotted several times in the area. They claimed he was wearing a green jogging suit and sported a ponytail and carried a blue bandana—similar to the one found stuffed in Christine Schultz's mouth.

Two nurses who worked at a nearby nursing home also implicated the jogger. They claimed that approximately thirty minutes after the murder took place they were walking through the nursing home parking lot and saw a man wearing a green jogging suit, lying in the parking lot coughing. He also had a ponytail. Fearing it may be someone who was injured or recently robbed, the women went back inside to call the police. When they came back out to check on the man, he was nowhere to be found.

Christine's neighbor, Ray Kujawa, filed a police report the day after the murder, claiming someone had broken into his garage and stolen a green jogging suit and a .38-caliber revolver. Something about Ray's story didn't sound right to investigators, but they decided against pursuing it.

And then, there was Laurie Bembenek.

Lawrencia Bembenek was born on August 15, 1959, in Milwaukee, Wisconsin. As Polish Catholics, the Bembeneks officially named their daughter "Laurie Ann" at birth. However, the latin version, "Lawrencia," mysteriously showed up on her birth certificate and they kept it. Laurie's father, Joseph, was a former Milwaukee police officer who spent a mere three years with the department. He left because of the constant corruption and cover-ups and decided to pursue a career as a carpenter instead.

Laurie Bembenek grew up to be a stunningly beautiful woman. Standing a statuesque five feet ten inches tall, she had blonde hair and blue eyes that made for a lucrative modeling career. However, Laurie was a staunch feminist. During her modeling days she refused to pose nude or in only underwear but, however, did a short stint as a waitress at a nearby Playboy Club. Belonging to several feminist groups, Laurie decided to pursue a career in law enforcement in the latter part of 1979 to early 1980. She knew the task would be a difficult one. Women were not widely accepted as police officers, and women actually serving on the force were few and far between. When Laurie was finally accepted into the police academy on March 10, 1980, she was ecstatic. However, she never dreamed at that time that her happiness would be short-lived.

Laurie was not exactly welcomed at the academy, but she did earn her notorious nickname—"Bambi"—there. With her bright blue eyes and attractive looks, the other officers said she looked like "Bambi in the headlights." The name stuck.

She and the few other women enrolled were subjected to ongoing taunts and harassment. She befriended one of the other female recruits, Judy Zess, and they did their best to get through it. For Judy, the academy was the beginning of the end. Before graduation, investigators alleged that a marijuana cigarette had been found underneath a seat where Judy had been sitting. After several long days of coercion, Judy signed a written confession that the marijuana belonged to her, and she was promptly fired from the Milwaukee Police Department.

Laurie saw what was happening and did her best to keep her mouth shut. When she ultimately graduated from the academy, she thought she'd actually made it. However, in August 1980, shortly after she began her official duties patrolling the streets of Milwaukee as a police officer, she was called into an office and told to hand in her gun and badge—she was being fired. Given no reason for her dismissal at that time, Laurie was one of three women fired that same week from the department. She later read in the newspaper that the police chief, Harold Breier, claimed the women were fired "for the good of the service."

Utilizing the services of the police union, Laurie later learned that Judy Zess had given a written statement alleging Laurie had smoked marijuana. When she confronted Judy with the claims, Judy admitted that she had lied and had been forced to give the statement under duress. Armed with a written statement by Judy, Laurie hired another attorney and subsequently filed a wrongful termination suit against the Milwaukee Police Department. At that time, the police union refused to help her anymore and her unemployment benefits were promptly canceled. With little hopes of getting her job back, Laurie enlisted in the United States Air Force. At the tender age of twenty-one, she thought she had plenty of time to salvage her future. That was until she met Fred Schultz.

It was November 1980 when Laurie met the newly divorced Milwaukee police detective through a friend of hers who was sleeping with Fred at the time. Finding him arrogant and distasteful at first, Laurie was surprised when Fred began to pursue her. She was even more surprised when she found herself having romantic feelings toward Fred that eventually led to an exclusive relationship between the two.

Still in the throes of her lawsuit against the Milwaukee Police Department, Laurie began to receive threats and had her car vandalized several times. Reporting each incident to the internal affairs division, Laurie was told there was nothing they could do about it. A further blow came when the air force told her that she would be unable to enlist as long as a pending litigation against a government agency was still active. She was told by the air force, "Either drop the suit, or don't enlist." With her and Fred's relationship blossoming, and considering all of the work she had put into the lawsuit, Laurie decided against going into the air force. In fact, Laurie and Fred married on January 30, 1981, only two months after meeting one another.

On the night of Christine Schultz's murder, Laurie maintains that she was home at the apartment she shared with Fred. Her parents visited for most of the evening, eventually leaving at 11:00 PM, just before Fred left for work on the night shift at 11:15. According to Laurie, as she lay in bed reading a book, Fred called her an unusual amount of times before she eventually fell asleep sometime before midnight. At approximately 2:40 AM, Laurie woke up to Fred's phone call informing her that Christine had been shot. Laurie was astonished when Fred showed up hours later to insist that he and Laurie go to the morgue to identify Christine's body, even though Stu Honeck had already done it.

Not keen on now having to raise two young boys, Laurie recalled the day after the murder when Sean and Shannon were watching the news about the crime. As the news reports continued to give the description of the killer wearing a green jogging suit, the boys yelled at the television, saying the reports were wrong—the killer had a green army jacket on. It was also shortly after the murder that Laurie learned Fred had been hiding a key to Christine's house, a piece of information he dismissed as nothing unusual when he was confronted about it. In fact, Fred expressed little to no emotion at all regarding Christine's death.

The days following the murder proved to be difficult for Laurie. Whether it was the underlying guilt of a murderess or the notion that an innocent woman was about to be accused of murder depends on who you ask. She ultimately obtained a job as a campus police officer at nearby Marquette University. But like her other job in law enforcement, this one was also short-lived.

On June 24, 1981, almost four weeks after the murder, Laurie was patrolling Marquette University when she realized that she had forgotten her radio. Arriving at the campus police station, she was met by two Milwaukee police detectives who advised her that she was under arrest for the murder of Christine Schultz. They had already—without a warrant—searched her locker and purse. Laurie was taken to the Milwaukee Police Department and subjected to intense questioning. She further learned an arrest warrant had not even been issued at the time of her arrest. She refused all questioning and requested an attorney.

Irritated with her refusal to answer questions, the detectives put Laurie into a holding cell where she spent the next three days. It was during this time that the detectives typed up a criminal complaint and an arrest warrant. They believed that Laurie was insane with jealousy over Fred's relationship with his ex-wife. Investigators maintained that Laurie, accustomed to a luxurious lifestyle from her modeling days, hated the fact that Fred paid child support, alimony, and saw Christine almost three times a week. While Laurie sat in jail, the detectives presented the district attorney with the case. Initially, he didn't want any part of it, claiming it was entirely too circumstantial. But with consistent prodding from the detectives and assistant district attorney who swore, "This is her, this is our killer," he conceded and filed the charges.

With her bail set at $10,000, Laurie's aunt put up the money and she was free—for now. Facing murder charges, Laurie retained renowned defense attorney Donald Eisenberg to represent her. Eisenberg assured her that the case would be dropped at the pretrial owing to an overwhelming lack of evidence. Laurie held out hope while she tried to keep her life and marriage together. On the outside, Fred appeared to offer his sincere support to Laurie, agreeing that the case would never go to trial. However, Fred was facing his own problems with the Milwaukee Police Department.

Convinced that he couldn't possibly be mentally equipped to handle both his wife's upcoming murder charge and his law enforcement duties, the department demoted Fred Schultz to a desk job, which he grew to loathe. Seemingly excommunicated from the department, Fred quietly began to blame Laurie for his own troubles. However, to the public, he still boisterously and vigorously defended his wife. Furthermore, Fred and Laurie lost custody of Sean and Shannon to Christine's sister, who had been working to get them away from a potentially violent situation.

On the day of her preliminary trial, Laurie was convinced that her case would not be bound over for trial and her nightmare would soon be over. But what happened during the hearing was a surprise to everyone. Eisenberg put forth an airtight defense, ridiculing nearly all of the circumstantial evidence presented by the prosecution.

When Sean Schultz, the only witness to the murder, testified that he knew for a fact the murderer wasn't Laurie, she thought for sure the judge would toss the case right into the garbage. Sean also vehemently defended his accounts of the killer wearing a green army jacket—not a jogging suit.

The prosecution aggressively portrayed Laurie as a jealous ex-wife. It claimed she had access to the murder weapon, her husband's .38-caliber revolver, although it was never determined that the shots were actually fired from that particular gun. Prosecutors also presented a black-and-white photograph of Laurie wearing a jogging suit, which the photographer testified was green. Laurie adamantly denied ever owning a green jogging suit, stating the suit she was wearing in the photograph was red. They claimed a brownish reddish wig was found stuffed into the plumbing of a neighbor's apartment in the same complex as Laurie and Fred. They theorized that on the night of the murder, Laurie jogged to Christine's, committed the murder, and jogged back to her apartment where she disposed of the wig. The prosecution discounted Sean's testimony by saying he and his brother were so distraught that they could've easily mistaken Laurie for a man, because of her above-average height.

Ray Kujawa, Christine's neighbor who claimed his home had been broken into the night of the murder, refused to testify to that fact, and the police report he filed was never submitted by Eisenberg.

Perhaps the most devastating blow came when Fred Schultz testified. Laurie expected him to take the stand and defend her character, but instead he invoked his Fifth Amendment rights and requested immunity in exchange for his testimony. Laurie was shocked—so was Donald Eisenberg. Taking the matter further, Fred, who had not once shed a tear over the death of Christine and openly stated that he never loved her, broke down in dramatic fashion on the stand. Once granted immunity, Fred began sobbing in front of the courtroom, explaining how much he loved his ex-wife and how devastated he was that she had been murdered.

Throughout the trial, the judge consistently overruled Eisenberg's claims of illegal searches, warrants, and arrests. Siding with the prosecution, the judge found that there was enough evidence against Laurie Bembenek for murder, and she was bound over for trial. Laurie was again arraigned on murder charges on November 9, 1981, but was allowed to be free on bail.

For the next several months, Laurie Bembenek worked expeditiously to prove her innocence. She was fired from her job as a campus police officer and did odd jobs to keep busy. Fred eventually resigned from the Milwaukee Police Department and began working at carpentry jobs with Laurie's father. Laurie's claims that she had been framed by the Milwaukee Police Department in response to her lawsuit fell on deaf ears within the criminal justice system.

On the outside, however, she was garnering quite a fan club. People from all over the country had been following the story of the beautiful cop who was a former model and Playboy waitress. She had become the center of tabloid stories and newspaper columns nationwide. Letters were sent and support groups were organized to help the "wrongly accused" female police officer.

Nonetheless, Laurie Bembenek's life continued on a downward spiral. While waiting for her trial to begin, Laurie was informed by Eisenberg that her marriage to Fred wasn't legal. With feelings of loathing increasing for Fred, Laurie wasn't thrilled about the idea of having to remarry him, but Eisenberg said they needed to keep the situation quiet. Most important, it would make Laurie look unquestionably guilty if Fred were to leave her before the trial started. Laurie conceded, and she and Fred had their second wedding. This time, it was less than a joyous occasion.

With the pressure of the upcoming trial looming and the fate of her future hanging in the balance, Laurie didn't give it much thought when Eisenberg requested to meet her—without Fred—ten days before her trial started.

Eisenberg's usually flamboyant demeanor was replaced by one that screamed the seriousness of the situation. Laurie was concerned.

Unbeknownst to Laurie, Eisenberg had a private investigator working every aspect of the murder case against her. He had found a man in Chicago who had credible information that accused Fred of a "murder-for-hire" scheme against his ex-wife. According to Eisenberg, the man in Chicago had strong ties to the actual hit man responsible for Christine's murder. Laurie was shocked and refused to believe the claims that her husband was involved in the murder. In what was most likely the biggest mistake on her part, Laurie refused to allow Eisenberg to propose the theory during her upcoming trial or to even bring the man from Chicago in to testify.

On February 23, 1982, Laurie Bembenek's murder trial began before a crowd of hundreds, most of whom were turned away. It was a media frenzy. There were those who were thoroughly convinced of her guilt and those who were unshakable in maintaining her innocence. Both sides vied for the right to be heard before the numerous news cameras and reporters, and the nation transfixed itself on the glorified murder trial taking place in Milwaukee, Wisconsin.

The trial was overseen by Judge Michael Skwierawski, a hard-nosed common pleas court judge who was known for being all business. During the jury selection, Laurie continuously expressed her doubt at the jurors who were selected. Laurie knew of the stereotypical uphill battle she would face if everyday housewives serving as jurors were confronted with an attractive professional woman. Despite her protest, the women remained, and the jury was officially seated.

The three-week trial proved to be in the prosecution's favor almost from the very beginning. Although Eisenberg did his best to trip up almost every witness on the stand, disproving their testimony and making them look like fools, Laurie felt increasingly frightened at what the trial's outcome would be. According to her, the blatant lies told by the witnesses on the stand while under oath were phenomenal. Like the previous judge, Judge Skwierawski denied every motion put forth by the defense, including the illegal searches of Laurie's locker and purse.

Toward the end of the trial, Laurie testified for almost five hours in her own defense. When the jury heard the final arguments and began deliberation, Laurie clearly didn't think she could bear the outcome. After three days with no result, she began to become hopeful, but her hope became instead incredulous when the judge refused to declare a hung jury. However, on March 9, 1982, she waited breathlessly as the jury returned its verdict. Laurie Bembenek was found guilty of the murder of Christine Schultz.

The judge acknowledged the jury's decision, and even went so far as to admit that it was the most circumstantial case he had ever seen, but he didn't hesitate to sentence her to life in prison.

Whisked away immediately by corrections officers and sent to Taycheedah Women's Prison in Fon Du Lac, Wisconsin, Laurie's first day was spent grappling with numerous thoughts of suicide. For those on the outside who felt that she had been wronged, support groups began to solicit as much money as they could to further her defense fund. Laurie spent her first few days in prison feeling instead like a caged exotic animal at a local zoo. Inmates and corrections officers alike would peer through her door constantly to gawk at the famous murderess who they had been reading about in the newspapers. Some would say loudly, "Is that one the police officer?" while others would simply smile and walk away.

Eisenberg met with her to discuss comments made by the

jurors after the verdict was returned. It was obvious that several held out, but it was the women Laurie worried about initially who persuaded the rest of the jury to find her guilty. One of the women blatantly stated that she thought Laurie's blouse was inappropriate for trial and thought something was definitely wrong with any woman who didn't want children.

As for Fred Schultz, he appeared to be committed to his wife—for a short while. After a few months in prison, while waiting to hear word on her appeals, Laurie began to hear rumors of Fred's numerous affairs with other women. Then she began to receive credit card bills in prison—in her name—that Fred had run up buying his girlfriends expensive gifts. Fleeing to Florida to find a job, Fred sent a postcard to Laurie in July 1982 that read simply, "Good Luck, and Goodbye." She was not saddened, but actually relieved to hear of his departure.

In February 1983, after being incarcerated for almost a year, Laurie began to hear rumors that Fred was publicly stating she was guilty. After passing a voice stress analysis test about her involvement in the murder, Laurie was again dissuaded by Eisenberg to file for a divorce from Fred. Around that time, Laurie began to have serious doubts about the attorney who was handling her case. However, she held on with high hopes. In August 1983, the medical examiner who had testified against Laurie during her murder trial wrote a three-page affidavit that suggested numerous irregularities in the case and how she now believed that Laurie Bembenek was innocent.

In December, Judy Zess wrote an affidavit that she lied during her testimony when she claimed she heard Laurie ask if there was anyone who could "take her out," the "her" referring to Christine. Laurie felt that both statements would be crucial to her in winning a new trial.

As the events leading up to this point predicted, the district attorney refused to reopen the case and all of her appeals were denied. Laurie decidedly had enough of everything, hired new attorneys to take on her case, and filed for divorce from Fred. Her divorce was official in June 1984.

During this time, Laurie's case was picked up by a private investigator and former police officer, Ira Robins, who was convinced of her innocence. As he continued to uncover hidden evidence and discrepancies in the case, he also began to receive numerous death threats aimed at him and his family. Refusing to succumb to the threats, Robins worked harder than ever on Laurie's case.

In 1989, while still incarcerated, Laurie began a relationship with Nick Gugliatto, a man she had met while he was visiting his inmate sister. A romance ensued and the two quickly became engaged, preparing for an August 1990 wedding within the prison walls. With new evidence uncovered by Robins, Laurie was more hopeful than ever that she would soon be a free woman with a new husband. Again her hopes were dashed when all her appeals were exhausted in July 1990. At that point, Laurie decided to give up and take her chances.

On July 15, 1990, Laurie Bembenek escaped the Taycheedah State Women's Prison through a laundry room window with the help of her fiancé. Laurie and Nick disappeared into the night, and a manhunt of enormous magnitude ensued.

The nation went wild over the escape of the attractive female police officer. Major news outlets, tabloids, and talk shows featured the story on a daily basis. The police department was flooded with citizens claiming that if Laurie were to show up at their front door, they would take her in and hide her—they believed she was innocent. Bumper stickers with the logo "Run Bambi Run" adorned cars across the United States and people wore T-shirts that read "Go, Lawrencia, Go!" inside local coffee shops.

After Robins released newly uncovered evidence that contradicted Fred Schultz's alibi on the night of the murder, and instead pointing toward him and other members of the Milwaukee Police Department including Judy Zess, the public screamed for a new trial. Again the district attorney's office refused, stating that Laurie's escape was a direct implication of her guilt.

After almost three months, the trail of Laurie and Nick ran cold. Rumors of the couple being seen in Mexico ran rampant, and the television crime show *America's Most Wanted* aired a segment in October asking the public's help in finding the duo. The segment proved useful.

Shortly after the show aired, the FBI received a tip from a man in Thunder Bay, Canada, who claimed he had been served by a waitress in a local restaurant who was a dead ringer for Laurie Bembenek. The Canadian police contacted the woman, who identified herself as Jennifer Lee Gazzana, and the authorities determined that she was in fact Lawrencia Bembenek. The police quickly located Nick and the two were jailed in Canada while awaiting extradition. However, to Laurie's shock, her extradition was delayed. The Canadian officials, after speaking with her, determined that she was unfairly convicted and faced certain persecution—and prosecution—if she were returned to the United States. The Canadian attorney hired to represent her filed a motion asking the Canadian government to grant Laurie refugee status.

Back in the United States, the system began to act in Laurie's favor as well. After hearing about the decision from the Canadian officials, coupled with the new evidence uncovered by Ira Robins, the murder of Christine Schultz was officially reopened as a John Doe Investigation. Laurie would now get a new trial.

For Nick, things weren't as promising. He was extradited back to the United States and sentenced to one year in prison for aiding Laurie's escape.

Laurie's new trial was to begin in early 1992, but it never transpired. Instead, the district attorney's office offered her a plea deal: plead "no contest" to second-degree murder, and be released on time served. A no-contest plea doesn't necessarily admit guilt, but admits that the facts of the case are accurate. Laurie, faced with the possibility of being found guilty during yet another trial, accepted the plea. For the first time in almost ten years, she was officially a free woman. However, Laurie Bembenek continues to maintain her innocence and has fought in the years following her plea to get her conviction overturned.

Her life after prison continued to spiral downward. She was arrested several years later for marijuana possession, fought an intense battle with alcoholism, filed bankruptcy, and contracted hepatitis C. In 2002, displaying one of the more bizarre aspects of her life, Laurie was scheduled to appear on the talk show *Dr. Phil*. The show offered to conduct independent DNA analysis that would officially clear Laurie of the murders. While waiting for the test results, Laurie claimed that she was confined in a hotel room by the show and was not free to leave. Panicked by an intense claustrophobia that she developed while in prison, Laurie jumped from a second-story window and ultimately had to have her leg amputated; she later filed a lawsuit against the television show.

In 2004, Laurie returned to Milwaukee in a repeated attempt to clear her name, but it was simply not meant to be. Nothing but a shell of her former self, Laurie's looks, intelligence, and to some, her sanity, had completely disappeared. She retreated to the Pacific Northwest where she now lives in seclusion.

Fred Schultz was found in 2002, living in Florida with a new family and working as a respiratory therapist—a quiet life. He refused to discuss the case, only stating that, in his opinion, Laurie undoubtedly murdered Christine.

The question of whether or not Lawrencia Bembenek committed the murder of Christine Schultz will always remain in the back of the minds of many. There are others, however, who insist her plea was a factual admission of guilt. Most don't doubt that Fred Schultz was involved somehow, but as for what really happened, only Christine Schultz—and the killer—know for sure.

CHAPTER 9

EVIL IN BLUE

ANTOINETTE FRANK
POLICE OFFICER, NEW ORLEANS, LOUISIANA

L ike her fellow officer Len Davis—who is featured in chapter 11, New Orleans police officer Antoinette Frank blackened the other eye of an already failing police system. Some claim that there are no comparisons between the two. Davis committed murder for money, while Antoinette Frank was pure evil to the core. On the day that Frank was charged with three counts of aggravated murder, it was clear that this female police officer was nothing but a stone-cold mass murderer.

In the early morning hours of March 4, 1995, while former New Orleans police officer Len Davis was awaiting his own trial of aggravated murder, twenty-four-year-old Antoinette Frank entered the doors of Kim Anh, a Vietnamese restaurant. Followed by eighteen-year-old thug Rogers LaCaze, Frank and her cohort proceeded to murder an off-duty New Orleans police officer, Ronnie Williams, who was working security at the restaurant, and two restaurant employees, Ha Vu, twenty-four, and seventeen-year-old Cuong Vu. Was it a robbery attempt gone awry? Or was it simply a barbaric act of revenge by a woman who no one dared cross? Investigators are fairly certain it was a combination of both. One thing they were convinced of—Antoinette Frank was a monster.

Antoinette Frank was born on March 30, 1971, to Adam and Mary Ann Frank in Opelousas, Louisiana. From an early age, Antoinette had high hopes of becoming a police officer. Not many people would know that, since she was typically overly shy and branded as a loner. What most people couldn't see were the wheels spinning in the back of her head for years. She was bound and determined to achieve her dream—no matter what the cost.

Her childhood was less than stable. Her older brother, Adam Jr., was a regular in the criminal justice system—a fugitive who was wanted for a separate attempted murder at the time Antoinette was arrested—and their father, Adam Frank Sr., was rarely home. However, Antoinette began her law enforcement career in high school as a junior police officer at the Opelousas Police Department. After transferring jobs, Adam Frank Sr. moved his family to the east side of New Orleans, where Antoinette eagerly joined the New Orleans Police Explorers—a group for teens who sought to become police officers later on in life.

With things not working out well in New Orleans, the Franks moved back to Opelousas. In June 1988, Antoinette obtained a job at the local Wal-Mart. She was fired six months later. The manager described her as unable to get along with other employees. When she graduated from high school in May 1989, Frank quickly left the small town once again for New Orleans, setting her sights on the New Orleans Police Department. Giving her a second chance, Wal-Mart again hired the attractive female at its New Orleans East store.

Franks rented a house and waited patiently for her twentieth birthday—the minimum age at which she could submit an application to the New Orleans Police Department for a police officer position. On the day she turned twenty, Frank launched an aggressive, and questionable, campaign to obtain the desired position.

After Frank was charged with murder, officials began a lengthy cycle of pointing fingers at one another since it was clear from the beginning that Frank should never have been hired to begin with. Someone had dropped the ball.

The problems started immediately with her application.

Anyone who is seeking employment as a police officer has to endure a stringent background check process. Any civil service department, like the New Orleans Police Department, first offers a written test to establish an orderly list of candidates. Frank had no problem here—she aced the test and found her name near the top. The department then assigns each applicant to a background investigator—an official who delves deep into the applicant's personal and professional life. This background check includes verification of past jobs, relationships, criminal records, and references. Then the applicant must pass a rigorous physical examination, drug screening, and a psychological evaluation.

Frank's background investigator immediately noted that she lied on her application. In her job history Frank had written that she was "transferred" from the Wal-Mart in Opelousas to the Wal-Mart in New Orleans East. She unequivocally denied being fired. An immediate red flag is raised to the background investigator when someone isn't truthful on his or her job application.

However, Frank's problems didn't stop there. Even though she sailed through her written and physical examinations with ease, it was the psychological tests that proved to end her career before it even started.

She did poorly on the first two series of psychological exams and failed miserably on the third. The last one, performed on September 1, 1992, by Dr. Philip Scurria, was an accurate summation of Frank's personality disorders. Dr. Scurria noted an immediate dislike for the aspiring young police officer, stating that within five minutes of their conversation (which she tried to control), she dropped ten to fifteen names of employees in the police department in an attempt to impress him. As for the blatant fact that she lied on her application, she looked Dr. Scurria right in the eye and said she was transferred, not fired. He classified her as "shallow, superficial, and dishonest." His ultimate report should have been looked at more closely: "[Frank] suffers from a narcissistic personality disorder with anti-social features. . . . She is not suitable for the job as a police officer."

Frank's background investigator immediately forwarded his own findings, coupled with the psychologist's report, to the chief of police. It was ignored.

Frank, sensing she would not be hired, set out on a vengeful self-marketing campaign that included numerous letters of recommendation from high-profile public figures— most of which were forged. Some of these letters were from judges and attorneys. There were even letters from the mayor of New Orleans and the chief of police. After her arrest, then-chief Arnesta Taylor was astonished to see a letter of recommendation signed by him in her file. He acknowledged that she approached him for one, but he quickly dismissed her without ever writing a letter.

Frank eventually found a loophole in the city's hiring practices. She had the option of obtaining her own independent psychological examination to counter the ones performed by the police department. On October 9, 1992, Frank sat down with Dr. Dennis Franklin for her psychological examination.

When making the appointment, she informed Dr. Franklin that she was referred to him by Judge Dennis Waldron. Later, under oath, Judge Waldron denied ever referring her.

This particular exam proved to be more promising for Frank. Dr. Franklin wrote that, although she did show traits documented by the other psychologists, "I feel this applicant could function in a position as a police officer. I see no major psychopathology." He said his conclusion was based on the "glowing" letters of recommendation written for Frank.

Still, the police department was hesitant. On January 20, 1993, Frank decided to meet with a private attorney to speed things up. Accompanying her to the appointment, Frank's father sat in the car and waited. After a couple of hours, Adam Sr. went into the building and asked the attending security guard if he'd seen Frank. Adam was promptly handed a letter with his name on it. It appeared to be a suicide note from Antoinette written to her father. It read: "I cannot live in this world the way I am, so I will not hold you down with me. I don't know where I will go but I want to be away from as many people as I can. I was doomed since the day I was born. I see that now, I hate myself and my life."

Adam Frank, who had since been living with his daughter, filed a missing persons report with the New Orleans Police Department. The note appeared to be needless since Frank showed up the next day with seemingly no explanation of where she'd been for twenty-four hours.

Astonishingly, after everything that had transpired up until this point, Antoinette Frank was officially sworn into the New Orleans Police Department two and a half weeks later. She was given badge number 628.

Frank lucked out with a police department that was frantic to hire females and minorities. Those responsible for hiring in the department felt their misgivings could be overlooked since she was not only black but also a female. Frank graduated from the police academy on February 28, 1993, and was assigned to the seventh district—the same district she lived in.

She began her duties as a police officer working second shift, 3 to 11 PM. As aggressive as she had been to land a job as a police officer, her aggression quickly dissipated when it came to the job itself. Her field training officer informed his superiors that Frank simply wasn't cut out for the job; she was clueless and too scared to perform the duties required. His recommendation of sending her back to the police academy for further training was ignored. The superiors knew that recommending a black female for termination or further training would be immediately shunned by the department, so Frank essentially squeaked through.

It was during her field training that Antoinette Frank filed a missing persons report on her father. On September 26, 1993, she came into the seventh district station on her day off and said that her father had simply vanished. The report was filed away and not much attention was paid to it—at least not for a while.

Finding Frank a partner proved to be a further problem for the seventh district. She claimed that every male officer she was assigned to sexually harassed her and that the female officers assigned to her were too mean. She couldn't get along with anybody and was quickly becoming a daily headache for the seventh district's supervisors. After a year, in which Frank was now protected by civil service, her superiors found themselves up against a brick wall. No one would work with her, and she wasn't competent enough to perform the job alone.

Eventually, they had to order someone to be her partner—an order that didn't sit well with the man selected to do it. Officer John Smith couldn't stand her. When they rode together, he had to do all of the driving because she caused accidents on an almost daily basis. He also couldn't count on her for backup. During one incident, Officer Smith wrestled with two armed suspects while Frank just stood there watching.

Smith did his best to work daily with Frank, even including her in an off-duty security detail he worked with another officer at the district, Ronnie Williams. Williams and Smith took turns working security at a local Vietnamese restaurant called Kim Anh. Most officers at the New Orleans Police Department needed the extra money, and twenty-five-year-old Ronnie Williams was no different.

Growing up in a middle-class neighborhood of East New Orleans, Williams spent the better part of his teen years working on cars. After meeting a police officer, he immediately knew, without a doubt, that he wanted to be one. He married his high school sweetheart, Mary, a year out of high school in 1989, and the couple had their first son, Christopher, later that year. Williams joined the New Orleans Police Department in 1991 and began working the Kim Anh detail when Mary was pregnant with their second child.

The owners of Kim Anh, the Vus, treated the officers who worked there like family. Antoinette Frank was no exception. In fact, they loved her like a daughter, buying her presents, giving her free food, and showering her with hugs when she came in. The Vus trusted the police officers—that was, until Frank started hanging out with Rogers LaCaze.

On November 25, 1994, Frank responded to a shooting in which the eighteen-year-old LaCaze was a victim. Born to Michael LaCaze and Alice Chaney, Rogers was no stranger to criminal behavior. After he fathered three children in his teens and dropped out of school in the tenth grade, his mother decidedly had enough. She threw him and his older brother, Michael, out of the house. Both the LaCaze brothers had a lengthy history of drugs and violence. Michael LaCaze was paralyzed and confined to a wheelchair after being shot during a bad drug deal.

Frank was one of the first officers to arrive at the shooting that sent Rogers LaCaze to the hospital and took the life of his best friend, Nemiah Miller. A few days later, when Frank went to the hospital to obtain a statement from LaCaze, their truly bizarre relationship began.

In the days after his release from the hospital, Frank began showing up at LaCaze's house, telling him to watch his back and that gangsters on the street and police officers she worked with were after him. LaCaze thought it was neat to have a cop alert him to those dangers. She immediately took LaCaze under her wing. Some say she sympathized with him because he was so small. Standing five feet nine inches and weighing 150 pounds, Frank towered over the little criminal who wore gold teeth. But from that point on, Frank and LaCaze were inseparable. She bought him clothes, phones, pagers, got him his driver's license, and even rented him a Cadillac.

Her new relationship with the career criminal raised the eyebrows of many officers within the seventh district. After the murders, many officers and citizens came forward to testify that LaCaze was normally in Frank's police cruiser with her while on duty when her partner was off. Several business owners recounted how she was so hell-bent on finding LaCaze a job, they were "bullied" by her into hiring him. One tow truck company owner recalled an incident with the frightening duo.

After handling a car accident, Frank, with LaCaze in her cruiser, followed the tow truck to the business's headquarters. Seeing the New Orleans police cruiser pull in behind the tow truck, the owner assumed Frank was there to provide him with paperwork about the car. After she approached him, with LaCaze (who was wearing street clothing), the owner became unnerved when Frank pointed at LaCaze and said, "This is my nephew. You need to give him a job." After informing the pair that he had no job openings at the time, the owner became increasingly frightened when they followed him into his office and stared at him. Sensing an impending problem, the owner told LaCaze to write his name and phone number down. He would call him if any openings arose. The uniformed police officer and her "nephew" finally left the office. The owner was left extremely shaken over the incident.

Some witnesses claimed they saw LaCaze driving Frank's police cruiser. However, even this wasn't enough to bring anyone in the department to say, or document, anything. But her brother, Adam Jr., would.

At the time, no one realized that Adam Frank Jr. was a fugitive from the law, wanted for attempted murder. Escaping the watchful eye of law enforcement in Opelousas, Adam moved in with his sister, believing her uniform and the protection of the big city would keep him under the radar.

Adam began to hang out at Kim Anh habitually. For the Vus, it was okay for a while—he was their beloved Antoinette's brother. However, they became increasingly leery around Adam and expressed their fears to Ronnie Williams. He took care of the problem immediately.

Seeing Frank at a call, Williams cornered her about her brother. He told her the Vus no longer wanted him at the restaurant and stated, "He's got to go!" Frank came unglued, exploding at her fellow officer: "Fuck you!"

She got into her cruiser with LaCaze as she continued to unleash on Williams: "Ronnie shouldn't have fucked me over like that! You don't mess with my family! I'm gonna get him. . . . I'll take him out!"

In the darkest parts of their imaginations, no one thought Frank would act out these threats.

In December 1994 officers discovered warrants for Adam Jr.'s arrest. Investigators contacted Frank, accused her of hiding a fugitive, and searched her residence. Like her father, Adam Jr. had simply disappeared. Most believe Frank helped him get out of town. However, the department was now keeping a close eye on Antoinette Frank.

In the early months of 1995, Frank and LaCaze went on an unbelievable crime spree that included several accounts of armed robbery. In one incident, Frank (on duty) pulled a car over that was occupied by two enemies of LaCaze. LaCaze exited the police car carrying an automatic TEC-9 handgun, and a fight ensued. The two men, seeing LaCaze with a police officer, made a desperate attempt to get away. However, they were apprehended by a former sheriff's deputy who happened to be driving by the incident. Frank immediately pointed at LaCaze and said, "He's the victim here." Frank booked the two men on charges of attempted murder of a police officer. Those charges were later dropped and the men were released.

Things remained tense between Frank and Williams after he expelled LaCaze from the restaurant. Williams didn't care; he thought Antoinette was just as much of a thug as the one she was hanging out with. He repeatedly voiced his opinion to the Vus telling them to stop being so nice to her.

On March 3, 1995, Williams was working at Kim Anh when Frank came in. She helped herself to a free orange juice before hugging members of the Vu family. She told them she was going to a late show with her nephew. While out she called and asked them to fix her some food, stating that the show wasn't that good, so she and LaCaze—finding that they were hungry—left early. They both came into the restaurant and sat down to a free dinner. Frank seemed distracted while in the restaurant, continuously getting up from her seat and walking around the dining room. It was closing time when they left.

Williams was incensed. He informed Chau Vu that they needed to stop giving Frank free food, and in fact, quit catering to her altogether. He told them that she was not a good police officer and insisted they needed to watch her carefully.

Sometime around midnight, Chau Vu stood in the closed restaurant counting the earnings for the night's business. Making her first priority to pay Ronnie Williams, she walked out to the front of the restaurant where he stood. It was at that moment Vu saw Frank's car pull into the parking lot for the third and final time that night. For reasons unknown, maybe it was the earlier warning issued by Ronnie Williams, Chau likely felt herself quickly growing uneasy at the sight of Frank coming to the restaurant again. Remembering the large amount of money she had been counting, Chau hurriedly ran back into the kitchen and hid the money inside the microwave.

Just as she was walking back into the dining area, Chau saw Frank and LaCaze at the front door. Initially feeling safe because the door was locked, Chau became alarmed as she watched Frank open the door with a key that had gone missing from the restaurant. Entering the building, the pair pushed Chau and other employees to the side as they headed for the kitchen. Ronnie Williams uttered his last words at that very moment.

"Hey, what's going on?" he demanded.

It was too late. Williams didn't see LaCaze behind him, nor did he see LaCaze raise the gun to the back of his head. Pulling the trigger once, LaCaze shot Ronnie Williams in the back of the neck. As Williams slumped to the floor, LaCaze shot him two more times—once directly in the head and once in the back. He wanted to make sure the officer was dead. In a further reprehensible act, LaCaze retrieved Williams's duty weapon and his wallet.

Chau, hearing the shots, pulled her brother, Quoc, and another restaurant employee into a nearby cooler to hide. Frantically worried about her other siblings, Chau held her breath as she heard Frank enter the kitchen, followed by LaCaze. They weren't alone; Chau's sister, Ha, and brother, Cuong, were in the kitchen with them. Frank was screaming at Ha to tell her where the money was. Ha didn't know, because she hadn't been in the kitchen when Chau put it in the microwave. Chau, fearful of what could happen, desperately tried to call 911 from her cell phone but had no signal inside the cooler. Instead, she and Quoc had to remain quiet while they listened to Frank brutally murder their siblings. Twenty-four-year-old Ha Vu was shot three times while she was on her knees, begging for her life. Seventeen-year-old Cuong Vu was pistol-whipped before he was shot seven times.

After ransacking the kitchen in a desperate attempt to find the money, Frank and LaCaze fled the restaurant. Terrified that the murderous pair was still inside, Chau and Quoc remained in the cooler for a short while longer before Quoc fled to a nearby residence to call 911. Chau remained in the cooler.

The 911 call came in at approximately 1:55 AM, March 4, 1995. As Frank and LaCaze were speeding down Bullard Boulevard, Frank heard the call come out over her police radio as a shooting. Seconds later, the call was changed to an "officer down" call. Frank knew with certainty that every police car within a twenty-mile radius would be screaming toward the restaurant. Dropping off LaCaze, Frank drove to the seventh district police station, demanded a department vehicle, and sped back toward the restaurant. Entering through a back door, Frank was determined to find the witnesses before the other officers arrived. Still not being able to find them, Frank stood in the shadows and waited.

Two narcotics detectives working in the area also heard the

call come out. Officers Wayne Farve and Reginald Jacques were first to arrive at the gruesome scene. They carefully parked their car in the lot before getting out. At this point, they had no idea what had transpired and didn't know if any suspects were still inside the restaurant.

From where she stood inside the cooler, Chau saw the men get out of their car, but she was frightened. Frank was a cop and had just slaughtered her family. Chau didn't know for sure if these men could be trusted. Only when she saw a marked New Orleans Police Department cruiser come into the lot did Chau run for the door. Just as she neared the door, Chau saw Frank step out of the dark and start toward her.

Outside, Farve, Jacques, and Farve's wife, Yvonne—the officer who was driving the marked police car—were startled to see the small Vietnamese woman come screaming out the front door. She was being chased by a woman wearing a black leather jacket. Chau was so upset she was screaming in Vietnamese, so the officers weren't able to understand her. Farve recognized the woman in the black leather jacket as Antoinette Frank and immediately asked her where the suspects were. "They're in the back . . . three of them wearing ski masks," Frank lied.

As Farve and Jacques walked through the carnage inside, Yvonne immediately noticed how upset Chau was around Frank. At one point, in English, Chau yelled at Frank: "You were there. You know everything. Why you ask me what happened? . . . Antoinette, why my brother and sister get killed, and Ronnie?" Chau sobbed.

"I don't know," replied Frank with masked concern.

It was most likely Frank's intention to make the grim scene appear as if she interrupted a robbery. However, the officers on the scene weren't able to instantly grasp that theory, specifically because of Frank's bizarre behavior.

Frank kept following Chau around, asking her where she had been hiding. Trying to comfort Chau, Yvonne Farve led her inside and sat with her at a table. At this point, Yvonne noticed that Frank was everywhere, pacing back and forth, walking into the kitchen, traipsing all over the crime scene. Yvonne had enough and grabbed Frank by the arm. "What are you doing?" she demanded.

"I'm a police officer," was Frank's only reply.

Frank had been ordered to remain at the scene and wait for the homicide detectives, an order that proved quite difficult for her to honor. Her actions grew increasingly strange to the other officers. "She acted trapped," recalled Yvonne, "like she was a caged animal."

At one point, Frank headed for the front door and was blocked by Yvonne, who again reminded her that she was the main witness and had to stay for detectives.

Going back to Chau, Yvonne did her best to get more information from the hysterical woman. So far, Chau had told her a little man with gold teeth had been responsible.

"Was he with anyone else?" Yvonne prodded.

"He came in with Antoinette," Chau responded fearfully, looking at Frank, who stood only a few feet away.

At that moment, Yvonne realized that Frank was not a witness, but a suspect, and quickly informed the other officers.

Homicide detectives Eddie Rantz and Marco Demma arrived on scene and were quickly briefed on Antoinette Frank. They sat down with her at a table and began asking her a series of questions about the events that led up to the shootings. Frank told them she came in with LaCaze to get food and he started shooting up the place (without her prior knowledge). Frank claimed she protected Chau and Quoc by hiding them in the cooler, and then drove to the seventh district station to report the murders. She had no explanation as to why she didn't pull her gun on the suspect, why she didn't use her police radio, and why she didn't call the police from the restaurant.

The detectives deemed her story ridiculous at best and placed Antoinette Frank in custody for murder. A warrant for LaCaze was issued, and he was found at his brother Michael's apartment.

During Frank's questioning, she changed her version of the story repeatedly and showed no emotion whatsoever. She admitted to killing Ha and Cuong, but maintained that LaCaze made her do it by holding a gun to her head. As shocked as the investigators were at Frank's cold-hearted demeanor, nothing prepared them for the question she asked at the end of her interview. "Sir, do you think I'm going to lose my job?" she calmly asked one of them.

They were incredulous.

Antoinette Frank and Rogers LaCaze were both indicted for three counts of aggravated murder on April 28, 1995. Both faced the death penalty. They were tried separately, and on July 21, 1995, Rogers LaCaze was found guilty and sentenced to death. At first, LaCaze claimed that Frank was obsessed with him, and that he had no other choice but to hang out with her. Later, he claimed he looked up to her, because he had also wanted to be a police officer since he was five years old. LaCaze is still on death row, awaiting his execution.

Frank's trial began September 5, 1995. Only one hour into the trial, Frank tried to fire her attorney and was quickly admonished by the judge. The defense's case was seemingly weak. During the trial, prosecutor Elizabeth Teel noted the emotionless demeanor of Frank. "She scared me. . . . She would stare at me and smile, and it would send the worst shivers up and down my back. . . . I think she is just an evil person."

It took the jury only twenty minutes to return a guilty verdict and forty minutes to recommend the death penalty. Frank stood stoically as the judge handed down her sentence: "I sentence you to death by lethal injection, and may God have mercy on your soul."

Antoinette Frank is one of two women currently sitting on death row awaiting execution.

In November 1995 a gruesome discovery was made under Frank's old home in New Orleans East. A neighbor, seeing his dog chewing on something in the yard, was shocked to see that the chew toy was actually a human spine. Officers responded and found a grave containing human bones under Frank's house. The grave had been covered in lime, and the skull that was found there had a bullet hole in it. Frank refused to answer any questions about the remains, but later claimed that her killing spree was a direct result of years of sexual and physical abuse at the hands of her father. These claims have laid the groundwork for several appeals. She's had two execution dates postponed so that the courts can further investigate this theory, much to the Williams and Vu families' dismay.

To date, the New Orleans Police Department has taken no action in identifying the bones, assuming they are the remains of Frank's father, Adam Sr.

To this day, those who remember Frank remember her as calculated, cold, and most important, evil. There are those who place the blame solely on the New Orleans Police Department; had they never hired her, the murders would never have occurred.

Chuck Hustmyre, who wrote the full story of Antoinette Frank in *Killer with a Badge: The True Story of Antoinette Frank, the Cop-Killing Cop*, had only one thing to say about the monstrous duo: "Frank and LaCaze deserve the death penalty, and I can't wait for justice to be served," he wrote.

As for the residents of New Orleans and the officers that remain at the New Orleans Police Department, they continue to try to erase Antoinette Frank from memory. Ronnie Williams's widow, Mary, and the remaining members of the Vu family continue to pick up the pieces while going on with their lives. In fact, the Vus and the Williamses have grown quite close since the incident. Kim Anh is still open for business, and Ronnie Williams's own son works there occasionally—just as his own father had over a decade ago.

PART III
THE MOST UNUSUAL

CHAPTER 10

HE KILLED HIS GAY LOVER

STEVEN RIOS
POLICE OFFICER, COLUMBIA, MISSOURI

Desperation rises to a significantly higher level in the case of Columbia, Missouri, police officer Steven Rios; twenty-seven years old, married to a young, attractive brunette named Libby, and father to a newborn son, Steven Rios was considered by many to be a fortunate man. However, Steven Rios felt differently underneath his uniform and empowering badge—he was suffocating.

A city of roughly ninety thousand people and home to the University of Missouri, Columbia, Missouri, certainly had its fair share of crime. Steven's assigned patrol area was the East Campus district of the university, a relatively low crime area, the infractions consisting of nothing more than college crimes: drunkenness, loud parties, disorderly conduct, and vandalism. However, on the afternoon of June 5, 2004, the university, residents of Columbia, and particularly Steven Rios, took notice.

At approximately two o'clock in the afternoon, the body of twenty-three-year-old university student Jesse Valencia was found in the backyard of a residence about a block from his own apartment. His throat had been viciously and savagely slashed.

For those close to Jesse, the crime was heart stopping. Growing up in Kentucky, Jesse transferred to the University of Missouri in 2002 from Earlham College in Indiana. Majoring in history, Jesse was described as a loving, friendly, and outgoing person who was driven to succeed in his endeavors. However, acquaintances and friends of Jesse began immediately to question whether his murder was the result of a hate crime, because Jesse Valencia was openly gay.

One of the aspects of Jesse's personality respected by his friends was his ability to embrace and accept his homosexuality. His family knew and supported him, and he made no attempt to conceal his sexual orientation. In fact, Jesse felt so strongly about the issue of legalizing gay and lesbian marriages, he wrote an editorial piece titled "The Maneater" on this topic for the college newspaper.

With looks that could no doubt land him a modeling career, Jesse went through his life with a strong sense of self-awareness, vigor, vivacity, and an outgoing personality that drew people to his side, earning him an enviable amount of friends. Jesse worked evenings as a hotel clerk and attended many social events afterward: parties, Internet dates, and frequenting the only gay nightclub in Columbia. According to friends, Jesse joked about the possibility of becoming the first homosexual president of the United States.

As social and outgoing as Jesse was, it was almost incredible to most of the people who knew him that he would keep a secret lover without them knowing. But in the days following his murder this would be proven true. Fortunately for Jesse's family and friends, he had provided enough information about his secret lover to a few people that the investigators on the case knew where to start looking almost immediately.

Rumors began to run rampant within the gay community that Jesse Valencia was secretly dating a cop. Chances are, investigators would have dismissed this theory, had they not been approached by fellow officer Steven Rios, who offered his assistance. This sort of gesture also wouldn't raise any red flags—except that Steven Rios was on his day off.

Anyone can understand how much most police officers value their time away from the job. It's the time they can spend with family and friends enjoying life inside the bubble—a place where normal people live. They can ignore the incessant criminal activity and inhumane violence they have to deal with on the other days of the week. Occasionally, an overly eager rookie comes along who lives and breathes police work, even while on his days off. However, Steven Rios, by all accounts prior to the night of the murder, did not fall into this category. What is astonishing about the events of June 5 is that Steven Rios acted out in a textbook manner that is clearly associated with a suspect's behavior.

He arrived at the crime scene on his day off, offering to help.

Regardless, this was prior to the rumors and witness statements, and although Steven's actions may have raised an eyebrow or two that day, no one thought much of it. Of course, what would anyone possibly think? That a gawky, twenty-seven-year-old cop with a receding hairline, glasses, and a family would have any connection to the dashing young college student? Most wouldn't believe that the two would have anything to do with each other.

Rios came forward on the day of the murder and offered to identify Valencia's body. Steven's demeanor was casual as he told a sergeant that he knew Jesse from arresting him at a party on April 18 for interfering with officers who were making another arrest. What he failed to add was that, after that night, he began visiting Jesse Valencia at his apartment—where they began a sexual relationship.

Steven sauntered over to the crime scene and was placed outside of Valencia's basement apartment to ensure that no one entered without permission. Perhaps it was the fact that he was at the scene of the heinous crime again, or that the reality of what happened finally sunk in—whatever it was, Steven's demeanor changed throughout the course of the day, catching the attention of fellow officer James Means later in the evening. Admittedly a good friend of Steven's, Means asked what was wrong. Steven merely said he was tired.

"Based on what I know of Steve, there was something wrong," Means recalled.

Of course, it's certainly plausible that Steven could have been tired. After going off duty at 3:00 AM, he joined his co-workers in a nightly ritual of drinking beer on the roof of the police department until 4:45 AM. Rios arrived at home around 5:30. His wife was awake, preparing a bottle for their son, Grayson, and they all went to bed around six. Waking up at ten, Steven drove to the nearest police substation to send out a memo to the other officers for a children's program that he was in charge of. However, Means had seen Steven tired before, and this was something entirely different.

In the days following the murder, and with little to go on, investigators reached out to Columbia's gay community in hopes of gathering information. They stopped at the famed gay bar SoCo Club and the Columbia Gay Pride benefit show, all the while distributing Jesse's photograph. It was crucial for the investigators to establish a timeline of Jesse's last hours prior to his death. This was done fairly quickly. They determined that after leaving his shift at the hotel, Jesse attended a college party on the East Campus, leaving around 3:30 AM. It was the statement made by Jesse's neighbor, Ryan Kepner, which proved the most useful to investigators.

Kepner was trying to go to sleep when he heard loud thumping noises coming from Jesse's apartment between 3:30 and 4:00 AM.

"I got the impression that he was trying to kick somebody out of the apartment that didn't want to go," Kepner recalled to a news reporter. "After awhile, I yelled back at the wall saying, 'Yeah, stop it,' because I couldn't get to sleep. Then it was over, the noise stopped."

Kepner told the investigators that he didn't wake up until 2:00 PM and soon saw that Jesse's front door was slightly ajar. Kepner later told reporters that he was going to apologize for yelling during the night because he didn't want any tension with his neighbor.

In the hopes of establishing a time of death, investigators swiftly began to account for any relationships Jesse was involved in, trying to learn if any threats were made against him. Soon after, numerous tips that claimed Jesse was involved with a police officer came flooding in. It became a long, tedious investigation. Jesse was also involved in numerous online chat rooms that investigators needed to learn about. At first, the evidence and information was difficult to sort out, but Steven Rios unknowingly made the investigation much easier.

Only days after the murder, Steven—upon hearing the rumors of Jesse's involvement with a police officer—approached detectives immediately to inform them that he was not the officer involved with Valencia. This was an odd move, considering that no one in the department had even mentioned his name as being the involved officer—at least not openly or publicly. The investigators working the case already had Steven's name and were slightly taken aback when Steven gave the names of two other officers in an attempt to incriminate them. At that point in the case, the investigators had several statements from Jesse's friends that gave eyewitness accounts of Steven's relationship with him, including a statement from a man named Andy Schermerhorn who claimed to have had sexual relations with Steven and Jesse at the same time.

Andy thought that he was going to jail. He was inside Jesse's bedroom when the door burst open and the harsh beam of a flashlight was trained upon them, alerting Andy and confirming his fear that the man holding the light was a police officer. Doing his best to hurry and put his clothes on, Andy was shocked when the officer told the lovers to continue what they were doing. What came next was beyond comprehension. The officer, Steven Rios, took off his gun and belt—and joined the duo in bed.

Regardless of Andy's statement, coupled with the others, for an officer to be involved in a homosexual affair certainly doesn't present a motive for murder. The county's own prosecutor, Kevin Crane, admitted to the press that there are other gay officers on the force. In Columbia, known as the most liberal city in the state, being gay doesn't make waves. Unfortunately, it weighed heavily on Steven Rios. Being gay isn't a motive for murder, but threatening to expose a man's homosexuality to his wife, his boss, and the community he works in is another story. And to top it all off, there were threats to out Rios.

According to Jesse's best friend, Joan Sheridan, three days prior to the murder, Jesse explained to her his plan to expose Steven. One of the biggest issues for Jesse was that Steven wouldn't come clean about his marital status. Jesse told Joan that he was going to confront Steven once and for all to find out if he was married or not, adding that he didn't want to be in a relationship with a married man. It was the end of Jesse's conversation with Joan that most likely proved fatal for the young college student. He was planning to tell Steven that he wanted him to dismiss the ticket Steven issued him the night he was arrested on April 18.

"If he doesn't, the police chief might learn a little secret," Joan recalled Jesse saying.

Jesse's mother, Linda, also told investigators that her son was terrified of Rios. She knew of their affair and claimed Jesse called her numerous times because he was too scared to break it off. She said she told him repeatedly to file a police report. However, no such report was ever filed.

No one but Steven knows if Jesse followed through on his threats. Considering the brutality of Jesse's murder, a strong assumption logically suggests that he did.

Armed with the incriminating statements, on June 9—four days after Jesse's body was found—investigators confronted Steven Rios about his intimate relationship with Jesse Valencia, a relationship he initially lied about. With the pile of statements made against him, Steven had no other choice but to admit that he had been sexually involved with Jesse. Steven requested a leave that day, went home and immediately told his wife, Libby, of the affair, and suggested they attend marriage counseling.

The chief of police later gave a statement to the media that an officer admitted to a relationship with Jesse Valencia, but he refused to give Steven's name or say that he was being considered a suspect. In fact, the police chief, Randy Boehm, went further and added that the officer had been thoroughly investigated and there was nothing tying him to the crime.

This wasn't good enough for the media; they wanted a name—and unfortunately for Steven, they found one. On June 10, after attending another interview with investigators, Steven Rios went home and turned his television to the local news. Stunned, he saw a picture of himself in uniform prominently displayed on the screen. After announcing that there was a "bombshell" in the Jesse Valencia homicide, Steven Rios's name was repeated over and over as Jesse's homosexual lover. At that point, the rising tension that had been building in Steven over the last five days finally exploded.

In a strange turn of events, Steven immediately got into his car and drove to Kansas City, Missouri. Using his cell phone, Steven called police back in Columbia and informed them that he had purchased a shotgun and ammunition. He was going to shoot himself. It took several hours for detectives to convince him to drive back to Columbia, where he was immediately taken into protective custody and placed in the Mid-Missouri Mental Health Center for a psychological evaluation.

With increasingly bizarre behavior exhibited by Steven, while continuing to deny him as a murder suspect, investigators focused on the Rios home the day after the suicide threat. Armed with a search warrant, investigators seized numerous items, which included clothing and the contents of his shower drain. Searching his home and vehicles, there was one item in particular that the investigators were desperate to locate: a four-inch-long serrated knife. During his previous interviews with investigators, Steven claimed that he didn't own a knife—a claim disputed by his fellow officers who allegedly saw Steven with it on several occasions. However, investigators couldn't locate the knife in question.

Only hours after the search of the Rios home concluded, Steven made an attempt to take his own life. In a blatant and ostentatious spectacle, Steven escaped from the mental health facility and was found on top of the fifth-floor parking garage, threatening to jump. While officers on the ground continued to shake their heads in disbelief at this and the other bizarre events of the past week, the crisis negotiation team and a family member struggled to talk Steven down. Steven stood, with his back to the ground below, for nearly two hours.

Steven Rios during suicide attempt. Photo reprinted by permission of *Columbia Tribune*.

Police blocked off surrounding streets, yellow crime scene tape was put up to prohibit pedestrians from nearing the scene, and emergency workers were inflating a giant air mattress to break Steven's fall should he choose to jump.

Again conceding to the demands of his fellow officers, Steven eventually stepped down from the ledge, was placed into protective custody, and was quickly spirited off to the mental health facility. Afterward, Chief Boehm explained to the media that none of the statements Steven made while on the ledge incriminated him in the Valencia murder investigation—he was still not considered a suspect.

Chief Boehm's play on words continued to unsettle the
media. After the events of the past several days it was clear to
any prudent person that Steven Rios was somehow connected
to the murder of Jesse Valencia. Soon realizing the incredulity
of the public and the media that existed as long as he denied
that Steven was a suspect, Boehm eventually saw the case
through new eyes when questions were raised as to whether or
not his department was capable of investigating their own.
Several days later, Boehm changed his tune.

Although he continued to say that at that point Rios still
was not a suspect, he maintained reservation when using the
word. "The term 'suspect' is usually reserved for someone
police are seeking to arrest, or someone officially charged with
a crime. Rios, at this point, does not fit that narrow defini-
tion," Boehm explained.

However, Boehm would admit that Rios was considered a
"person of interest" in the case and that two investigators
from the state highway patrol were assisting investigators.
While Boehm's statement that Steven didn't incriminate himself as he stood on the ledge preserved Rios's innocence, the
conversation that Steven had with Detective Jeff Westbrook
after the fact did not.

Detective Westbrook told Steven that he wanted the truth
about his involvement in the murder of Jesse Valencia.

"If I killed Jesse Valencia then I'd kill myself," Steven responded.

"But you almost did kill yourself," Detective Westbrook
countered.

"Yes, but I couldn't go through with it."

Some may consider Steven's response a "shadowed" confession. However, what most didn't know at the time was that
although they had plenty of circumstantial evidence tying
Steven Rios to the murder, Chief Boehm was waiting for the
smoking gun—physical evidence.

Within two weeks of Jesse Valencia's murder, investigators interviewed hundreds of potential witnesses that led to the questioning of dozens of people, costing the department approximately 750 hours of overtime. Investigators reviewed 266 leads in the case, produced 10,000 lines of text, and composed 276 reports—undoubtedly one of the largest cases the Columbia Police Department has ever seen. Sorting through the case very carefully, investigators continually returned to Steven Rios as a suspect.

Rios officially ended his career as a police officer on June 16 when he had his attorney deliver his written resignation to Chief Boehm. Not listing any reason for quitting, Rios essentially went into hiding.

Consequently, the smoking gun that Chief Boehm was waiting for arrived in the form of DNA retrieved from underneath Jesse Valencia's fingernails and from hairs found on his chest. Both indisputably matched Steven Rios. On July 1, 2007, Special Prosecutor Morley Swingle formally charged Steven Rios with first-degree murder and armed criminal action in the murder of Jesse Valencia. Steven was being held in the more secure Fulton State Hospital at the time the charges were filed. Citing him as a "danger to himself and the community," Circuit Judge Gary Oxenhandler denied Rios bond.

Friends and family of Jesse Valencia cried tears of relief over the arrest and waited anxiously for the trial to begin. Linda Valencia wanted justice—and the insanity surrounding the case to stop. Throughout the investigation, Linda rode a nonstop emotional roller coaster. While receiving numerous calls from friends and strangers offering their prayers and support, she also received several e-mails and phone calls providing just the opposite. Some of the brutally harassing messages contained vile attacks aimed at her dead son.

"You will suffer in hell because your son was gay. . . . He deserved to die," was but one of the more disturbing messages.

After her Kentucky home was burglarized and several of Jesse's things were taken, Linda was ultimately fired from her job at a local hotel because of the incessant reporters and other media people who constantly harassed her.

On the other hand, Steven Rios appeared to be quite optimistic about his upcoming trial. In August 2004, while still incarcerated at the Fulton State Hospital, Steven contacted a local reporter and criticized the media's interpretation of his involvement.

"It's totally wrong," he declared, "I still have friends in Columbia that support me. . . . Just remember, there's another side to this, and people out there have information."

When asked if he expected to be set free, Steven simply said, "yes."

The murder trial of Steven Rios began on May 17, 2005. The prosecution presented a battery of witnesses for the trial, including Valencia's former lover Jack Barry.

Jack testified to Jesse's personal hygiene. Since Steven claimed he hadn't been with Jesse in five days prior to the murder, the question of whether or not Jesse washed regularly was important to the prosecution. The DNA expert who found Steven's DNA under Jesse's fingernails claimed it was "highly unlikely" the DNA would still be there five days later, even if Jesse hadn't washed. Jack Barry dated Jesse off and on for approximately two years and was quite accustomed to his personal habits. Holding Jesse's manicure kit, which was submitted as evidence, Jack testified that Jesse filed his nails down rather than clean them. And, although Jesse only showered every other day, he washed his hands and face daily.

Afterward, the Boone County medical examiner, Valerie Rao, gave detailed testimony to the jury about the injuries

Jesse received the night of the murder. Not only was his throat slashed, but he had also been beaten fiercely. He had severe hemorrhaging on his chest, bruises all over his body, and numerous abrasions. The prosecution proceeded to show the jury nearly fifty photographs of Jesse Valencia's dead body.

What was anticipated by the defense as the "ace in the hole" witness failed to influence the jury or put reasonable doubt in their minds as had been hoped. Called as a prosecution witness, Ed McDevitt had met Jesse Valencia two days before the murder at a gay nightclub. Engaging in sexual relations afterward, Ed and Jesse had planned to meet again on the night of his murder. In fact, Ed McDevitt was the last person to talk to Jesse or see him alive. What furthered the defense's hopes was that McDevitt's DNA was also found on Jesse and in his apartment—more than Steven's DNA was. Another key factor was McDevitt's roommate, Eric Thurston. With a lengthy criminal history, Thurston was incarcerated and wearing a prison jumpsuit at the time of his testimony; a visual most would concur gives a jury an immediate negative opinion of the witness. The defense laid the theory before the jury that Thurston was jealous of McDevitt's relationship with Jesse and that it was either Thurston or McDevitt who went to Jesse's that morning—not Rios.

The prosecutors shredded this theory when they put another witness on the stand, Kevin Harmon, who testified that he picked Thurston up at 3:30AM and brought him back to his apartment, where he stayed until 10:00 AM. This was the only witness to testify to Thurston's alibi.

The defense came back again, questioning Detective Westbrook about the conversation he'd had with Rios immediately following his suicide attempt. Westbrook admitted that Steven told him what his habits were when it came to Jesse. On any given occasion, Steven wouldn't visit Jesse that late because he was expected at home by his wife. Taking care of a household and a newborn baby, Libby relied on her husband for much-needed breaks at the end of a long day. Furthermore, Steven would only stop at Jesse's when he saw the bedroom light on.

The ultimate hope for the defense was Steven's own testimony. Dressed in a crisp blue suit, Steven blatantly denied any role in Jesse's murder. When asked why he logged into the dispatcher's CAD system the morning the body was found, Steven claimed it was "by habit." He merely wanted to see what was "going on out on the street." He never sent the memo he had intended because he got distracted by coverage of former president Ronald Reagan's death. As for the knife, Steven maintained he never owned one, disputing numerous officers' testimony to the contrary.

Several officers testified that Steven carried a serrated knife, including one he carried on a canoe trip the day the tip came in about the victim dating a married police officer. As the officers were joking around about the new information, Steven claimed he was sick and needed to go home. Steven contended that the knives he was seen carrying either belonged to other officers or were taken from suspects. As for initially lying to investigators about his relationship with Jesse, he said he had wanted to tell them the day of the murder, but the "brutal gay jokes" made by the other officers at the crime scene stopped him from doing so. He was humiliated and knew the consequences should he come forward.

Steven offered no explanation as to why he left the canoe trip to go home and tell his wife that he was afraid of being implicated in an affair with the victim. His paranoia seemed less than rational.

Incredibly, testimony that was not allowed at the trial further damned Steven in his bizarre behavior. Earlier in the trial, Officer Ted Anderson testified that he had responded to two noise complaints at Jesse Valencia's apartment. On both occasions, Steven jibed to him about "being at your gay lover's house." Anderson further testified that after the murder Steven laughed at him and said, "I see your gay lover is dead." The officer stated he was confused by the ongoing joke and didn't know what Steven meant by it. Anderson was shocked to learn that he was one of the two officers who Steven had initially named as suspects during his first interview with detectives.

Furthermore, the prosecution had several individuals prepared to testify that Steven told Jesse his name was Anderson, and even wore a badge with the name emblazoned on it when visiting Jesse's apartment. Ted Anderson reported his name badge missing earlier that year, and it still had not been located at the time of the trial. Considering this was hearsay, the testimony was not allowed.

During Steven's testimony, there were more than one hundred friends and acquaintances of Jesse packed into the courtroom to show their support for Linda Valencia.

Perhaps the most damaging of all testimony came from Joan Sheridan in recounting the conversation she had with Jesse and learning of his threats to expose Steven to the police department. This was the key point when the prosecution established its motive.

Finally, the testimony of Libby Rios proved emotional for both sides. Even Linda Valencia expressed sadness for her, even though Libby supported Steven diligently throughout the entire case. She testified to the fact that Steven never owned a knife and remembered that he had asked for one the previous Christmas. Since they were expecting a baby, she said they couldn't afford it at the time. When asked if she'd forgiven her husband for the affair, she said, "no." For either side, it was hard to imagine the roller coaster of emotions suffered by Libby Rios. What appeared in her eyes as a picture-perfect life had been ultimately shattered—before the public, to make matters worse.

Steven Rios listens to verdict. Photo reprinted by permission of *Columbia Tribune*.

On Friday, May 20, closing arguments were heard and Steven Rios's life was officially in the hands of the jury. On Saturday, May 21, after nine hours of deliberating, a verdict was reached—guilty on all counts. When questioned afterward, the jurors claimed Steven's credibility was sociopathic and his emotions were "just for show." His own testimony was the most damaging. While deliberating, some jurors claimed to have doubts. The alleged ringleader of the jury, Jared Buchan, admittedly told them "He's a cop, he can get away with anything," until they were ultimately convinced. Also, they didn't like Rios's own testimony and deemed him "unbelievable." Additionally, Joan Sheridan gave them the perfect motive.

Linda Valencia's words were just as harsh for Steven. Although she acknowledged a slight sense of compassion for Libby Rios, Linda made her thoughts well known on the courthouse steps following the verdict: "I hope every day he's in

Linda Valencia addresses reporters after verdict.
Photo reprinted by permission of *Columbia Tribune*.

prison, he suffers. I never felt compassion for him while I looked at him because he had no compassion for my son."

Steven Rios received an automatic sentence of life imprisonment without parole. In another move, Prosecutor Morely Swingle, in his usual manner of grandstanding, asked for a second life sentence for the sole purpose of sending a message to other law enforcement officers that "there will be a ton of bricks dropped" if they break the laws they are sworn to uphold. There was no second life sentence added.

It would be logical to assume that the case was finally put to rest and that the family and friends of Jesse Valencia would be able to go about their lives, grieving and remembering Jesse fondly—all images and thoughts of Steven Rios forever removed from their minds. Once in awhile, Rios would remind everyone that he was still there. In the first interview that he gave since his sentencing in October 2005, Steven still upheld that many facts were not given in court, and he was very confident in the appellate process. "I just want to get back to being a dad and living my life," he told the reporter.

His arrogance angered many, while others laughed at his wishful thinking. Regrettably, the city of Columbia, Linda Valencia, and others received the shock of their lives on April 27, 2007: Steven Rios's conviction had been completely overturned and thrown out by the Missouri Court of Appeals. He would automatically receive a new trial.

The three-judge panel on the court of appeals ruled that Joan Sheridan's testimony to the conversation between she and Jesse, a conversation that established a motive for the prosecution, was hearsay—completely inadmissible during a trial. Allowing Joan's testimony tainted the jury, the court ruled. In the actual ruling, the court stated:

The trial court erred in admitting the two hearsay statements made by the victim because the statements did not indicate intent to perform an act in the immediate future and, therefore, did not fall within the future acts exception to the hearsay rule. In addition, because the statements were offered by the State to provide Rios a motive for murder, admission of the statements prejudiced Rios . . . because the trial court erred in admitting two statements made by the victim, and the admission of those statements prejudiced Mr. Rios, the trial court's judgment is reversed and the case is remanded for a new trial.

The state of Missouri attorney general's office immediately filed a request with the appellate court to rehear the appeal or to transfer the appeal to the Missouri Supreme Court. Both requests were denied. With the new trial set for August 1, 2008, the case proved to be one of the most watched in Missouri's history.

However, in August 2008, the trial was again delayed until December of that year. Most continue to wonder if the case was simply about a man, husband, and father who caved to the standards of social acceptability, becoming humiliated at his homosexual tendencies. Others believe it was a case of a calculated, trained, and vengeful police officer who used his badge and authority to take the life of another.

In December 2008 Stephen Rios was again convicted of murdering Jesse Valencia.

CHAPTER 11

SHE FILED A COMPLAINT, SO HE KILLED HER

LEN DAVIS
POLICE OFFICER, NEW ORLEANS, LOUISIANA

They were the years that "The Big Easy" turned into "The Big Sleazy." Jokes trumpeted across the pages of city newspapers: a solution to the massive crime problem within the city of New Orleans, Louisiana—"Want Less Crime? Hire Fewer Policemen!" Of course, the satirical suggestion failed to amuse city officials or those residents feeling the brunt of the rising crime rate. These were the years before Hurricane Katrina. The 1990s—a time when New Orleans was no longer known for its historical intrigue, famous Mardi Gras, great food, and spectacular movie locations, but for its overwhelming number of corrupt cops on its payroll and murders in its streets. It was the case of convicted murderer and former New Orleans police officer Len Davis that exposed the heart of corruption within city hall.

In 1994, New Orleans was branded the unwelcomed title of "Murder Capital of the World." Ending the year with 421 murders ranked it as the city with the highest per capita murder rate in the nation. Understanding that the taste for rich Cajun food or the dubious honor of earning beads during Mardi Gras wasn't worth one's life, tourism industry revenue dropped to a record low. Conventions went elsewhere and businesses pulled out. Organizations from large to small boycotted the city, demanding action from the powers that be.

And if the murder and crime rates weren't bad enough, New Orleans received another unsavory distinction—the highest police brutality rate in the nation. In fact, on October 31, 1994, CBS showcased the tainted police department in an hour-long segment on the popular show *60 Minutes*. If the majority of the nation hadn't been aware of the seedy workings of one of the country's largest cities, they were now. New Orleans mayor Marc Morial was furious over the CBS show, calling it "as stale as a six-month-old loaf of French bread."

However, it was murder number 341 in 1994—a murder the mayor was unaware of at the time of the CBS show—that catapulted the darkest, most evil secrets of the NOPD to the frontlines. It was the murder of thirty-two-year-old Kimberly Groves.

A single mother of three, the attractive Groves was a part-time security officer who supported her family by working at the Louisiana Superdome. Before the rest of America had even heard of places like the Ninth Ward and the Superdome during Hurricane Katrina, Groves worked at the stadium and returned to her children in the low-income and high-crime area of the city's Ninth Ward. However, it was a decision made by Groves on October 11, 1994, that proved fatal.

She happened upon two New Orleans police officers, Len Davis and Sammie Williams, as they mercilessly beat a citizen. The officers were literally pistol-whipping a young man, Nathan Norwood. Although she wasn't a police officer, Groves felt strongly about her position as a security guard and knew the incident that she witnessed was criminal. She felt it was time someone took a stand against the ongoing police brutality that invaded her neighborhood, so she promptly filed a complaint with the NOPD internal affairs division.

For the most part, Officer Len Davis was accustomed to complaints filed against him. He was also accustomed to the complaints merely "going away" because witnesses were too scared to come forward—or they simply, and conveniently, couldn't "remember" what happened. A common scenario that Davis made sure of.

A seven-year veteran, Davis had over twenty complaints filed against him for a variety of reasons. The six-foot, two-hundred-pound Davis usually laughed these charges off, which ranged from brutality and intimidation to theft. One of the few times he was disciplined occurred when he was accused of hitting a woman over the head with a flashlight. Davis received a fifty-one-day suspension from his duties.

He was, perhaps, as close to the criminals as one could get, since he ironically grew up with most of them in the Ninth Ward. In fact, Len Davis was hired by the New Orleans Police Department while carrying his own history of criminal behavior. Convictions of battery, urinating in public, and other misdemeanors were quickly expunged from his record.

During the 1980s, the NOPD began feeling the pressure from civil rights watchdogs and community groups regarding their lack of minority hiring. In a city with a 65 percent black population, the groups felt the department was overlooking qualified candidates of color. Unfortunately, the NOPD held a strict residency standard that required all of its policemen to reside within the city limits—limits that contained the highest areas of crime. Therefore, administrators at the NOPD thumbed their noses at the groups in a "you want it, you got it" manner and lowered hiring standards, recruiting known criminals from areas such as the Ninth Ward and bypassing other, more qualified black applicants. Some of these criminals who were given badges and guns had horrific crimes on their records, which ranged from armed robbery to rape. These records were expunged. Len Davis was one of these recruits.

Beginning his career with a pattern of criminal behavior that started when he was suspended from the police academy for "unspecified disciplinary problems," Davis was ultimately suspended four more times in his short career and received one written notice of disciplinary action. On the flip side, Davis received two medals of commendation, one for chasing down and catching an armed robber—essentially, for doing his job.

Davis was ultimately transferred to the Fifth District, known as "The Bloody Fifth." Most of the officers who accrued a lengthy disciplinary record or caused too many headaches for the department were assigned there—the NOPD's own form of exile. With 145 of the 421 murders occurring within the Fifth District, it was as if the NOPD was throwing a pack of wolves into a lion's den; utter chaos and violence was the only possible result.

Frequently visiting and terrorizing the Desire and Florida low-income housing projects within the district, Davis became known as "Robocop" to some due to his size, but he was "the Desire Terrorist" to most. Even though the residents were used to the criminal behavior of the police officers in their district, Davis was the worst. Reporter James Gill of the *Times-Picayune* summed up Davis's career in the district accurately: "Though the competition is tough, Len Davis may just be the most dangerous criminal ever to have worn the uniform of a New Orleans police officer."

This statement, of course, was made prior to the arrest of Antoinette Frank.

Davis's intimidation and brutalization of the majority of the residents within the projects caused local ministers to stand up and complain to the NOPD. However, the complaints fell on deaf ears. It wasn't unusual for Davis to end his shift at a seedy bar in the Ninth Ward, laughing at the complaints with his criminal friends. One of those friends was Paul "Cool" Hardy.

Hardy, a notorious twenty-eight-year-old drug dealer, was arrested twice previously for murder charges. Feared on the streets as a cold-blooded killer, Hardy was known to have an arsenal of weapons within his reach. It was rumored, and later confirmed, that Hardy and Davis negotiated numerous drug deals together, with Davis covering up their trail. Hardy welcomed the protection Davis provided, and Davis welcomed the money that Hardy generated.

It was no secret that the New Orleans police officers were some of the lowest-paid men and women in uniform in the entire country. Starting out at a meager income of just $15,000 per year, the department found over 80 percent of its officers working extra duty details just to survive. Even its high-ranking members found their income of $25,000–$30,000 per year just below what most of the country's officers were starting at. The nation's lowest-paid police officers in the city with the nation's highest crime proved to be a volatile combination. The old adage "you get what you pay for" earned new meaning and caused morale and public trust to run at a record low. Most officers were too tired from their extra duty details to put forth a valiant effort during their regular shifts, and most maintained an unusually high stress level due to financial burdens that, ultimately, led to marital problems. For most of the fifteen hundred honest, hardworking officers at the department, extra duty was the only way to survive. For others, like Len Davis, cutting corners and negotiating with the local criminals was far easier.

In fact, the NOPD received a significant amount of blame

when it came to connections with Len Davis and other officers. To some, hiring a man of Len Davis's character was comparable to appointing John Wayne Gacy as a Boy Scout troup leader. It was inevitable, given his past criminal history, that handing him a badge and a gun would only allow him to cover and commit his own crimes, rather than fight crime. Regardless, all of the complaints and finger-pointing failed to slow the momentum of Davis's corrupt life as a law enforcement officer—for a while, that is.

On October 11, 1994, Kimberly Groves filed a complaint against Davis for police brutality. By October 13, 1994, less than forty-eight hours later, she was dead. Davis's own partner, Sammie Williams, proved crucial in testifying against him.

According to Williams, during the late afternoon hours of October 13, 1994, he and Davis were on duty and stopped at a red light in their police cruiser. Another car pulled up next to them, also stopping. Inside the vehicle was Groves, with several other people. Groves, upon spotting Davis and Williams next to them, started alerting the other occupants of the car, pointing at the officers and mouthing the words "that's them! that's them!" She had clearly informed the people she was with about her complaint two days earlier.

Davis was furious. Pointing out the window at Groves, he yelled at her, "I see you, too! I see you, too!"

Davis couldn't believe the woman had the audacity to challenge him on the very streets he controlled, especially with others watching. At that point, completely irate, Davis picked up his pager while making an alarming statement: "I could get 'P' to do this whore! We can handle the 30!" he blurted, angrily.

Williams knew "P" to be Paul Hardy, Davis's cohort in crime. A "signal 30" was police code for homicide. As Williams understood it, Davis wanted Hardy to murder the woman.

Davis and Williams would be the first responders to the homicide, subsequently eliminating any incriminating evidence at the scene. A short time later, Hardy responded to Davis's page. By later that evening, Davis was calling Hardy with a description of the intended murder victim, and her address.

By 10:15 PM, Hardy, accompanied by two other known criminals, Damon Causey and Steve Jackson, was en route to Grove's home in Jackson's 1991 blue Nissan Maxima.

Lying in wait, Hardy watched as Groves pulled into her driveway and walked toward the front door. In execution style, Hardy walked up to Groves and shot her directly in the head.

Fleeing the scene, Hardy threw the cylinder of the gun into a nearby canal and replaced it. Handing the weapon over to Causey, he instructed him to hide it in his apartment. Causey complied. The first order of business afterward was to call Davis and inform him the hit had been carried out. Davis was overjoyed. "Yeah, yeah, yeah! It's rock'n' roll time!" he allegedly yelled.

Calling his partner, Williams said that Davis simply informed him, "Signal 30 NAT." Williams understood this to be "homicide complete—necessary action taken." After the crime scene was "cleaned up,"—essentially, tainted—the officers celebrated with the murderous group at a Ninth Ward bar.

Despite the three young children now left without a mother, the murder of Kim Groves garnered little to no attention other than a short obituary. Groves had been involved for years in an abusive relationship with Sylvester "Jimmy" Jones, a likely suspect in her murder. But with only a few witnesses claiming to see a young man driving from the scene in a blue car, and little interest from law enforcement, the case went cold. With the highest percentage of murders in the city consisting of "black on black" crime, Groves's murder was simply filed away with the rest.

It was truly more of an accident, not hard-core investigative work, which led to Davis's involvement in the murder. It also had to do with the spotlight on the newly appointed police chief, Richard Pennington. Tired of the criticism and harsh focus on his city as corrupt and dying, Mayor Morial launched a nationwide search for a new police chief who would clean up New Orleans. He found his prime candidate in Pennington.

Formerly the assistant police chief in Washington, DC, Pennington was known for his tough tactics in policing his own. In fact, prior to his swearing in, Pennington took it upon himself to drive around the streets of New Orleans while undercover. Watching the criminal acts carried out by the cops with his very eyes, Pennington knew he had a lot of work ahead of him. However, nothing prepared him for the scope of the problems until the night of his swearing in. Thay night happened to be October 13, 1994.

Pulled to the side by an unassuming FBI agent, Pennington was informed that the FBI was currently in the midst of a large sting—over fifty officers from the New Orleans Police Department were being investigated. Hearing that the allegations ranged from drug dealing and stolen property to shaking down nightclub owners, Pennington was breathless. He told a local reporter what was going through his mind on his first night as police chief. "My God, what am I getting into?" Pennington thought.

Little did he know that only eight hours into his new position the first murder on his watch would be committed by one of his own police officers.

In fact, it wasn't until almost December when the FBI, while listening to numerous recorded phone calls and wire taps, came across the voice of Len Davis. It was a phone conversation between Davis and Hardy, in which Davis gave a physical description of Kimberly Groves, along with her address. The investigators were listening to a police officer give an order to commit murder.

By the end of December, Len Davis and nine other New Orleans police officers were indicted for corruption—accepting over $100,000 in bribes to protect large-scale cocaine operations—and for violating federal laws. Davis was charged under federal law for murder and witness intimidation. He faced the death penalty.

As news of Groves's murder by a police officer spread throughout the city, and eventually the nation, residents were shocked, but not altogether surprised. The tension had been building between the city's residents and those who were sworn to protect them for a long time. They hoped to see retribution, but they didn't like the fact that an innocent woman had to lose her life to achieve it. In the end, almost sixty police officers within the New Orleans Police Department were indicted and tried for a variety of charges ranging from drug trafficking and money laundering to simple thefts. However, none of the charges compared to those that Len Davis faced.

In April 1996, flanked by Paul Hardy and Damon Causey, Davis's trial began in federal court. The prosecution laid out an airtight case against the men, referring to them as a "police death squad." The defense contended that the murder was most likely committed by Groves's abusive boyfriend, Sylvester Jones. Regardless, the jury didn't buy it. All three men were found guilty of murder, and Davis was sentenced to death.

Shockingly, The US Fifth District Court of Appeals overturned the witness tampering conviction in 1999, but allowed the murder conviction to stand. However, the court ordered a new sentencing trial for both charges. Again, Len Davis was sentenced to death. In a message from US Attorney Jim Letten, he stated: "This case involved the murder of a citizen for filing a complaint against a police officer. . . . Two juries have said loudly and clearly that this behavior will not be tolerated and will be punished in the most severe manner."

For the citizens of New Orleans, justice was finally served. In the decade that followed Len Davis's conviction, an extraordinary effort was made by the city of New Orleans to reestablish the public's trust in its law enforcement officers. With more stringent hiring standards and background checks, not to mention higher salaries, the men and women patrolling the streets there have unquestionably earned the public's respect. As the nation watched the aftermath of Hurricane Katrina, the respect given to the officers rose to an entirely new level—one that the city could only be proud of.

Ignored by the rest of the nation for two days, the New Orleans officers endured unimaginable horrors. Some committed suicide, while others left the force afterward, but most stayed behind to protect New Orleans and the citizens that called it their home. Had Katrina occurred in the darker days of the New Orleans Police Department, the potential aftermath of that situation could have been even more disastrous than anyone could imagine.

Consequently, as Assistant US Attorney Michael McMahon appealed to the jury during the end of the Len Davis trial, the citizens can move forward from those dark days, but they will never be forgotten. His words were eerily reminiscent of the words spoken by millions across the nation as they watched the horrifying aftermath of Katrina—the bodies floating down the streets, the looting, the confusion. Americans never imagined it would happen here, just as McMahon spoke for the residents of New Orleans about their dark days of police corruption:

"What happened on that day to that poor woman, a citizen of the United States, should not have happened in this country; maybe somewhere else—but not in the United States. Because what the evidence showed, what we proved to you . . . was the existence of a police death squad in New Orleans, Louisiana," McMahon passionately pled to the jury. "Kim Groves had to die like a dog on the street because she got in Len Davis's way. . . . She deserves a little justice right now because in life she didn't get any. . . . We are not supposed to have death squads in the United States of America."

CHAPTER 12

NO PARKING

RICHARD DiGUGLIELMO
POLICE OFFICER, NEW YORK CITY, NEW YORK

The majority of cases included in this book are clear-cut cases of murder beyond a reasonable doubt. However, the circumstances surrounding the case of former New York City police officer Richard DiGuglielmo undeniably cast a small shadow of a doubt on his murder conviction. He was included in this book because he was ultimately convicted of murder by a jury of his peers, rendering his version of events unbelievable in the eyes of the twelve men and women who held the power to decide his fate. His defense team clearly spun a different tale of events—a tale of an innocent man sacrificing his own life to save his father's. In an unpredictable turn, several of the prosecution's witnesses felt the same, not during the course of the murder trial, but at the time of the murder—and even now.

The question of whether or not thirty-one-year-old New York City police officer Richard DiGuglielmo was justified when he shot and killed Charles Campbell is being posed in appellate courts to this day. The actual facts of the case vary depending on who is asked.

What are not debated are the general facts. On October 3, 1996, in Dobbs Ferry, New York, thirty-seven-year-old Charles Campbell pulled his prized black Corvette into a parking space directly in front of Richard "Ritchie" DiGuglielmo's father's store: the Venice Deli.

Ritchie's father, Richard DiGuglielmo Sr., was known for his strong enforcement of his prized parking spaces. The complex that the deli was in housed three businesses and only afforded eight parking spaces. Richard Sr. had erected signs that read "Parking for Venice Deli Patrons Only" in front of his three designated parking spaces, and he monitored them closely.

Upon seeing Charles Campbell leave his vehicle and not enter the deli, but instead start toward the pizza shop across the street, Richard Sr. exited his store and told Charles to move his car. Pointing to the "No Parking" signs, Richard Sr. informed Charles that if he did not move his car a "No Parking" sticker would be placed on his windshield. Since the issue of parking had become such a problem within the business complex, the Dobbs Ferry Police Department allowed the business owners to place such stickers on the windshields of violators.

No one would say that Charles Campbell was being rude or violent at this point. In fact, he informed Richard Sr. that when he was finished picking up his pizza, he would buy soda at Richard's store—his own attempt to diffuse the situation and appease Richard Sr.

Upon entering the pizza shop, Charles ordered one slice of pizza and asked the man working behind the counter, "What's up with that guy and his parking?" The employee told Charles that he always confronts nonpatrons when they use his spaces before putting stickers on their cars. Charles also told the employee that he was planning to purchase a soda from the deli but added, "If he puts a sticker on my car I'm gonna kick his ass." Pointing to the window, the employee alerted Charles to the fact that Richard Sr. was indeed placing a "No Parking" sticker on the windshield of Charles's beloved Corvette at that very moment.

Visibly agitated, Charles left the store (and his slice of pizza), walking directly toward Richard Sr. Hearing and seeing a heated exchange of words, Ritchie and his brother-in-law, thirty-eight-year-old Robert Errico, came out of the deli. Ritchie immediately went to his father's defense, squaring off with Charles. According to witnesses at the trial, both men began punching each other "simultaneously." Coming to the aid of their family member, Robert and Richard Sr. joined in the melee, the three men eventually pinning Charles down on the pavement of the parking lot. While Richard Sr. and Robert held Charles's arms as he lay on his back, Ritchie commenced mercilessly beating his face. At one point, Ritchie resorted to using Charles's own cell phone to aid in his attack—beating Charles in the head with it before the phone broke into pieces. To Ritchie, at that very moment, the fear of consequence was obsolete.

There was also no dispute about what transpired next. Charles no longer resisted or tried to fight back. Breathlessly, he simply said, "Enough." Believing that their brief encounter with Charles Campbell was over, the men stood up and allowed Charles to walk away. Ritchie and Robert went back inside the deli, but Richard Sr. continued to pursue Charles.

Disoriented and reeling from the vicious attack, Charles Campbell took this brief opportunity to arm himself. In his mind, he was not yet in the safe zone and still faced the possibility of another brutal assault. Grabbing his car keys, Charles Campbell opened the trunk of his car and retrieved an aluminum baseball bat. With Richard Sr. now only a few feet away and still walking toward him in a threatening manner, Charles felt he had no other option but to swing the bat at Richard's knees in an attempt to get him to back away. Struck in the area of his right knee, Richard leaned over and groaned in pain. Regardless, it was only mere seconds before Richard Sr. was standing straight and again coming for Charles. However, Charles didn't swing again. He kept the bat over his shoulder in a "batter's stance" as he walked backward, and away from Richard Sr.

It was only a matter of seconds upon seeing Charles swing a bat at Richard Sr. that Ritchie and Robert were back outside confronting Charles again. Ritchie attempted to pull at Charles's arm to no avail. Running back inside the deli, Ritchie grabbed a .32 revolver with nine rounds in the cylinder before going back outside. With no verbal commands or warning, Ritchie fired three shots into Charles Campbell—killing him almost instantly.

This was the version presented by the prosecution. But a different account of the day's events began to poke serious holes into their case, and the allegations of prosecutorial and police misconduct put both agencies on defense.

During the trial and the subsequent appellate documents that followed, the Westchester County District Attorney's Office portrayed Charles Campbell as a respected employee and a loving father. Charles was employed by the White Plains Sanitation Department and worked part-time at St. Christopher's home for abused children in Dobbs Ferry. He organized sporting activities, field trips, and was well liked by the staff and children. An amateur boxer, Charles was in good physical shape and worked out regularly. Charles was also an African American, a fact that would affect many facets of his murder case.

The day of his murder, Charles picked up his paycheck from

St. Christopher's at approximately 4:00 PM. Described as being in his usual good mood, Charles even stayed a bit to talk with some of the children. Around 5:00 PM, Charles entered the Bank of New York in Dobbs Ferry to cash his check. Giving in to his increasing hunger pangs, Charles decided on that particular day to have a slice of pizza. At 5:05, he pulled into the parking space in front of the DiGuglielmo deli. At 5:43 Charles Campbell was pronounced dead at a nearby hospital. None of these facts were under dispute. The witnesses, however, painted a very different picture—in the beginning.

Kevin O'Donnell found himself caught in the middle of a made-for-television movie the day he was driving his company's cable truck in front of the Venice Deli. His passenger and trainee, Michael Dillon, proved to be a pivotal and controversial witness throughout the entire case. O'Donnell, Dillon, and several others found themselves in the middle of a high-stakes game of race cards.

In his first statement, given to police detective Joseph Ellman only two hours after the murder occurred, Kevin O'Donnell completely shredded the airtight case that the prosecution later presented at trial. In his own words, O'Donnell stated:

> The black male became very boisterous to all three white males and was making gestures with his hands, and then he walked over to a black Corvette that was parked in front of the Venice Deli. The black male opened up the rear hatch to the Corvette and removed what appeared to be a yellow carpet rolled up. The three white males were about ten feet from the black male, on the passenger side of the Corvette, they were all exchanging words. At this time, the black male had unrolled the carpet and took out a gold and black aluminum baseball bat. The black male made like a hurried up motion toward the three white males.

This contradicts the prosecution's story that Charles was backing away as Richard was moving forward in a threatening manner. O'Donnell, who undoubtedly was in the best position of any of the witnesses to see what occurred, defended Ritchie's actions.

> The black male took a batter's stance and struck the older white male in behind the left knee area and thigh. He struck him twice. At that time, the other two white males tried to grab hold of the black male. . . . The black male was able to get free and again took a batter's stance and was about to strike the second white male who was trying to regain his balance. . . . *I was out of my van* trying to get behind the black male to take the bat away from him so he would not hit anybody . . . *when the black male was shot, I was five feet from my truck and two feet from the black male.*

Exactly five days later, after the district attorney's office filed second-degree murder charges against Richard DiGuglielmo, the Dobbs Ferry police brought O'Donnell in for a second interview. In his statement, given on October 8, O'Donnell drastically changed his story.

> I noticed four men arguing in the parking lot of the Venice Deli. . . . I saw the black male, Charles Campbell, walking to his black Corvette. . . . He was being followed by three white males. . . . Charles Campbell removed a yellow carpet and removed a gold and black aluminum baseball bat. . . . Mr. Campbell then struck Richard Sr. across the legs. . . . *I guess the reason that he struck Ritchie Sr. was that Richie Sr. was threatening him.* . . . I saw Mr. Campbell walking backward in the parking lot. . . . They were walking toward Mr. Campbell who was in a batter stance. . . . *He appeared to be getting ready to defend himself.* . . . *While I was still sitting*

in my vehicle with my trainee Michael Dillon, Richie Jr. appeared in front of my truck with his right arm extended. . . . Mr. Campbell never swung the bat. . . . I then exited my truck. . . . I told one of the officers that it was my opinion that he had no right to shoot him. . . . He wasn't threatening anybody. . . . The reason for the change in this statement from the original is due to that I was nervous and excited . . . when I left the police station the first time I was thinking that I may have left some details out and the statement wasn't a hundred percent accurate.

If Kevin O'Donnell's statement was the only one that changed so drastically, it might have been overlooked. But when his passenger, Michael Dillon, emerged from the Dobbs Ferry Police Department after giving his second statement, a statement that mirrored O'Donnell's, the defense attorneys screamed police coercion and misconduct by the prosecutors. Three witnesses supported Richie's claim of defending his father. All three of those witnesses were brought in repeatedly by the Dobbs Ferry police only to emerge as solid witnesses for the prosecution—except for one: James Brendan White.

White vehemently refused to change his statement. It was difficult to question his credibility since he was the son of a former FBI agent. Making matters more uncomfortable was White's three brothers—one was also an FBI agent, one was a district attorney for Westchester District Attorney's Office, and the other was a police officer for the Dobbs Ferry Police Department. White found himself in quite a predicament but tenaciously stuck to his story.

However, White's father was extremely ill and begged White not to "go against the police and talk to defense attorneys." Under certain pressure from his siblings as well, White refused to talk to DiGuglielmo's attorneys and the prosecution would not call him as a witness. After a change of heart, White ultimately testified for Richard DiGuglielmo in an appeals hearing. His statement, given on June 5, 2007, never deviated from any of his prior statements on his version of the events that occurred on October 3, 1996. Here is the actual statement given by James Brendan White:

Transcript of Statement of James White—June 5, 2007

James White states: on 10/3/1996 I was employed as a teacher at Morris High School in the Bronx. After school/work that day I exercised at Court Sports gymnasium in Yonkers. After my workout I went to the Venice Deli @ 225 Ashford Avenue, Dobbs Ferry, to purchase items for dinner. At about 5:15 PM, I witnessed Charles Campbell in the act of swinging a bat at Rich DiGuglielmo's head before Campbell was shot by Rich Jr.

I have reported on other statements that Campbell was the aggressor in this incident and that is the way it happened. There is no question that Campbell was swinging the bat, advancing on the elder DiGuglielmo, when the shots were fired. Following the shooting, I was required to remain at the scene and later at DFPD for questioning. I explained to detectives that the shots were fired in self-defense and that the shooter had no choice. I explained to detectives that Campbell was enraged, aggressive, and advancing on DiGuglielmo Sr. swinging the bat at the elder DiGuglielmo, and my recollection is vivid and clear.

I was not allowed to leave. I was questioned for many more hours. Detectives who questioned me knew I was related to a Dobbs Ferry detective and even so, they were not very nice to me. I can only imagine how they may have treated me if I were not related to a detective. Detectives kept asking me the same questions relating to the fight started by Campbell which ended with shots fired. They kept asking me the same questions . . . repeatedly showing me different scenarios of the shooting I witnessed, scenarios that were ridiculous.

These scenarios included Campbell retreating instead of advancing, Campbell not swinging the bat instead of swinging the bat, etc. I told them again and again how it happened but Dobbs Ferry detectives tried to get me to back off my initial statement and describe DiGuglielmo as the aggressor, which he was not. They tried to get me to describe Campbell as a victim instead of the aggressor. The detectives continued to paraphrase versions of events told by other witnesses in an effort to suggest to me that my recollection was wrong. After the night of the incident I was required to return to DFPD at least two more times on separate days/evenings for further questioning.

I feel very strongly that the DFPD detectives didn't like what I said about the events. The detectives were very serious. It felt more like an interrogation. I strongly felt, and still believe, that the DFPD wanted me to change my version of the events to a version that did not justify DiGuglielmo's actions. It was clear that they wanted another statement from me that would help convict DiGuglielmo. The detectives told me my statement didn't "match" statements of other witnesses. I wanted to get out of the interview room but they kept harassing me in attempts to get me to change my recollection. They were continuing to suggest other scenarios as I described above.

I didn't like what they were doing. They paraphrased the sworn statements of other witnesses while showing me diagrams of the scene. It is ridiculous to suggest that Campbell was retreating and that is what they wanted me to say. They continued to badger me and it was clear that they weren't happy that wouldn't change my statement or version of events. After I refused to change my statement at least four, or possibly five, times, I was told that I was libeled in local newspapers as a drunk. I refused to change my statement. The DFPD insinuated that I was drunk on the afternoon of the incident. I was not.

I have read all three pages and it is true to the best of my memory.

[Signed]

James Brendan White

If what James White alleges was true, the detectives would find the task of proving him intoxicated on the day of the murder quite difficult. Since he left work/school and immediately went to the gym before arriving at the deli to purchase dinner, White would have to be a chronic alcoholic with a hidden stash and possess the ability to exercise while drunk—an unlikely talent.

Perhaps the most damaging testimony against Richie came from a Dobbs Ferry nurse, Marianne Wekerle. At approximately 5:15 PM on October 3, Wekerle pulled into the parking lot of the Venice Deli to buy cigarettes. Driving up on the parking lot brawl that was at that point in full swing, Wekerle ran into the deli, requesting the Hispanic clerk behind the counter to call the police. Immediately following the shooting, Wekerle attempted to render aid to Campbell, and requested those around her to retrieve towels from the deli.

Nonetheless, like the other witnesses, Wekerle was subjected to numerous interviews with Dobbs Ferry detectives. And, like the others, her final statement deviated from her statement given the day of the murder. On October 3, Werkerle described the black and gold aluminum baseball bat as "wooden." She also stated that Charles Campbell swung the bat at Richard Sr.'s shoulder and head, referring to the swing as "the first time he swung," indicating that there were other swings. In her statement on October 7, Wekerle omitted a description of the bat, claimed Campbell swung at Richard Sr.'s shoulder only, and said Richard Sr. immediately continued walking toward Campbell. Wekerle's statement disputes every single witness statement given in the case. The other witnesses were consistent with the fact that, once struck across the legs by Campbell, Richard Sr. stayed at the rear of the car, groaning in pain. Wekerle never even mentioned the leg strike, indicating she was distracted by aiding the male at the counter in making the 911 call. None of the witnesses, in their final statements, stated that Campbell ever swung the bat at Richard Sr.'s head, but Wekerle did. This statement seemingly added weight to Richie's claim that he was protecting his father.

Regardless, it was the statements that Wekerle claimed to have heard that proved to impact the jury the most during the criminal and civil trials. In her final statement, never before mentioned, Wekerle stated that while she was tending to Charles Campbell and requesting towels, she distinctly heard Richie say, "Fuck the towels, I'm not touching that piece of shit!" Immediately after this, Wekerle claimed that Richard Sr. told her, "Get out of here! You didn't see anything!" Jurors questioned after the trial concluded stated that these statements were crucial in their decision.

It may seem that this chapter is leaning toward the defense of the suspect, but, in this case, it is completely factual that many questions are left unanswered. Although Richard DiGuglielmo was found guilty of murder, the persons responsible for investigating and prosecuting the case are also guilty—they are guilty of corrupting the system they chose to enforce and uphold. What was it about this particular case that caused the "good guys" to throw their ethics and conduct out the window? Most speculate that the phenomenal media attention and the arrival of civil rights advocate Reverend Al Sharpton played a major factor in the district attorney's decision to prosecute. However, what the public didn't know was that the decision to charge Richard DiGuglielmo with second-degree murder was noted in Assistant District Attorney Patricia Murphy's notebook only twenty-five minutes after arriving on the scene of the murder. This was after statements given to Murphy by O'Donnell, Dillon, and White that claimed DiGuglielmo was defending the life of his father. But, ultimately, the decision to charge Richie was made by the Westchester County district attorney herself—Jeanine Pirro.

Pirro had been constantly under fire and accused by citizens that, due to her Italian heritage, she would be lax in prosecuting organized crime. It seemed to many people that certain cases involving Italians, including the DiGuglielmo case, were prosecuted with a bloodthirsty vengeance. Jeanine Pirro wanted to prove the allegations wrong, especially during a time when she was preparing for reelection.

Pirro, no stranger to controversy, found herself playing the part of defense when she came under fire for withholding 376 pages, 52 boxes, and an enormous amount of audiotapes and videotapes that exonerated Anthony DiSimone, a man who she had prosecuted and sent to prison for the stabbing death of Louis Balancio. Included in this hidden evidence was a confession by the actual killer of Balancio—Nick Djonovic. After withholding the evidence for thirteen years, Pirro was forced to present it in federal court, which resulted in the release of the seven-year-imprisoned DiSimone.

In most law enforcement agencies across the country, "the prosecutor is God." The upper echelons of the most well-known police departments, from the sergeants to the chief of police himself or herself, will scurry and scramble at the slightest hint of dissatisfaction from the district attorney's office. Most district attorneys, specifically those elected, scoff at police departments as unworthy—mere peons—pawns in their narcissistic realm of authority. Of course, and not to stereotype, there are always prosecutors out there who respect and work well with law enforcement. Rarely will a high-ranking member of a police department stand up to a district attorney to express the notion, "Hey, something just isn't right here."

Considering the power over law enforcement held by district attorneys, the question of whether or not the Dobbs Ferry Detective Bureau should be held responsible in this street carnival of an investigation remains unanswered. The then thirty-five-year-old Dobbs Ferry police chief, George Longworth (still an infant in the span of a law enforcement life), proved no different than most when he bowed to the whim of the Westchester County District Attorney's Office. For those of lower rank there wasn't much choice. These people had families to support, and they relied on their jobs.

Anyone who is told by the powers that be to "make it happen" really doesn't have much choice. Or do they? Should they sacrifice everything to do what is right, or just go home at night, continuing to provide for their families and telling themselves "its part of the job—politics rule?"

For the detectives investigating the DiGuglielmo case, one can only assume what kind of a nightmare transpired when they are ordered, prior to learning all the necessary facts of the case, to investigate—and "make it good"—the case as a legitimate homicide. Even worse, when questioned about the unethical tactics on the witness stand, visibly uncomfortable, Patricia Murphy claimed to have no knowledge on the repeated interrogations and "transformed" witness statements, essentially hanging the detectives that she ordered around out to dry.

What is so disturbing about the prosecution's case is that

the prosecutors seemed to miss the simplest angle of the murder, instead focusing on the borderline absurd. In his Affirmation in Opposition to an appeal filed by Richard DiGuglielmo in 2006, Westchester Assistant District Attorney Robert K. Sauer stated that DiGuglielmo made "no attempt to disarm Campbell" nor did he "fire a warning shot out of concern of innocent bystanders." Furthermore, Sauer stated that DiGuglielmo was "not acting as a police officer or attempting to protect himself, but only trying to protect his father."

Unfortunately, there are serious problems with the statements presented by Sauer. First, by questioning as to why Richie didn't try to disarm Campbell, Sauer not only acknowledges Campbell as a threat, but the entire concept itself is ridiculous. There are very few people, police officers included, who will walk up to an agitated amateur boxer wielding a baseball bat and then attempt to take it away from him. An aluminum baseball bat is considered an "impact weapon," and when faced with impact weapons officers are trained nationwide to immediately resort to their firearm—a key level in the use of force continuum. Most prosecutors know the use of force continuum and other officer procedures like the back of their hand. Apparently, Sauer did not.

Second, I am not familiar with any state in the entire country that allows officers to fire warning shots. In fact, it is illegal, and most officers would be prosecuted for doing so. It is outrageous that Sauer would even raise this issue.

Last, any sworn officer certified by his or her respected state is a peace officer twenty-four hours a day, seven days a week. The oath taken upon commencement of their career is to uphold law and order—no matter what the circumstances. If Richard DiGuglielmo walked into a bank robbery and halted it while off duty and legally armed, he would be hailed as a hero for taking control of the situation and apprehending the criminal(s). If he walked into the bank robbery, off duty, and legally armed, and failed to take any action at all, he would most likely be disciplined. Most important, in Sauer's last statement, he acknowledged that DiGuglielmo was "not protecting himself, but protecting his father." This completely contradicts the prosecutor's entire case.

Again, the case could have been very simple for the prosecution. Did Richard DiGuglielmo commit murder? Yes; the reason—a duty to retreat. There is enough case law on that topic to fill a small barn, yet the Westchester County District Attorney's Office and the Dobbs Ferry Police Department failed to make it the main issue. If, in fact, Charles Campbell crossed the street from the pizza shop and approached Richard Sr. in an aggressive manner, Richie and Robert would certainly be compelled—and justified—to rush to the aid of their fifty-four-year-old relative. As an investigator, the following questions should have been posed: *As Charles Campbell was crossing the street, did you feel he was a threat toward your father? As a police officer, didn't you feel it was imperative to call 911?*

The next window of opportunity for the prosecution, and perhaps the most important, was seemingly ignored. The investigators focused on whether Campbell was, or was not, swinging the bat. What they should have focused on was the moment Charles Campbell was being beaten and conceded, "Enough." At that point, Richie, Richard Sr., and Robert released Charles and he began walking toward his Corvette. There was no longer a threat, and the opportunity to retreat and contact law enforcement commenced. The three men, had they felt as threatened as they had claimed, had the opportunity at that point to retreat into the deli, lock the door if needed, and wait for law enforcement to arrive. However, they didn't. Richard Sr. continued to follow Campbell and engage in an altercation, at one point ripping off Campbell's shirt. It's that simple.

Instead, the district attorney's office focused on whether or not the bat was swung—where, and how many times—and whether or not Campbell was moving forward or backward, a difficult fact to nail down when dealing with numerous witnesses at different vantage points.

As flimsy as its case was, the prosecution prevailed. Richard DiGuglielmo was sentenced to twenty years to life for second-degree murder. Again, the statements of Marianne Wekerle proved potent when the lack of remorse or guilt in the statements of Richie and Richard Sr. were presented to the jury. Regardless, continuous appeals are being filed to this day. It only takes one judge to determine that the police coercion and prosecutorial misconduct are enough to warrant a new trial for Richard DiGuglielmo. So far, that judge hasn't been found, but it's only a matter of time.

In a financial blow to the city of New York, Campbell's brother William, and son, seventeen-year-old Vaughn, were awarded $4.5 million in a civil suit brought against the DiGuglielmo family and the city of New York. Again, Marianne Wekerle's testimony convinced the jury. One of the jurors explained that hearing Wekerle testify to Richard Sr. saying, "You didn't see anything" was the final straw. "It pretty much undermined the testimony of the DiGuglielmos," the juror said.

Regardless, an undeniable fact in the murder case of Charles Campbell still remains, something that presiding judge even picked up on—the case against Richard DiGuglielmo raises many questions, questions that, to this day, still haven't been answered.

CHAPTER 13

MAFIA COPS VOW OF OMERTA

LOUIS EPPOLITO AND STEPHEN CARACAPPA
POLICE DETECTIVES, NEW YORK CITY, NEW YORK

There are brothers, and then there are brothers in blue. In law enforcement, finding one's partner—one's true brother—*can* have detrimental consequences, such as evidenced in the case of New York City police detectives Louis "Lou" Eppolito and Stephen Caracappa: "The Mafia Cops."

In the end, after being on the Mafia's payroll for more than twenty years, Lou and Stephen would spend the rest of their lives in the same prisons that held the criminals who they helped put away—some legitimately, some not. On the outside, they were award-winning veteran officers who sometimes rubbed elbows with the rich and famous. On the inside, they were cold-blooded murderers.

Lou Eppolito began his career with the New York City Police Department on August 1, 1969. A former body builder, Lou's size proved useful in his "cowboy" approach to catching criminals, an approach that earned him a significant number of medals and awards. Strangely, Lou's family ties were seemingly ignored throughout his background investigation as he was being hired. Although he later reported that he was very honest about his family with the investigator, there was never a shred of documentation found to prove it. Lou was related to the Mafia. His own father, Ralph, used to be a soldier for one of the most famed families in organized crime—the Gambinos. His uncle, Jimmy "the clam" Eppolito, was also a soldier for the family at the time of Lou's hiring. Lou's cousin, Frank Santora Jr., was loosely associated with both the Gambino and the Lucchese families. Apparently, this fact somehow slipped by the background investigator. Still, Lou claims he was upfront about his family and the department hired him anyway.

Stephen Caracappa was hired in the same year as Lou. After two years of service in Vietnam, joining the police force at age twenty-seven made him one of the older recruits. However, unlike Lou's, Stephen's own background investigation came into question. The investigator assigned to perform Stephen's background wrote on his application "absolutely do not hire." He based his recommendation on the fact that he uncovered a highly complex burglary that Stephen was involved in during his teens. Although the record was expunged, the investigator felt that the planning and complex nature of the burglary proved Stephen very dangerous. The warning was ignored.

Lou and Stephen were polar opposites in both appearance and personality. Lou was a large, husky man who was loud and boastful. Most who knew Lou say he took pride in bragging about his awards, newspaper write-ups, and connections to rich and famous people. He rarely shutup, which later proved to be the duo's downfall. Stephen was tall, thin, and very quiet. He kept to himself for the most part, with the exception of Lou. In any case, both men's taste for corruption began early in their law enforcement careers—especially Lou's.

It was 1979 when Lou first caught the attention of investigators. A young man, John Sciascia Jr., was looking at a substantial amount of time in prison for armed robbery. While he was awaiting trial, Lou contacted the suspect's father, John Sciascia Sr. At that time, Lou said he could get a police lineup of mug shots that looked very similar to John Jr. They would be very useful in causing reasonable doubt to a jury. For the right price, Lou would give the lineup to John Sr. so he could give it to John Jr.'s defense attorney. Although he was nervous about the situation, John Sr. agreed—but taped his conversation with Lou to be on the safe side. When he turned over the lineup to the defense attorney, along with the tapes, the attorney said, "No way," and turned everything over to the New York Police Department's internal affairs division. For two years, the department investigated the matter before simply setting it to the side and forgetting about it.

Also in 1979, Lou approached Maria Provenzano with an offer. Maria's brother had died suspiciously and she was hell-bent on finding out who was responsible. The murder had occurred in Las Vegas, and she was having a tough time obtaining the files from the Las Vegas Police Department. Lou, who was casually dating Maria at the time, said that he would easily obtain the files for her. But as time passed without any files, Maria became curious. At that point, Lou told her that she would have to pay for the files. Maria thought this request was outside the realm of normalcy. Not only did she refuse to pay for the files, she ended her relationship with Lou.

Later, Maria became an informant for the Drug Enforcement Agency. Remembering her bizarre partnership with Lou, she informed the agent she was working with about it. He passed it along to New York Police Department's internal affairs division where, like most of the complaints regarding Lou, it was ignored.

Lou and Stephen were partnered up in the robbery division

as detectives, and quickly became friends. Prior to their meeting, Stephen had his own share of troubles. He had worked heavily in the narcotics division undercover for years. After the death of his daughter, who was not quite a year old, he began drinking heavily and taking amphetamines. At one point Stephen overdosed, marking the end of his career in working with drugs. He worked in various other divisions within the department, including robbery, where he met Lou, before landing a position in the most elite division of the New York City Police Department—the Major Crimes Squad.

Lou, on the other hand, was finding that he had a real taste for shaking people down. In June 1982, gangster Salvatore Gravano took part in the gunning down of a business associate in front of a nightclub. Lou was assigned to the case and quickly formulated Gravano as a suspect. Knowing what a wealthy businessman Gravano was, Lou arranged for Gravano to pay him five thousand dollars to make the case go away. Gravano happily paid the money.

In 1984, Lou found out he was the subject of an intense investigation that brought his corruption out into the open. The FBI had just raided known crime family member Rosario Gambino's home. In the garage, they found a large file that contained a substantial amount of information on the Gambino family. The file was the property of the New York Police Department. Question was, how did Rosario Gambino get his hands on a confidential police file?

The FBI quickly tracked down the last person to sign out the secret files, Detective Lou Eppolito. It would appear that Lou was backed into a corner. One would assume that there would be no possible excuse for Lou to come up with, but he did. Lou acknowledged that he signed out the files, but said he turned them back in and had no clue how they got into the hands of Rosario Gambino.

The department had enough of Lou's shenanigans and sus-

pended him for five months without pay. Lou fought the suspension, was found not guilty by the commission, and was
reinstated with back pay. Up to this point, Lou always managed to escape criminal charges or discipline. Looking forward
to again working in his old precinct, he received somewhat of
a shock when he learned that he had been transferred out. The
chief of detectives no longer wanted Lou Eppolito under his
command, and he wanted Lou out of the Mafia neighbor-
hoods. This time Lou went directly to the police commissioner.
He was placed in a nearby precinct—which was still in the
same area as the mob.

Things began to quickly heat up for Eppolito and Caracappa when they were introduced to businessman Burt Kaplan.
Kaplan, a shady character who ran an upscale clothing business, had met Lou's cousin, Frank Santora Jr., in prison. Kaplan
was a well-known associate among the powerful crime families.
A navy veteran, Kaplan was deep into gambling and owed large
debts by the time he was twenty-five years old. Fencing stolen
property to pay his debts, Kaplan's million-dollar clothing business was actually legitimate—for a while.

When they met in prison, Kaplan was serving a short stint
for drug trafficking while Frank was in for stealing from a
restaurant owner on a regular basis. The two developed a
friendship after they realized they had connections to the same
crime families. Frank suggested that Kaplan put Lou and
Stephen on his payroll in case he needed any information or
muscling. Kaplan thought this a splendid idea, and went ahead
with it. He never wanted to go back to prison again.

It was in 1985 that Kaplan found himself truly requiring
the services of Lou and Stephen. He had been doing a lot of
business with Anthony Casso, boss of the Lucchese crime
family. In fact, Casso was now earning a small percentage of
Kaplan's business. Frankie Santora also worked there.

Casso had recently given Kaplan a stolen Treasury bill worth a half million dollars. Casso wanted Kaplan to sell it and they would split the money. Of course, finding someone to buy a stolen Treasury bill would be difficult. After going through several different people, Kaplan found an intermediary, Israel Greenwald, who could sell the bill overseas. The men made money, and Kaplan thought the plan worked out beautifully—until the FBI started nosing around his associates and inquiring about the Treasury bill. Kaplan was sure someone was talking—a rat. Most important, Kaplan didn't want Casso to know they were close to being caught. Desperate, he requested Lou and Stephen find out who the snitch was. Using their contacts, it was only a matter of time before they all figured out it was Greenwald who had been working with the FBI. Kaplan wanted him gone—immediately.

Lou and Stephen pulled Greenwald over in an "official" manner before taking him to a nearby auto body shop. By then, Frankie had joined them and they murdered Israel Greenwald before burying his body in the floor of the garage. It would be twenty years before his body would ever be found.

In 1986, Stephen Caracappa helped form the Organized Crime Homicide Unit. With the families at war and the streets now a battleground, the New York Police Department was overwhelmed with murders due to organized crime. Within the unit, two men were each assigned one of the five crime families. Caracappa, not surprisingly, chose the Lucchese family. At the time, with the same man on their payroll in charge of investigating them, the Luccheses may well have been one of the most protected families in New York.

That same year, an incident occurred that proved to be a pivotal point for Anthony Casso. While standing outside of a bar frequented by the Mafia, Casso and others were alerted to a disturbance at a nearby restaurant. The owner had run over to the men and told them that two thugs with a vicious dog were in the restaurant scaring customers and roughing up the place. Casso sent some of his men to retrieve the thugs. Casso recognized one of them as twenty-six-year-old Jimmy Hydell, a two-bit criminal in the neighborhood. Hydell's girlfriend had recently disappeared after breaking up with him. Casso, trying to confront Hydell about his behavior, became increasingly annoyed with repeated interruptions from the barking dog. He told Hydell several times to shut the dog up, but to no avail. Casso decidedly had enough. He walked into the bar, got a gun, and shot the dog to death right there on the sidewalk. Hydell was devastated, and was told to leave immediately.

It wasn't until several months later that Hydell's name resurfaced. Casso was inside his vehicle in a parking lot waiting for an associate to arrive for a meeting. The meeting never took place because two separate vehicles pulled into the lot and began shooting up Casso's car. Unfortunately for the shooters, Casso survived—and there would be hell to pay. He wanted the names of all the people involved in his attempted murder, and Lou and Stephen would help him find them.

It didn't take long for them to provide Casso with a couple names: one was Nicky Guido. Casso, enlisting the services of his murder-for-hire cops, tracked down a Nicky Guido to an address in the city. Lou and Stephen warned Casso that they weren't sure this was the right one, but Casso didn't care. This particular Nicky Guido, who was never part of the mob nor knew anyone involved, was shot dead in his car right in front of his house. Casso had gotten it wrong. The real Nicky Guido got wind of the murder and fled town. For now, Casso had his eyes set on another name responsible for his attempted murder: Jimmy Hydell.

Casso and his underboss, Vittorio "Vic" Amuso, instantly got ahold of Hydell. For hours, they beat and tortured him in the basement of a house before ultimately murdering him. His body remains missing to this day.

Lou and Stephen were getting more and more comfortable in their roles as hitmen and informants. In 1986, a jogger saw a man in a dark sedan dump the body of a prostitute in a parking lot. Lou was the first to get ahold of the jogger, since the man responsible for the homicide was a business associate of the Lucchese family. Driving the jogger around, Lou was adamant about finding a viable suspect who the jogger could identify. Finding a man sitting on his front porch stoop, Lou pointed out to the jogger that the man fit the description of the suspect. The jogger said absolutely not—the man was not the same man he saw dumping the body.

After intimidation and a series of threats against the jogger, he finally conceded and said that the man on the stoop, Barry Gibbs, was the man responsible for the murder. He knew Gibbs wasn't the murderer, but the jogger was fearful of his own life. The innocent man, Gibbs, was sentenced to life in prison for murder. The only thing he was guilty of was sitting on his front porch at the wrong time.

In early 1987, the body of Pasquale Varriale, a well-known criminal, was found in the middle of a road—another who lost his life to Lou and Stephen.

One of the worst, most incomprehensible crimes one could commit inside of the Mafia was to be a snitch. Anyone who was fingered as one would ultimately pay with his life. In 1987, career criminal Otto Heidel found himself in that role. Heidel was a top-notch electronics expert and could disable any alarm system, so it was natural for the Mafia families to use him frequently. It was after a burglary at a Bulova Watch warehouse that Kaplan began to have suspicions of a possible snitch. Kaplan was having a hard time selling off the stolen watches because people who normally bought from him were getting visits from the FBI. At this point it was apparent that someone was clearly talking, and Kaplan urged Frankie to have Lou and Stephen find out whom it was. Kaplan's suspicions were later confirmed: it was Otto Heidel.

On October 12, 1987, as he left racquetball practice, Otto Heidel was gunned down as he was getting into his car. He died instantly.

Frankie Santora never took part in Otto Heidel's murder; he was murdered just one month before by Anthony Casso—accidentally. Casso had ordered a hit on Carmine Varriale, the brother of already deceased Pasquale. Casso had no idea that Carmine would be walking down the street with Frankie when the hit was supposed to take place. Lou was furious, but he was unaware Casso had ordered the hit on his own cousin.

Now, with Frankie no longer the go-between for Kaplan and the two dirty cops, they began to deal directly with each other. They negotiated a $4,000 per month deal with Anthony Casso. For that amount, Lou and Stephen would provide Casso with all available information, including the status of investigations, wiretaps, and undercover officers. It was a mobster's dream, and Casso quickly agreed to the deal. It was one of the better decisions Casso had made.

In May 1988, wealthy businessman Pete Savino became an informant for the FBI. The owner of a prominent window business, Savino was involved with most of the crime families. For the next two years, he recorded the most damning conversations that resulted in a slew of federal indictments, including those of Anthony Casso and Vic Amuso.

Just prior to the indictments, Casso had ordered the hit on union boss Jimmy Bishop because Lou and Stephen were adamant that he was an FBI informant. They quickly relayed this information to Casso, and Bishop was immediately murdered. Also prior to the indictments, Casso had a disagreement with Anthony DiLapi. Lou and Stephen tracked down DiLapi's address in Los Angeles and gave it to Casso. DiLapi was also subsequently murdered.

In December 1989, Lou decidedly had enough of the New York City Police Department. He had personally met actor Robert DeNiro and scored a bit part in the mobster movie *Goodfellas,* playing a gangster named "Fat Andy." With stars in his eyes and a book deal about his family Mafia history, Lou now wanted to be famous. He retired after almost twenty years. In April 1990, Lou's friends in the Mafia threw him a large retirement party at the main hangout of all the mobsters. Apparently, no one from the New York City Police Department thought this was unusual.

The FBI raided the Mafia families and associates on May 30, 1990. The two men at the top of the FBI list, Lucchese family boss Anthony Casso and underboss Vic Amuso, were nowhere to be found. Having been tipped off by Lou and Stephen, the two mob leaders began a long period of hiding.

During the summer, Lou requested Casso's help. A man named Bruno Facciola was pressuring the guy who owned the auto body shop—the same shop were Israel Greenwald was buried—for money. Lou wanted to keep the shop owner on his good side, so he asked Casso to get Bruno to back off. Casso said he would take care of the problem. It was a short while later that Lou came to Burt Kaplan and said that Bruno was still a problem and was convinced Bruno was working for the feds. Burt relayed this information to Casso, who, at first, didn't believe believe the association because he personally knew Bruno. Casso decided to take Bruno out based on Lou's word since Lou had always been right before. On August 30, 1990, Bruno Facciola's body was found in the trunk of his car, which was parked right on the street. Officers on the scene noted something in Bruno's mouth. When they examined further, they saw it was a dead canary.

Casso was still on the run in November 1990 and very angry about the attempt on his life years before. He had taken care of Jimmy Hydell, but the other two men responsible were either in prison or under government protection. Casso's logic was that the order for the hit had to be placed on the highest ranks of the Gambino crime family, in order to make the entire family pay. The closest he could get to the top was Gambino family soldier Eddie Lino—a man who worked strictly for the Gambino boss, John Gotti. Lino was one of the soldiers who executed former boss Paul Castellano outside of a Manhattan restaurant. Gotti was next in line to run the family, so they took Castellano out of the equation.

Casso called upon his trusty cops, Lou and Stephen, to commence the hit on Eddie Lino. It was easy for the duo. They followed Lino onto the Belt Parkway toward Brooklyn. As they tailed Lino, the crokked cops activated their rotating dashboard light. Lino thought he was being stopped by the cops and pulled over onto the shoulder of the road. Lou and Steven went up to the car and fired repeated rounds into Eddie Lino's head. Casso paid the duo $70,000 for the job.

During the summer of 1991, while still in hiding, Casso ordered the hits on a slew of gangsters around the city. He felt that there were too many snitches on the streets and that many of them had volatile information on him. Lou and Stephen carried out or provided information for many of these murders. Vic Amuso had been apprehended after being on the run for a year.

It was only a matter of time before the FBI started focusing in on Burt Kaplan. His name was consistently linked with some of the top players of the Mafia factions. Burt continued in his dealings, many of which with snitches wearing wires. At that point, Burt was selling more designer knockoffs than ever, as well as moving several hundred pounds of marijuana through his warehouse every day.

Lou's book, *Mafia Cop*, made it big, rising on the *New York Times* best seller lists. Lou appeared on several talk shows promoting the book, including *Sally Jesse Raphael*. That particular show proved to be the downfall for Lou years later. A woman who watched the episode, Betty Hydell, immediately recognized Lou as one of the police officers suspiciously sitting on her street the morning her son Jimmy disappeared. She was terrified. At that moment, she didn't feel secure enough to push the issue out of concern for her son Frank's safety. However, she filed the information in the back of her mind.

After *Mafia Cop* had been optioned for film rights, Lou packed up his family, said goodbye to Burt, and set his sights on Las Vegas. He was going to make it big.

In January 1993, Anthony Casso was finally captured at his girlfriend's house in New Jersey. At first he remained silent, but the notion of spending his life in prison seemed to wear on the lifelong criminal. By 1994, he agreed to give everybody up in exchange for a lighter sentence. Casso gave up Lou, Stephen, Burt, and everybody else he knew who was involved in organized crime. Burt was tipped off that Casso was talking—and panicked. Leaving his wife and daughter behind, he fled New York City, moving from city to city under assumed names before joining Lou and Stephen (who also moved) in Las Vegas. There he was known as Barry Mayers.

Lou's and Stephen's names were splashed all over the newspapers. They were now being accused of being hitmen and cronies for the top organized crime families. Lou quickly played it down and had an excuse for every accusation. Interestingly enough, the allegations faded away. Nothing seemed to come of them at all.

In Las Vegas, Burt picked up where he had left off in New York. He started a clothing business again, frequently loaning money to Lou to jump-start his screenwriting and movie-producing career. Kaplan still kept tabs on New York, wondering just how wanted he really was.

By mid-1995, the government had enough of Casso's flip-flopping and lies. They were especially taken aback when Casso admitted to plotting to murder the city prosecutor. They withdrew the plea bargain and the news spread throughout the country that one of organized crime's top bosses was going down. To Burt Kaplan, it was music to his ears. He felt that if the authorities didn't believe Casso, then he was in the clear to return to New York. This is precisely what he did in the spring of 1996.

Unfortunately for Burt, his freedom was short lived. He had only been in New York for six months when he was arrested by the DEA and the NYPD. They had everything: his drug transactions, taped conversations, snitches—everything. There was just a small catch, though. If Burt gave up Lou and Stephen, all his charges would go away. Scoffing at the notion of being a rat, Burt adamantly refused—against the wishes of his wife and daughter. On January 9, 1998, Burt Kaplan was sentenced to twenty-seven years in prison.

For almost six years, Burt sat quietly in prison while Lou and Stephen lived a life of luxury in Las Vegas. Then something happened that would change their lives forever; Jimmy Hydell's older brother, Frank, was killed. Now Betty Hydell had nothing to lose. Picking up the phone, she called the FBI.

Before long, Betty Hydell was sitting at a table in a room filled with investigators from numerous law enforcement agencies. After hearing her story, they quickly launched a complete and in-depth investigation into Lou Eppolito and Stephen Caracappa. What they found was astonishing.

From their employment applications, to Lou selling mug shots, to unauthorized computer entries, to allegations of murder, the investigators were dumbfounded that the two detectives had managed to work so many years in the nation's largest police department without so much as a misdemeanor charge against them. The investigators were on a mission. This time, Lou and Stephen were not going to get away with anything.

The investigators started as far back as the duo's applications in 1969 and worked their way forward, uncovering the blood-splattered and corrupt trail of the dirty cops, eventually finding their way to Burt Kaplan.

US Attorneys Mark Feldman and Robert Henoch and DEA Agent Mark Manko met with Burt in prison in August 2004. At first, Burt still wouldn't talk. However, the continual pressure from his wife and daughter finally took its toll. He was too old to be in prison and decided that he had nothing to lose. He told the authorities about everything, including the murder of Israel Greenwald, which they knew nothing about. The investigators were again sickened that these two men who were supposed to live their lives by a higher standard were in actuality nothing more than street thugs and emotionless murderers.

Burt signed a formal agreement in October and the agents began tracking down the former owner of the since defunct auto body shop where Israel Greenwald was buried. Burt was never at the scene of the murder, so he wasn't sure where the body shop was. In the meantime, the agents enlisted the aid of a shady accountant, Steve Corso, to help them nail Lou and Stephen once and for all.

Corso was in Las Vegas and had done some minor business with the two and was found to have millions of dollars in tax thefts and evasions. It was put to him point blank by the feds: work for us, or go to jail. Corso agreed to help.

In the late months of 2004 to the early months of 2005, Corso, wearing a wire, regularly met with the two and talked business deals. In the meantime, he would try to get the two to open up about their past. Lou wanted a large amount of money from investors to help produce a movie from a screenplay he had written. Corso, under the direction of the feds, said he could get Lou the money, but it would be drug money. Lou didn't care where it came from—he just wanted it. These conversations were all taped. Lou also set up a drug deal with Corso where Lou's son delivered methamphetamines to Corso's office; again, all under the watchful eye of the feds.

By March 9, 2005, the FBI and the DEA had more than enough. Swooping in on a restaurant parking lot, they arrested Lou Eppolito and Stephen Caracappa. This time, there would be no going back.

Search warrants for the Eppolito and Caracappa homes provided the feds with a wealth of information, including a file found in Lou's home of the murdered prostitute the jogger found—the murder for which Barry Gibbs was serving a life sentence in prison.

On April 1, 2005, the body of Israel Greenwald was exhumed from the floor of the auto body shop. On April 21, Lou Eppolito and Stephen Caracappa were arraigned on eight counts of murder and conspiracy to commit murder, attempted murder, obstruction of justice, kidnapping conspiracy, witness tampering, bribery, money laundering, and drug trafficking.

In July 2005, Barry Gibbs was released from prison and his record expunged after it was determined that Eppolito threatened the sole witness in the trial. The only thing Gibbs was ever guilty of was sitting outside when Eppolito drove by.

The trial of Lou and Stephen began March 15, 2006, in front of worldwide media. People were fascinated with the case, a real-life *Goodfellas* unfolding before their very eyes. Regardless, the families of the victims were clearly not fascinated. It was especially hard for them as they listened to the defense present the two men to the jury as credible, lifelong, and award-winning police officers who were guilty of nothing and should be exonerated. Burt Kaplan testified against his longtime partners, and, in the end, it took the jury just ten hours to come to a verdict.

An era of police corruption and Mafia brotherhood had finally reached its end. Louis Eppolito and Stephen Caracappa were found guilty on all counts. Since Lou and Stephen continued to deny their guilt and showed absolutely no remorse, they were both sentenced to life in prison without the possibility of parole.

Even though her son's body had never been found, Betty Hydell could now find some peace and closure.

CHAPTER 14

HELLO, DELIVERY HERE!

KEITH WASHINGTON
POLICE OFFICER, PRINCE GEORGE'S COUNTY, MARYLAND

He was known for having a temper. The "hothead" of the
Prince George's County Police Department in Maryland,
he had a lengthy history of altercations, both verbal and physical, when confronted—or when not confronted. Most felt it
was simply best just to stay away from police corporal Keith
Washington, forty-six, and there are those who truly believed
that he had no business working within the scope of a police
officer to begin with. Twelve years prior to shooting two deliverymen, Washington was diagnosed with a laundry list of
mental instabilities after a psychological examination.

Some of these conditions included depression, post-traumatic
stress disorder, and paranoid state and adjustment disorder. One
psychiatrist wrote that Washington was "a potential danger
because of his impulsivity and generalized fearfulness." This
seems to repeat the mantra of wondering why he was allowed to
continue serving in law enforcement. In fact, any law enforce-

ment agency that employs an individual with such blatant and questionable behavior seems almost archaic or backward in this day and age; or so it would seem. Regardless, if Washington's erratic behavior was a certainty, so was the propensity for the Prince George's County police to cover it up—they had his back, repeatedly.

Prince George's County was no stranger to high-profile crime, or any crime for that matter. In 2006, the county had the highest crime rate in the entire Baltimore–Washington DC metro area. Known for being the birthplace of such celebrities as Goldie Hawn and Sugar Ray Leonard, the area is most famous for being the escape route that John Wilkes Booth took after shooting President Lincoln. At the time of Washington's murder trial, there were two other trials pending that involved public officials. The State Attorney's Office clearly had their hands full.

On January 24, 2007, Keith Washington grew more impatient by the hour while waiting for the delivery of his bedrails. It was during this wait that he retrieved his department-issued duty pistol, a Beretta 9 mm, and tucked it into his waistband. The bedrails he had recently purchased were scratched, and the replacements were to be delivered early that afternoon. At one point, approximately six hours before the deliverymen arrived, Washington called the store to inquire about the arrival time. According to court testimony, he screamed, complained, and yelled obscenities at the employee. As each hour ticked by slowly, Washington's blood boiled hotter and hotter. The deliverymen, Brandon Clark, twenty-two, and Robert White, thirty-six, arrived sometime before 7:00 PM at Washington's home in the quiet neighborhood in Accokeek.

Washington was like a time bomb ready to explode. All he needed was a few words to trigger him, and Clark and White unknowingly obliged. Clearly agitated, Washington let the men into his home and led them upstairs to the master bedroom. His wife, Stacey, and six-year-old daughter remained downstairs. As they walked down the hallway toward the bedroom, Washington claimed he turned around and only saw one man behind him. When he asked where White had gone, he claimed that Clark backhanded him in the chest and said, "I got him, Shorty, I got him." At that point, Washington claimed that White emerged from his daughter's bedroom and that he felt extremely "uneasy."

When the trio entered the master bedroom, words were exchanged, and Washington ordered the men to leave his home. According to him, he told the men approximately three times to leave, and they refused. In fact, they started beating on him, Washington claimed. They were in the hallway and had Washington down on his knees as they were punching him in the head and neck. He had no other choice but to pull his gun and shoot. This was Washington's claim.

White explained the story much differently. He stated that when the men went upstairs, they went directly into the master bedroom. Clark questioned Washington as to why the current bedrails had not been disabled. Apparently this was all it took to set him off. "You telling me what to do in my own fucking house?" Washington screamed at the men.

It's not exactly known what transpired from that point up until the shootings, but Clark was able to make a phone call to his supervisor to report the problem. "He's looking for a fight," Clark told him, referring to Washington.

At that point, after Washington had just shoved Clark three times, White suggested to Clark they should just leave to avoid any further confrontation. Washington completely unraveled. As the men were walking down the hallway to leave, Washington began yelling. "I know how to get you the fuck out of my house!" he screamed.

Washington then opened fire on the two men. His wife,

Stacey, was the first to call 911. "I think someone's been shot! They were beating my husband in my house!" she claimed.

As the dispatcher tried to obtain more information, Washington picked up an extension phone from upstairs and dialed 911, unaware that the dispatcher was already on the line. Communicating with the dispatcher, Washington immediately identified himself as a police officer and gave his badge number. He reported the incident as a "departmental shooting," and stated, "I was jumped by two guys in my house." And, with an eerie calmness, Washington provided more detailed information, revealing what he was most concerned about: "Two shot," he repeated. "They're in my house. Bleeding on my carpet!"

Washington, whose voice was cool and calm after having just been attacked, was overshadowed by the moans of the men in the background. Brandon Clark's last words were recorded on the 911 call.

"Oh, God!" he cried out.

"The ambulance is on its way!" Washington snapped back at him.

When asked where the men had been shot, Washington claimed he didn't know, but thought he had hit one in the leg. He repeated that the men had been assaulting him and refused to leave, and added his own thoughts of the matter: "You've got to be pretty bold to come into someone's house and jump on them," he told the dispatcher.

In the beginning, no one thought to question the sixteen-year veteran officer. In fact, both Clark and White were considered to be in custody for assaulting Washington while in the hospital. Clark, however, was unconscious and remained that way until he died nine days later. He was never able to give a statement. White was able to recover from his wounds.

The shooting quickly made the papers, prompting those

who knew Washington to say silently to themselves, "I told you so." As more details about the incident began to emerge, so did information on Washington's past—and temper.

Born in Houston, Texas, Keith Washington joined the army when he was eighteen years old. Even after leaving the military, he stayed in the reserves, where he was trained extensively in the area of counterterrorism and held the rank of lieutenant colonel. Most important, he had friends in high places. And those friends became a serious issue in the investigation.

Perhaps the most exclusive in Washington's circle of friends was County Executive Jack Johnson. During Johnson's campaign, Washington served as his driver, and when he was elected, Johnson quickly promoted Washington to the position of county homeland security officer. This raised the eyebrows of many, but surprised few. Washington even ran his own campaign, unsuccessfully running against County Councilwoman Marilynn Bland in 2002 for her position. Washington was always protected. He had been plagued with several lawsuits, excessive use of force complaints, and verbal and physical altercations.

On November 1, 1997, Washington was investigating a traffic accident involving attorney Paul Essex, who was clearly at fault. Being overly rude and confrontational during the investigation, Washington served Essex with several tickets and began to search him. A short time before, Essex had called his friend David Maslousky to tow his car for him. When Maslousky arrived, he saw Washington "roughing" up his friend and kindly asked the officer to take it easy. Washington set his sights on Maslousky for daring to question an officer of the law. He quickly arrested Maslousky for interfering with police business before transporting him to jail. During the ride, Washington told Maslousky that "Bubba is waiting for you at the jail." After their arrival, Maslousky was subjected to a humiliating and unconstitutional strip search.

After the complaint was reviewed and Maslousky's criminal charge was immediately dropped, he angrily sued Washington and the Prince George's County Police Department. During the trial, even the state's attorney admitted that Washington was "pompous, arrogant, and rude," but added that "no one has the constitutional right to a cordial police officer." However, it wasn't enough to sway the jury. David Maslousky was awarded $260,000 in damages. As for the internal investigation by the Prince George police, they cleared Washington and felt that he had done nothing inappropriate.

In another lawsuit, Washington, DC, police officer Robert Johnson was walking across a restaurant parking lot when he was stopped by Washington. Johnson claimed his fellow officer physically constrained him and placed him under arrest with no justification. The case was dismissed only because Johnson was killed in the line of duty during a traffic stop. Again, Washington was cleared by internal affairs.

In a more public incident, Washington attacked a fellow board member of the homeowner's association for which he served. This time, he was criminally charged with a misdemeanor, but it, too, was later dismissed.

After the details became public, much blame was placed on Jack Johnson and the police chief, Melvin High. They were accused of covering for Washington over the years—covering up behavior and actions that led to the death of an innocent man. Since there was no focus on Washington right after the shootings, people assumed this, too, would be covered up. Once indicted, Washington's only defense was that the prosecution was politically motivated, a claim they vehemently denied. Of course, Washington's high-ranking friends, like Johnson, threw him far under the bus once the charges were filed. Johnson claimed, "I barely even knew him."

Interestingly enough, months went by without any charges

against Washington. Most anticipated there wouldn't be any, and, like before, he would walk away scot-free as usual. However, a second incident on April 5, 2007, prompted the state attorney's office to reevaluate Keith Washington.

At approximately 9:30 AM, real estate appraiser Kevin King parked in front of Washington's home. With his company's name boldly printed on the vehicle, King mistakenly had the wrong house. Still in his vehicle, King watched as Washington pulled into his driveway, almost hitting his own mailbox, before going in through the front door. King claimed he waved at Washington, to say "Hi." A few minutes later, King noticed Washington was standing behind his vehicle. Before he could say anything, Washington walked to the rear of his house.

King then took some street-view photos of the home and finished his paperwork. At that point, he knocked on Washington's front door. According to King, Washington opened the door and immediately stuck a gun in his face. Horrified, King began walking backward while explaining that he was an appraiser and trying to show Washington the appraisal order form. Washington kept yelling obscenities and threatening King. Realizing he had made a mistake and was at the wrong house, King drove up the street to the correct address and called 911. King wasn't aware whom he was dealing with until a neighborhood resident informed him. "Considering what happened to those guys from the furniture store, I felt both terrified and grateful that I wasn't killed," he said.

King further added that Washington never identified himself as law enforcement, and that the assault was completely unprovoked and unjustified. The state's attorney had finally had enough of Keith Washington's temper. The day after the King incident, he was formally charged with first-degree assault, second-degree assault, and use of a handgun during a violent crime. Washington turned himself in, and his bond was set at $75,000, which he posted later that day.

The night of the incident, Chief High finally decided to suspend Washington with pay and confiscate his badge and gun while internal affairs conducted another separate investigation from the shooting of Clark and White.

Still on the payroll, Washington was indicted on June 14, 2007, for the incident with Kevin King. On July 31, 2007, he was indicted on charges of second-degree murder and attempted second-degree murder for the death of Brandon Clark and the shooting of Robert White.

With the trial slated for February 2008, residents were astonished when Washington was allowed to retire from the Prince George's County Police Department with benefits, as opposed to being terminated. The scope of the early retirement was classified as an "undisclosed medical injury."

The eight-day-long trial began in February to a packed courtroom. To several people, it was a matter of whose story one was to believe; the veteran police officer and his wife, or the furniture deliveryman with a lengthy criminal record. The prosecution made it crystal clear that the victims were clearly not saints, but that having a criminal record does not give someone the right to murder them.

Washington stood strong with his own version of events. However, it was the testimony of the Fort Washington emergency room physician Karen Dixon that proved to be most damning to Washington. Her testimony shredded his claims that he was being beaten so savagely by two large men that he had to kill them. Immediately following the shooting, Washington had requested that he be transported to the hospital for injuries suffered from the beating.

"I did not see evidence on his head of trauma," she testified. She further added that there were absolutely no bruises or scratches anywhere on Washington's body. Registered nurse Nilda Concepcion, who also treated Washington that night, stated she recorded his original complaint of pain in his neck, his face, and his head. Concepcion noted that Washington's blood pressure was 138/76 and his heart rate was 84, extremely calm for someone who had just been through such a traumatic event. Like Dixon, Concepcion saw no visible injuries on Washington.

However, Lt. Charles Walls of the Prince George Police Department testified that the photographs he took of Washington's face after he left the hospital did not show the redness that he claimed to have seen.

In his closing arguments, Assistant State's Attorney William Moomau wanted to drive the point home to the jury that Washington was nothing but a no-nonsense bully and thug. Moomau took the weapon that Washington used in the shooting and stuck it in his waistband, just as Washington did the day of the delivery. Parading in front of the jury that way, Moomau explained how this was what Washington did on the day that two men lay bleeding and dying in his home. Moomau said the gun was a symbol of Washington's "police bravado" being threatened.

Defense attorney Mike Starr was adamant that the jury should believe both Keith and Stacey Washington, not a felon with a history of sex crimes like Robert White.

"White said Washington wanted them to leave, but shooting them won't make them leave and if they're already leaving, why does he shoot them?" Starr questioned. "Keith Washington was the police. And what Stacey Washington did when she saw him was call the police, and the only reason why was because she saw he was helpless."

Even though Washington's past incriminations and damning psychological evaluation were not allowed into the trial, the jury deliberated for only eleven hours before reaching a verdict. On February 25, 2008, the jury returned with a verdict that actually acquitted Washington on the murder charges. They found him guilty on lesser charges of involuntary manslaughter, two counts of using a handgun in a crime of violence, and two counts of first-degree assault. Washington showed virtually no emotion as the verdicts were read, knowing he could possibly spend upward of seventy years in prison. As he was led out of the courtroom, he mouthed, "I love you," to his wife.

It seemed that trouble followed Keith Washington no matter where he went, even in jail. Only three days after his conviction, Washington was found with a handcuff key hidden in his county jumpsuit. According to the prosecutors, Washington became combative with corrections officers who were attempting to search him before transferring him to another county jail: "The shirt was pulled from the defendant's grip, and the handcuff key was found in the pocket of the defendant's jail shirt," they wrote. "Defendant stated that he found the handcuff key approximately two hours earlier and placed same in his pocket."

The prosecutors filed the incident in a motion asking the judge to deny the defendant's request that he be released on home detention pending sentencing. They stated the handcuff key was proof positive that Washington was a flight risk.

"Defendant's actions further show his danger to the community, as the possession of the handcuff key reflects a clear intention of escaping his current circumstances." The judge agreed, and Washington remained incarcerated until his sentencing.

On May 27, 2008, Judge Michael P. Whalen sentenced Keith Washington to forty-five years in prison—five more years than the prosecutors had asked for. He explained his sentence, stating that there was absolutely no evidence that supported Washington's story. "There wasn't one discernible injury on you to any of the medical personnel that examined you," he said.

After the sentencing, utilizing his opportunity to address the court, Washington launched into a bizarre sermon that included quotes from historical figures like Sojourner Truth, Thomas Jefferson, and George Washington before speaking directly to the victim's family; still not taking responsibility for his actions. "I did not murder your son!" he said to Brandon Clark's mother. "I feel your pain, no parent should ever have to bury a child. . . . I don't want you to go away thinking some monster shot your son and is indifferent to his death."

However, to most, Washington *is* a monster, one who has abused his authority over the years to threaten, bully, and intimidate anyone he could. For the family of the victims, having him off the streets doesn't compare to the loss that they suffered—but it'll certainly do.

"I don't understand all those second-degree, first-degree murder charges," Brandon's mother Marilynn told reporters. "I just know that my son is dead, so I just look for him to get locked up."

CHAPTER 15

EXCUSE ME, MA'AM

CRAIG PEYER
STATE POLICE OFFICER, CALIFORNIA HIGHWAY PATROL,
SAN DIEGO, CALIFORNIA

"People are safe with law enforcement officers."

Rory Divine, a female reporter for Channel 39 in San Diego, California, quickly jotted down the words proudly spoken by California Highway Patrolman Craig Peyer. Riding in Peyer's police cruiser for a news story on the dangers facing women on the highways, Rory felt that Peyer was very informative.

Two days prior to her ride-along with Peyer, the body of twenty-year-old college student Cara Knott was found in a remote area of a dead end road; she had been driving on the highway, coming home from her boyfriend's house. Her death was immediately ruled a homicide. With all of the paranoia by the public following the incident, Divine felt the story would be well received. After putting in her request with the California Highway Patrol (CHP), she was placed with the agency's spokesperson, Officer Craig Peyer—one of their best. At the time, Rory paid no mind to the scratches on Peyer's face.

December 27, 1986, began in the usual holiday-spirited manner for the Knott family. Sam Knott felt the Christmas season was one of the most amazing times of the year. They were the days when nothing but quality time was spent with his wife, Joyce, and their four children. On this particular Saturday, it was business as usual for the Knotts. They gathered in the family room of their El Cajon home to watch one of Sam's beloved Disney movies. Flanked by Joyce; his eldest daughter, Cindy—and her husband, Bill Weick; his second eldest daughter, Cheryl; and their youngest and only son, John, Sam felt a fleeting sense of disappointment that Cara wasn't with them. Cara, his youngest daughter, had gone to the home of her boyfriend, Wayne Bautista, in Escondido to care for him. Forty-five minutes away, Wayne was suffering from a nasty flu. Cara took an overnight bag the previous day so she could care for Wayne while he was sick. Still, she called frequently, updating the family on Wayne's progress. Since the young couple had been dating for almost three years, Wayne was affectionately viewed as another son, and brother, in the Knott family. There was no doubt the couple would marry soon.

Cara, a beautiful blonde, tan, and athletic college student, was destined for success. She was headstrong and resilient, and Joyce always referred to her youngest daughter as "my buddy."

At approximately 8:15 PM, Cara called her family with good news. Wayne was feeling much better and she was leaving to come home. A close, tight-knit, family, the Knotts were overjoyed that Cara would be joining them for the rest of the night. However, their joy quickly dissipated.

After the movie was finished, Joyce noticed it was after 10:00 PM. "Cara should have been home by now," she remarked to Sam.

Sam, becoming alarmed, quickly grabbed his car keys to go search for Cara. Some may think his actions were a knee-jerk response, but Sam Knott knew his daughter. Cara Knott was one of the most responsible people he knew—if she were going to be late, she would have called. Sensing Sam's urgency, Joyce called Wayne and confirmed that Cara had left his house shortly after calling home.

Sam set out on a mission—to find his daughter. For several hours, Sam and Joyce drove north toward Wayne's home in hopes of finding Cara. Wayne feared that Cara had broken down somewhere. Feeling hopeless, Sam spotted several CHP cruisers parked along the side of the road. He stopped to ask for their help in locating his daughter, but he was quickly dismissed. She had to be missing for twenty-four hours before they would take any action at all. By 2:00 AM, the family reconvened in the Knotts' home. Cheryl, in a panic, called 911, and, like Sam, was directed to various different police departments and quickly dismissed. Cheryl and Cara were as close as two sisters could be, and Cheryl feared the worst.

Knowing they were on their own, the Knott family set out again in hopes of finding Cara. Exhausting all of the possibilities by calling Cara's friends and other family members, Sam went out to the highway while instructing Cindy and Bill to check all of the exits off I-15.

Sometime near dawn, Cindy and Bill happened upon the Mercy Road exit. An undeveloped, dead-end road, the area had been turned into nothing more than a path for bicycles and joggers. A large "Road Closed" sign blocked the path to vehicles. Sam had pulled in earlier, but dismissed the idea of driving down Mercy Road—he couldn't imagine Cara driving down there alone. However, Bill and Cindy drove around the sign and continued down the bike path/road. The road was long and took them down a steep hill into a canyon. There, they saw Cara's white VW parked along the side. In shock, but hopeful, Cindy ran to the car, finding nothing but a gas receipt, purse, and clothes—but not Cara.

After searching the immediate area for several minutes and calling Cara's name, Bill and Cindy drove back to the interstate to find a pay phone to call the police. This time, the San Diego police said they would respond.

Sam Knott was still on the interstate searching for his beloved daughter at the time Cindy called the police. Call it luck, or call it fate, but Sam, at his wit's end, saw a San Diego police car speeding down the interstate. Determined to make them listen and file a missing person report, Sam started after the cruiser, running red lights, honking his horn, and flashing his headlights. Strangely, the officer didn't stop. Sam continued his pursuit of the police officer to the end of Mercy Road where Cindy and Bill were waiting.

Sam's heart thudded in his chest as he saw Cara's white VW Bug abandoned on the desolate road. After Sam quickly informed the officers on the scene that Cara was last seen wearing purple sweatpants with white leather boots, a white sweatshirt, and white leather jacket, San Diego Police Department Officer Jim Spears quickly set out to inspect the car. Immediately noticing a smudge of blood on the door, Spears knew something was wrong. So wrong, in fact, he called in numerous other members of the San Diego Police Department, including search dogs. Unfortunately, the dogs wouldn't be needed.

Sergeant Bill Maheu heard Officer Spears's request for more officers. Maheu, already aware of the situation, decided to drive in the opposite side of Mercy Road to take a look around. Familiar with the area, Maheu searched the bike path before going on an old abandoned highway bridge. Instincts forced him to look over the side of the bridge, and down.

There, lying on a bed of rocks sixty-five feet below, was the body of Cara Knott. Hearing Knott's clothing description earlier, Maheu saw the white leather boots, purple pants, and white sweatshirt—it was undoubtedly Cara.

Maheu drove back to the area of the abandoned VW and quietly informed Officer Spears of his findings. Together, they drove back to the bridge and walked down to the body. Lying face up, Cara's left arm was across her chest. The officers immediately noticed the thin red abrasions that were prominently displayed across her neck. Her blonde hair was soaked with blood, as was the right side of her sweatshirt. Her hair was pulled back into a ponytail, and there were deep, dark bruises over her right eye and near her mouth. Finally, on her brand-new leather boots, a Christmas present from her mother, was a single drop of blood.

Tests would later confirm that Cara Knott died from strangulation. She had a fractured skull, her face had been smashed in, and she also had a broken right collarbone, ten broken ribs, lacerated lungs and liver, a fractured pelvis, and multiple cracks at the base of her skull. Cara Knott had been beaten unmercifully.

With obvious signs of death, and no pulse, Maheu dreaded having to tell the worried, already grieving family that their loved one was dead. Regardless, this was his first priority. Sensing the worst, Sam stood stoically as Officer Spears delivered the words that are every parent's worst nightmare: "We've found your daughter . . . she's dead."

"So, this is it," Sam muttered, clearly in shock. "My daughter . . . she was an angel."

As Sam, Cindy, and Bill made the dreaded drive home to tell the rest of the family, including Joyce, that their worst fears had been realized, the detectives from the San Diego Police Department had a long day ahead of them. With the crime scene investigation unit on scene, the lengthy and timely task of collecting evidence commenced. Unfortunately, there wasn't much evidence to be found.

There were tire tracks, approximately thirteen feet from where Cara's body had clearly been dropped; these were photographed and measured. Approximately eight to ten feet long, the left track was shorter than the right, indicating the vehicle turned around at a high rate of speed. The distance between the tracks was fifty-three inches, giving the indication of a large or heavy vehicle. No casts of the tire tracks were ever made for comparison. Investigators also found three half-empty cans of beer, still moderately cold, underneath the bridge only a short distance from where the body was. Finally, a single, blonde hair was found on the edge of a concrete rail by the bridge.

The San Diego Police Department had over thirty unsolved homicides within the last two years, most of which were possibly at the hands of the Green River Killer—a serial killer who terrorized the West Coast for years. Fortunately, investigators quickly determined that the Cara Knott murder was an isolated instance. The Green River Killer targeted mostly prostitutes and displayed a common method of murder between the victims.

With the scene processed and little evidence found, the strenuous task of finding a suspect began. Unknowingly, television news editor Mike Workman received the first tip on the true killer within two days. A young woman, Terri Green, told him that she had a frightening experience with a CHP officer in November, and that the incident occurred on Mercy Road. Workman immediately passed the information on to the San Diego Police Department and the California Highway Patrol. Regrettably, the tip was put to the side and ignored—at first.

Completely unaware that they had received crucial information so soon after the murder, investigators set out on an exhaustive search for the killer. Almost instantly, the case began receiving a significant amount of media attention. Like the story aired by Rory Divine, the notion of a pretty, athletic, all-American girl found brutally murdered for no apparent reason struck the chords of parents and college students statewide, and soon the entire nation was engrossed in the case.

It was during Cara Knott's burial in Bonita, California, that investigators happened upon their first suspect. After everyone had left, detectives noticed Wayne Bautista's father, Jaime, standing at Cara's casket, alone and unusually grief stricken. Granted, emotions were at an all-time high that day, but his overwhelming display of anguish piqued an interest with officers. They already knew that Jaime was the last person to actually speak to Cara on the phone. Shortly after Cara phoned her parents, informing them that she was coming home, Jaime called to check on Wayne—and spoke to Cara. At that point, investigators decided to quietly look into Jaime Bautista.

Further information revealed that Cara had worked for Jaime at his health food store the prior summer. Jaime was known by neighbors as having "an eye for the women." Shortly after, a tip came in that a gold Cadillac was seen in the area of Mercy Road the night of the murder. The tip also gave information that a blonde woman was seen in the Cadillac, hanging over the passenger seat. At that point, investigators felt confident they had their man—Jaime Bautista drove a gold Cadillac. Neighbors informed detectives that Jaime had become abnormally depressed after Cara's murder. Consequently, when they received a call from a close friend of Jaime's notifying them that Jaime was overly upset and had something to tell them, they eagerly drove to the Escondido home with hopes of an arrest. Unfortunately, the investigators were wrong. Confronted with the fact that he was a suspect in Cara's murder, Jaime quickly provided an airtight alibi in the form of phone records. Jaime was well over an hour away at the time of the murder. After confirming this, detectives were back at square one.

They still had other tips. Specifically, witness accounts of a suspicious hitchhiker in the area of Mercy Road, but, like Jaime Bautista, this information failed to pan out. Frustrated and under intense scrutiny by the media and the Knott family, investigators received a promising new tip.

Cheryl Johnson, a young nurse, had been pulled over by a CHP officer on Mercy Road. Like Cara, she also drove a VW. The officer told Cheryl she had a cracked headlight and kept her on the stop for almost an hour and a half—the entire time Cheryl claimed that she had a "bad feeling." Quickly remembering a similar tip, investigators found the message left by Mike Workman. The account of the other woman, Terri Green, was eerily similar to Cheryl's. Most important, they named the same officer—Officer Craig Peyer.

Known by the nickname "Hot Pencil" for all the traffic citations he wrote, CHP Officer Craig Peyer was a thirteen-year veteran of the state's most elite police agency. Described as overly neat, and a consummate professional, Peyer was born in Minnesota and moved to California when he was a year old. A Vietnam veteran, Peyer was currently on his third marriage, a relationship that began when he started having an affair with his married next-door neighbor, Karen. Peyer's brown hair was rarely out of place, and he polished his uniform brass and boots excessively. For this reason, the CHP frequently made Peyer its spokesperson. With two young children and a stepson, Peyer appeared as the ultimate family man.

While detectives at the San Diego Police Department were putting two and two together regarding the phone tips, the CHP was quietly forming its own conclusions.

CHP Sergeant John McDonald was the first to suspect

Peyer. While giving information in the Cara Knott murder to his officers at roll call, a past complaint briefly interrupted his thoughts. He immediately remembered a complaint filed against Peyer by a woman whom he stopped on Mercy Road—an area that was his beat. The woman claimed she had been held at the stop entirely too long. Nothing ever came of the complaint, but McDonald decided to take a look at Peyer's activity log and traffic tickets the night of the murder. Shockingly, he found one of the ticket's times had been purposely altered. Furthering his search, McDonald found an "injury on duty" report filed by Peyer that same night. Peyer claimed that, while pumping gas at the CHP pumps, he slipped in spilled fuel and fell into a wire fence. Peyer claimed facial abrasions as well as right arm, right foot, and shoulder trauma.

Investigators at the San Diego Police Department were shocked to learn the information. Secretly meeting with the top officials of the CHP, they devised a ploy to search Peyer's cruiser. It would be a difficult task since Peyer was very possessive about his car. Officials decided to tell Peyer that since his cruiser was kept in such immaculate condition, they wanted to use it for a promotional video. Peyer was none the wiser.

The cruiser was inspected inside and out. Investigators were beginning to feel a slight sense of defeat until one of the detectives lifted Peyer's spare tire out of the trunk. Underneath were dirty yellow plastic ropes, three in total—ropes that weren't issued by the department. In light of the fact that the coroner determined Cara's strangulation was probably done with a rope, and based on the markings on her neck, both law enforcement agencies felt it was time to bring Craig Peyer in for questioning. The agencies decided to take a few days to get all of their facts together, but the interview would come much sooner. Several of the officers at the CHP tipped Peyer off that his cruiser was being searched and he approached his superiors and questioned as to why. At that point, he was informed that he was a suspect in the murder of Cara Knott.

Peyer was extremely eager to cooperate and agreed to speak to San Diego detectives. During the recorded interview on January 8, 1987, Peyer continued to protest his innocence, giving various explanations to questions asked. "Human being to human being, highway patrolman to highway patrolman, I didn't do anything," he pleaded. "I didn't murder anybody—I wasn't raised that way. I have never killed a human being or ever will kill a human being; I never even used my gun as a highway patrol officer!"

The interview went on for hours, draining the energy and patience of the investigators. They decidedly had enough of Peyer's games and threw out the smoking gun. "What about the ropes, Craig?" One of the detectives asked.

His answer shocked them and confirmed their beliefs that they had their killer. Peyer gave up information only the investigators knew. No one had ever told Peyer ropes were located in his trunk. "Those are only two ropes, I don't know about any other rope," he stated matter-of-factly.

In the days following the interview with Peyer, more complaints came in from women who had been stopped by him on Mercy Road.

Approximately two weeks before Cara's murder, Kathy Deir had been driving along I-15 late at night. Like the others, she was nervous at being stopped by the police. However, it was Peyer who ordered her on his speaker to drive off the exit down Mercy Road. He informed her she had been stopped because her headlights were "out of alignment," a strange equipment violation, but Deir thought it best to keep quiet. Deir claims she was terrified when Peyer asked her to get in his car, but complied. Even more terrifying was the fact he continued driving, away from I-15, down into the canyon. Stopping at the bridge, he engaged in unusual conversation before taking her back to her car and letting her go. Deir claimed she had been with Peyer well over an hour.

On December 26, 1986—one day before Cara's murder—Shelly Sacks was also driving on I-15 when she was pulled over in her Honda CRX by Peyer. He claimed she had a crack in her headlight. Sacks also stated she was extremely scared when Peyer ordered her back into his vehicle.

With similar complaints coming in daily, detectives decided enough was enough. On January 15, 1987—almost three weeks after the murder, CHP Officer Craig Peyer was arrested and charged with murder in the first degree. Although overjoyed that an arrest had been made, the Knotts family was horrified to learn the suspect was a police officer. However, Peyer's arrest answered a lot of questions for Sam Knott. "Who else but somebody in authority would my baby stop for?" He reiterated Cara's sense of responsibility to safety. "She was so good. She wouldn't stop for anybody. Isn't that what we told you all along? I thought it might have been some service station guy; somebody who we were depending on."

Like the Knotts, the nation was outraged. Someone people had been told to respect and obey had abused his power to take the life of a promising young girl. Surprisingly, there was a considerable amount of people who believed in Peyer's innocence—something Peyer himself vehemently maintained. His wife, Karen Peyer, stood by him, believing he could never commit such a brutal, coldhearted act.

On January 21, 1986, Peyer was arraigned on the charge of murder. For the first time, Sam Knott was able to look into the eyes of the man who stripped his family of their loved one and crippled their lives forever. At that time, bond was set for three hundred thousand dollars, low enough for Peyer's wife to post. However, as Karen Peyer was collecting the money, District Attorney Joe Van Orshoven announced new evidence had surfaced and the bail was raised to one million dollars—the highest bail in history for a non–death penalty case. Apparently, three gold fibers had been found on Cara's sweatshirt: fibers that matched the gold thread in the CHP uniform patch.

Throughout it all, Karen Peyer was unsuccessful in raising Craig's bail. She wrote countless letters asking for assistance, but each request was denied or ignored.

On January 4, 1988, almost one year and one week after the murder, the case of *The State of California vs. Craig Peyer* went to trial. Van Orshoven was trying the case for the prosecution. Peyer's attorney, Robert Grimes, was a local defense attorney with a reputable track record. The Knott family expressed disdain several times at the way Van Orshoven was handling the case, specifically his handling of the jury selection. The Knotts felt there was one juror in particular who should have been struck down immediately. After promising to take care of the matter, Van Orshoven told the family he simply forgot.

His presentation of the case was fierce. One by one, Van Orshoven offered each piece of evidence to the jury, confident there would be no question of Peyer's guilt. He explained how the measure of the tire tracks found at the scene matched the wheelbase of a CHP cruiser, and the threads found on Cara's sweatshirt unquestionably came from a CHP patch. He further presented a couple who testified to seeing a CHP cruiser speeding off Mercy Road at approximately 9:30 PM the date of the murder. Finally, the single drop of blood found on Cara's leather boot was presented. An expert testified the blood type of the drop was the same as Craig Peyer's, and had two matching DNA markers. Also, a gas station worker testified that Peyer entered the station the night of the murder with fresh scratches on his face. The worker also testified to watching Peyer stand at the trunk of his cruiser and wipe down his flashlight and nightstick. "It looked like he had been in a fight," the worker testified. "I noticed claw marks on his face. The one on his left was bleeding. . . . He told me he had 'one hell of a night.'"

However, the defense blasted all of the evidence as circumstantial and the witnesses as less than credible. Grimes pointed out that if Cara inflicted the scratches to Peyer's face, DNA would have surely been found under her fingernails. There wasn't any DNA found there. He also pointed out the fact that there were no drag marks by the bridge—if Peyer killed Cara as the prosecution stated, there surely would have been numerous marks in the dirt. Grimes also shredded the theory of the DNA. He confirmed with the expert that only two matching markers meant it could have come from 1 in 161 Caucasian people within the state of California, leaving the pool of other possible suspects rather large.

The issue of the rope fared no better for the prosecution when it came to the defense. Grimes's questioning of the pathologist who performed the autopsy revealed that the ropes taken from Peyer's cruiser were never tested for blood and skin. He further caught the pathologist lying about the liver temperature—all in front of the watchful eyes of the jury. He humiliated the witnesses after they admitted to waiting for months after the murder to give their accounts to the police, discrediting them on the spot. He further added there was no plaster cast made of the tire tracks for comparison, and the police completely ignored a footprint found at the scene. As for the gold fibers found on Cara's sweatshirt, Grimes contended they could have come from any factory-made piece of clothing.

Finally, one of the most damning testimonies came from Wanda Dobbie, a nurse. Dobbie claimed that she spotted a white VW just south of Mercy Road. Describing a white female whose description matched Cara, Dobbie claimed a Hispanic male had his hands on her shoulders, holding her up against the car. A brown Datsun was parked in front of the VW, blocking it. The most damning part of the story was the time. Dobbie insisted she witnessed the incident at 11:30 PM—nearly a full hour after Peyer was off duty and home with his wife and children.

Unquestionably, Grimes's tactics worked. On Thursday, February 25, 1988, nearly ten days after convening, the jury returned and announced its findings to the horrified prosecution and Knott family: "Your honor, we are a hung jury."

The announcement set the courtroom into a frenzy; screams and sobs emanated throughout. The Knotts were in unmistakable shock. The man they believed had brutally murdered their daughter and sister was going free. The district attorney's office was flabbergasted and knew they needed to work quickly to begin proceedings for a retrial. Obviously, the outcry from the public at the district attorney's office was large and loud.

While Peyer spent his few months of freedom working as a pool cleaner with a friend, the district attorney's office appointed a new attorney to handle the retrial of Craig Peyer. Paul Pfingst, formerly a prosecutor in New York, had successfully convicted fifty-three murderers. With little time to prepare, Pfingst was elated when an anonymous letter was received by his office: *"Look for 3 Mexicans who were under bridge and saw it happen. They came to fast food place near there and ask for ride north. They were scared and said they had to get out of this place as they saw a policeman kill a lady. They spoke fair English and worked in a packing plant in Escondido."*

Pfingst put his best investigators on the information. While they were following up on this, a new lead came in.

Traci and Scott Koenig had been traveling down I-15 the

night of the murder. They claimed they passed a state patrol car that had pulled over a white VW at the Mercy Road exit. Traci distinctly remembered seeing the young blonde driver and commenting, "Boy, is she busted."

Pfingst asked them why they waited so long to come forward with their information, letting them know bluntly that their testimony may not be credible in the eyes of the jury. The Koenigs stated that they were getting married the week after the murder and would be taking their honeymoon soon after. They'd heard an arrest was made and assumed their testimony was "nothing" and knew by getting involved that their wedding plans could be compromised. They figured the police had all the information they needed—until they saw the hung jury verdict. Regardless, Pfingst was ecstatic. He now had two credible eyewitnesses who placed Peyer with Cara Knott. Unfortunately, the investigators weren't so lucky with the anonymous letter. With so many immigrant workers and numerous factories in the San Diego area it was impossible to locate the witnesses, those who most likely left the beer cans at the scene.

Nonetheless, on May 17, 1988, Pfingst began the retrial of Craig Peyer with confidence. Presenting an airtight case for the prosecution, Grimes found, unlike the first trial, he would have a difficult time countering the prosecution's theories. The testimony of the Koenigs proved to be the smoking gun. On June 23, 1988, Craig Peyer was found guilty for the murder of Cara Knott. During his sentencing in August, the presiding judge outwardly chastised the California Highway Patrol for ignoring warning signs exhibited by Peyer. And, as Joyce Knott read from her victim's impact statement, Peyer sat stone-faced.

I awaken every morning, often against my will. Whether I like it or not, my life goes on. I would give anything to trade places with Cara. I think every mother would give her own life to save her child. Without a moment's hesistation, I would give my life to bring Cara back. I only wish I could have the chance.

Cara's murder by a law enforcement officer, one she had been taught to respect and turn to in time of need, is beyond anything my mind and heart can accept. My days are filled with thoughts of Cara, missing her, wanting to hold her in my arms and take away the pain and fear I know I suffered.

My nights are long and agonizing as I am haunted by Cara's terror, her pain, her dying. There can be no true justice because Cara cannot be returned to life. The only semblance of justice we have available is to assure that her murderer is imprisoned for the rest of his life. It isn't enough. It isn't just. It's all we can do.

As for Sam Knott, he embarked on a new calling in life and determined to fix the justice system that had initially failed him. Because of Sam, the twenty-four-hour wait to file a missing person report was abolished. He became a true victim's advocate at heart. Each day of his life was spent finding justice for Cara and others. Sam later dedicated a park to crime victims near the Mercy Road exit where his daughter spent the last minutes of her life. He also gathered two hundred people to plant oak trees—like the one Cara is buried next to. He changed policies, laws, and ignored criticism. He cared for the victims and scorned the criminals. In 2000, Sam Knott sadly died of a broken heart. Some may say the years of grief and fight in him brought on the fatal heart attack, but his family and friends know better.

In 2004, a new company offered Craig Peyer a DNA test for the sole purpose of exonerating him. He refused. At his parole hearing the same year, a member of the parole board asked him why he didn't submit to the test. Craig Peyer remained silent. Acknowledging his "exceptional disregard for human suffering," the board denied Peyer's parole. His parole was again denied in 2008.

The Knott family lives on, carrying Sam's quest and Cara's memory. They are always present at the parole board hearings, along with Wayne Bautista, to ensure the man they refer to as "the monster" will never see the light of day again.

CHAPTER 16

SHE INSISTED ON BEING BURIED IN THE WALL

RICHARD WILLS
POLICE OFFICER, TORONTO, CANADA

Imagine Charles Manson with a badge. It's certainly a frightening thought, but it was the theatrical antics during the trial of former Toronto police officer Richard Wills that led to a deep comparison to the infamous killer of the 1960s. Wills is remembered largely for his gross mockery of the Canadian judicial system, since his despicable crime seemingly took a backseat during the "circus" of a trial.

Fifty-year-old Richard Wills, a twenty-five-year veteran of the Toronto Police Department, was convicted of the first-degree murder of his longtime lover, forty-year-old Lavinia (Linda) Mariani. The body of Mariani was found stuffed inside a plastic garbage bin and buried behind a false wall in Wills's Thornhill, Ontario, home. Wrapped in plastic, Mariani's body was so badly decomposed that investigators literally poured her remains onto the autopsy table.

Wills, a traffic services officer within the police department, was married with three children when he began the nine-year love affair with his wife's close friend in 1993. Mariani was also married, to husband Dominic, and they shared a teenage son. Dominic thought nothing of the fact that his wife and Wills ran a school for power skating together, where she held a position as a bookkeeper. Dominic considered Wills to be a friend as well.

Often dubbed "the man with too much chin" by reporters who covered his murder trial, Wills stood a little over six feet tall, had dark hair, and was usually described as clean-cut by his fellow officers. However, his Boy Scout appearance proved to be merely a facade to the citizens he came in contact with during the course of his law enforcement duties. Officer Richard Wills was known for being rude and belittling to citizens. And if one faced the unlucky venture of committing a traffic violation in front of him and getting away, Wills would spend the entire day looking for the driver—ignoring everything else. He was controlling, and he was driven.

These unfavorable traits tended to spread into his personal life, ultimately causing the demise of his marriage. With allegations of severe verbal and moderate physical abuse, Richard and Joanne Wills officially separated in 2001. Most police officers, when faced with the prospect of divorce, have an overwhelming fear of financial pressure due to alimony, child support, and half of their hard-earned pension disappearing. They often end up working double shifts and extra-duty details. But Richard Wills wasn't like most police officers. Financially, his net worth was estimated to be around $1.5 million.

Finally free from the confines of his marriage, Wills looked forward to spending every waking moment with Linda. Unfortunately for Linda, she didn't echo his sentiments. Nine long years of controlling and jealous behavior proved to be too much for the married mother of one. Linda decided to end her relationship with Wills. Friends claimed he was already angry with her for not leaving Dominic. Wills felt that he took the first step in ending his own marriage, and Linda should have done the same. Not only did Linda fail to leave Dominic, there were new rumors that she was involved with someone else— someone other than Wills.

On February 15, 2002, Wills and Linda met for the last time at his home in Thornhill. According to Wills, he had left a Valentine's gift for Linda at the top of his sprawling spiral staircase. Furthermore, he maintained that Linda tripped as she bent forward to pick up the gift and went sailing down the stairs, striking her head and dying instantly.

Obviously, Wills was asked why he didn't call for an ambulance or notify police at that very moment. However, his responses to these sorts of questions were just a few of the bizarre and unbelievable actions that permeated the case. He claimed there was a love pact between him and Linda. They had decided long ago that if they died, they would be buried together by a cottage on nearby Wasaga Beach. His answer for not calling in medical help was alarming—he had to go to work.

"Had it been my day off, she would have gone off to the cottage," Wills referred to Linda's dead body, reminding everyone he had to leave for work that day. "That was her wish. I'm stuck with her body. She died. Where am I going to put her?"

He put her in the wall a few hours before his shift.

Surprisingly, it was Wills who contacted police the following day, February 16, to report Linda missing. However, it was Wills's intention to immediately direct investigators toward Dominic. He indicated that Dominic might have poisoned Linda. In a further shocking move, Wills invited the York Regional Police to search his home, and stripped his clothes off right in front of officers to show them he had no defensive wounds. He wanted to "assure" officers that he wasn't a suspect and that Dominic was. While officers were searching his residence, Wills insisted they look in the basement, right by the wall where Linda was buried, as if mocking them. Wills also mentioned "the brotherhood" approximately thirty times during his initial contact with police.

As the search for Linda Mariani continued, Wills left a series of messages on her cell phone, some of which—considering the heinousness of the crime—would be shocking to a jury. Most of the calls from Wills were calm and joking in nature. The jury in his trial would not be as amused. One of the first calls referred to a piece of chocolate he had found: ". . . I ran over it in the driveway. Was that you?" Richard cooed.

Some of the other messages were intended to direct investigators to Dominic, but were dripping with enough sarcasm to make those listening recoil. "I love you, Lavinia baby. *Smack! Smack! Smack!* Kisses for you! Where are you, baby? . . . Dom giving you a hard time? Call me. Call me. Call me. I loooove you baby! *Smack! Smack! Smack!*"

After Dominic voluntarily submitted to a polygraph, investigators quickly eliminated the worried husband as a suspect of any wrongdoing. With no other evidence pointing to Wills, the case ran cold for several months.

The investigation by the York Regional Police, dubbed "Project Willpower," took a strange turn in June 2002. Richard Wills was known for his belief in psychics. The investigators decided to use this to their benefit and placed an undercover officer in the position of a psychic named "Yousef." Using Linda Mariani's good friend, Janet Amare, as a liaison between Yousef and Wills, she would relay messages to Wills that Linda was in contact with the psychic, and wanted him to know the body should be moved because police were close.

The day before Linda's body was discovered, Wills visited his close friend, Tony Jackson, making startling claims. "Tony, throw me over the balcony. Linda is dead. Kill me, kill me, kill me!" Wills exclaimed.

For reasons that may be construed as panic or disbelief, Wills agreed to meet Yousef at a local doughnut shop to obtain more information. But Wills never showed. Instead, he turned himself into the York Regional Police and led them to Linda Mariani's body.

In perhaps one of the most gruesome crime scenes ever encountered by the Canadian law enforcement agency, Linda Mariani's remains had become almost liquefied by her environment inside the false wall.

Found inside a green sixty-gallon garbage can, Linda Mariani had been wrapped in plastic. An aluminum baseball bat and her identification, cell phone, and pager were also found inside. Wrapped around her neck was a child's skipping rope.

Wills, accompanied by his first of many lawyers, immediately tried to negotiate a manslaughter charge. He was quickly dismissed. His claims of an accidental death were clearly disputed. Investigators found that Wills had purchased bolts, a tarp, caulking, and the garbage can several days prior to the murder, materials used to entomb Linda Mariani's remains. Wills also removed the battery from her cell phone and pager, on the slight chance they might ring while someone was near. Coupled with the numerous phone messages Wills made in the days following, investigators had an airtight case for first-degree murder.

The autopsy confirmed Linda had a massive skull fracture. Because the remains were so badly decomposed, investigators theorized Wills hit Linda in the head with the baseball bat and then strangled her with the rope to ensure death.

What followed Richard Wills's arrest was a series of measures taken by the emotionless murderer to corrupt and delay the criminal justice system for as long as possible. Immediately transferring his six homes, $1,900 per month pension, and a lump sum of $120,000 to his ex-wife, Wills claimed that he was broke and applied for legal aid. After several months with the lawyers, Wills fired them, deeming them incompetent, and filed a motion with the government insisting they pay for an attorney that was well known and had more experience with murder trials. The government complied, footing Wills's legal fees.

Of course, the brutality and heartless nature of the crime brought into question Richard Wills's mental state. After his arrest, Wills claimed he had multiple personalities, depression, and also heard voices.

Wills was taken to the Whitby Mental Health Care Center for an extensive psychological evaluation by Dr. Jeffrey McMaster. As during his murder trial, Wills displayed his usual dramatic character. Growing his now graying hair out, Wills also appeared for his first interview with Dr. McMaster sporting a long gray beard. McMaster noticed that Wills appeared far older than his age. Wills consistently tried to "get in the face" of the doctor and control the interview. He was constantly rude to the staff, tried to tell them how to do their jobs, and was generally inconsiderate toward other patients.

Claiming to have frequent memory loss, Wills could only cite one particular incident—forgetting to put his laundry in the dryer. Dr. McMaster determined Wills to have average to above average intelligence. Dismissing Wills's other claims that there were "two to three Ricks," the doctor determined that Richard Wills did not suffer from any mental illness at all, other than narcissistic personality disorder.

More of a description than a diagnosis, McMaster determined that Wills patterned his life in a world of grandiosity, believing he was superior, special, and unique, and expected others to view him as such. Wills was entitled, arrogant, and consistently devalued others. McMaster stated Wills's emotional coldness and lack of reciprocal interest was typical in a snobbish, disdainful, and patronizing personality that Wills exemplified. However, he added that in having a narcissistic personality, Wills could be very sensitive to criticism and defeat, reacting with rage or a counterattack.

Regardless, McMaster said that Wills's claims of mental illness was "far-fetched and of low probability." Wills knew right from wrong. In the end, Wills showed no signs of thought disorder, multiple personalities, or any other mental problems—he was completely sane and able to stand trial.

It was somewhat difficult for those attending the murder trial to keep the above diagnosis in mind. Wills's antics ranged from annoying and unsettling to downright stomach churning.

After a series of motions to delay the trial were exhausted, the murder trial commenced, lasting almost six months and costing the taxpayers $1.3 million. At the end, Wills had hired, and fired, seven high-salaried attorneys—paid for by the citizens. Each time he fired one, the trial was again delayed for the new attorney to review the case and prepare a defense. All the while, the court accommodated Wills, allowing him special treatment at the jail and ignoring his courtroom antics.

Constantly rolling his eyes and yelling at witnesses who were testifying were a couple of the minor intrusions Wills threw into the trial. Burping, farting loudly, and telling Court Justice Michelle Fuerst, "you're a biased and fucking cunt!" in the middle of the courtroom also failed to garner the attention Wills was seeking. During the earlier trials, he called Justice Joseph Kenkle "asinine," and told another justice to "pull up your socks!" On six separate occasions, while being transported to his trial in new police cruisers, Wills purposely urinated in the backseat. His rants, for a short time, got him placed in a nearby room, dubbed the "rubber room," where he could watch the trial from a monitor. But the court ultimately allowed him back in and his tirades continued.

He would purposely pass out during testimony, but he would be transported to the hospital and deemed "fine." He publicly referred to his final lawyer, Zambian-born attorney Munyonzwe Hamalengwa, as a "pompous nigger, an uppity, fall-down, nigger."

Wills loved to shock the jury and found entertaining ways to do so. During one of his eleven days of testimony, he spontaneously reached over and grabbed the sixty-gallon garbage can that was meant to represent the one Mariani was found in. Holding it above his head and shaking it back and forth, Wills yelled out, "Hey! it's heavy duty!" The jurors' jaws dropped to the floor in shock.

When asked during his testimony about the manner in which he disposed of Mariani's body, Wills smiled, and said, "I hadda do, what I hadda do!"

Perhaps one of the more disturbing displays by Wills was on a particular day of the trial when for some reason he was prone to more outbursts than usual. The court ignored him—as usual—and Wills began yelling that the suit provided to him by the court "smelled like shit." Not receiving the attention he was seeking, Wills proceeded to stick his hands down his pants before holding them out—covered in excrement. Apparently he thought defecating in his pants would direct the court to pay attention. Wills's lawyer had the unpleasant task of delivering the news to Justice Fuerst: "I am told that Mr. Wills has excrement on his hands, your honor," Hamalengwa informed the court.

"Get him some hand sanitizer and Kleenex," the justice instructed the baliff, "now, let's move on."

The court had learned to take a hard-nosed approach when

it came to dealing with Richard Wills. Acknowledging his antics would further prolong the already lengthy trial. Regardless, in the end, in October 2007, five years after the murder, the jury found Richard Wills guilty of first-degree murder and sentenced him to life in prison without the possibility of parole for twenty-five years.

For the first time in almost six months, Richard Wills was quiet.

CHAPTER 17

THE FIRST

CHARLES BECKER
POLICE LIEUTENANT, NEW YORK CITY, NEW YORK

There's always a first for everything. And in the category of homicidal police officers, New York City police lieutenant Charles Becker holds the shameful and historic first slot. He was the first police officer ever executed for his crimes, which, of course, included murder. However, Charles Becker never pulled the trigger, nor was he present at the murder scene—facts no one disputes.

The phenomenon of Charles Becker occurred shortly after the turn of the twentieth century, a time when immigrants were flooded New York City in droves, believing that the streets were "paved in gold." Just as the commission looking into the disaster of the RMS *Titanic* was winding down, New York's Lower East Side was becoming the most densely popu- lated area in the world. Children were lucky if they could find a few square feet to play in. Because of the massive population and few jobs, structured gangs began to make their presence known on the streets of New York City.

The summer of 1912 proved to be one of the hottest on record, and the city saw almost thirty homicides in the month of July alone. With more horses on the street than cars, it was not an unusual occurrence to see horse carcasses lying along the sides of the streets, dead from the intense heat.

In July 1912, after the *Titanic* disaster had loomed on the front pages for months, a new headline emerged and dominated the city for the next three years—the case of New York police lieutenant Charles Becker.

Charles Becker was born July 26, 1870, in Calicoon Center, Sullivan County, New York. His youth was spent working hard on the family's farm, which did nothing but bolster the young man's size. The son of Bavarian immigrants, Becker left the farm when he was eighteen years old, his sights set on the big city of New York. Becker first found a job at a bakery, but his broad stature, huge shoulders, and hands that some claimed were so large that they looked like hams hanging from his arms caught the attention of a local German bar owner. He wanted Becker to be a bouncer, eliminating any riffraff that might have started trouble. Becker happily obliged and took the job seriously. Becker was known for a quick, no-nonsense temper, which could be easily provoked. With Becker standing over six feet tall and weighing around 215 pounds, not many tried. However, it was this opportunity as a bouncer that led him straight through the doors of Tammany Hall and to the New York City Police Department.

Tammany Hall was the Democratic political machine that purportedly held New York in its grips for years. A heavyweight player in the city's political realm, it initially began to help immigrants rise up in politics—mostly the Irish. It controlled most of the Democratic Party's nominations and patronage until its weakening, and eventual collapse, in 1934. But Tammany Hall will forever go down in history as a synonym for political corruption.

It was at his job as a bouncer that Becker was introduced to, and befriended, a well-known gangster, Edward "Monk" Eastman. Monk was highly regarded and credited with bringing organized crime and gangs over into the twentieth century. It was Monk who introduced Becker to one of the highest-ranking officials of Tammany Hall—Timothy D. Sullivan, a member of the state senate. With the help of Sullivan's strong arm, Charles Becker was appointed to the New York City Police Department in November 1893.

Becker's career began almost as tumultuously as it ended. The department was repeatedly inundated with complaints of brutality, false arrests, and threats made by Becker. Regardless, fellow officers looked upon him as an active, impressive officer who happened to have had excessive zeal. His first suspension came after only two years on the job.

Becker and his partner were chasing a burglary suspect when Becker pulled out his pistol and began unloading in the direction of the thief. Unfortunately, Becker's hail of bullets missed the burglar and hit an innocent civilian who was leaving a nearby store. Becker promptly covered the incident up and claimed the dead man was an accomplice to the burglar. However, an investigation into the matter revealed that Becker had lied and his victim had no criminal record. He was suspended for one month. Today, if an officer were to act in such a manner, he would consider himself lucky if he didn't spend the rest of his life in prison.

Becker's problems seemed to escalate from that point on. Less than a month after the hearing of the burglary shooting, Becker was under investigation again—this time for false arrest of a prostitute. According to the arrested woman, Becker walked right up to her and slapped handcuffs onto her wrists. When she began to protest, he responded with, "I know a whore when I see one!" Unfortunately for Becker, the woman was talking to a man who at the time turned out to be a most credible witness. The man was none other than literary marvel Stephen Crane, author of the best-selling book *The Red Badge of Courage.*

Little did the public know that an inner battle had been brewing between Crane and then police commissioner Teddy Roosevelt. Crane had been a critic of the local law enforcement's tactics for some time. During the investigation into Becker, Crane wrote Roosevelt a letter demanding a formal hearing. Consequently, it was a large mistake for Crane. After the longest departmental hearing in history, Charles Becker was exonerated. For Crane, life was unbearable after that particular embarassment. The harassment and threats from the police department afterward proved to be too much, driving him to leave the city for good.

Becker's behavior failed to change, and he was frequently featured in the news. The next incident reported started out very positive, but ended quite differently. Becker had received the Medal of Heroism for saving a drowning man by a nearby pier. Shortly after the award was given the man came forward with claims that Becker had paid him fifteen dollars to jump in the river because Becker needed some "good press." But, as could be predicted, Becker was cleared, forever protected by Sullivan.

Anyone who thought Becker's career was nearing its end at this point was sorely mistaken. Not only was he cleared in all of his disciplinary hearings, but he was promoted to sergeant in 1901. Now thirty-one years old, Becker was transferred to "The Great White Way," now known as Times Square. Before the *New York Times* building was erected, the area was clogged with casinos, restaurants, and bright lights. Known then also as the Tenderloin District, the area was the only place in town where one could go to get a good cut of steak, hence the name.

Becker's promotion angered a few seasoned officers who

were passed over for Tammany Hall's poster child. Becker's tour in the Sixteenth District proved quite profitable. He began to shake down most every casino and restaurant within his district, demanding 10 percent of all profits earned in return for little police presence and intervention; most casinos—which were illegal—and restaurant owners happily obliged. Becker did the collecting himself and earned an astounding $8,000 in payoffs in his first year, far exceeding his $1,500 per year salary. Becker's dealings within the district were simply known as "the system."

Becker's personal life was almost as damaging as his professional one. He was married three times. His first wife died of tuberculosis, and his second wife left him to marry his younger brother, Paul. He eventually married his third wife, Helen, a schoolteacher who would be most loyal to Becker during his future misfortunes.

In 1909, Democratic nominee William Jay Gaynor was elected mayor of the city on the promise that he would lift the blanket of corruption. However, his promises fell silent when a failed assassination attempt less than a year later left a bullet lodged in his throat.

In 1911, a new police commissioner was appointed. Rhinelander Waldo was young, naive, and highly inexperienced, raising eyebrows at Gaynor's competency as mayor. Gaynor had been acting irrationally since the attempt on his life. Waldo was frequently ridiculed in political cartoons for his poor decisions, one of which was the appointment of the new police lieutenant, Charles Becker. Becker, the corrupt prince of New York City, was just handed the keys to castle, thanks to Waldo.

Waldo organized three special units to oversee the citywide crime. Today called *strike teams* or *vice squads*, they were referred to in 1911 as *strong-arm squads*. Waldo promoted Lt.

Charles Becker to head the squad of the Sixteenth District, encompassing all of the Tenderloin District. Becker was now in charge of everybody and only answered to the commissioner himself—a terrible mistake on Waldo's part. All Becker had to do was occasionally raid a low-grade casino or restaurant to appease Waldo. Realizing, in his high position, that he could no longer be bothered with the simple task of collecting payoffs, Becker hired an acquaintance to shake down the district—the head of a Jewish gang—"Big" Jack Zelig.

Zelig employed four of his gangsters to do the weekly collecting: "'Gyp' the blood" (Harry Horowitz), "Dago Frank" (Frank Cirofici), "Lefty" Louis (Louis Rosenberg), and "Whitey" Lewis (Jacob Siedenscner).

During the first ten months of their endeavors, the thugs collected an astonishing $640,000 for Becker—almost $10 million in today's economy. Apparently, no one thought it was odd that a police lieutenant was driven around daily in a chauffeured limousine.

Life was good for Charles Becker and his cronies, until Herman "Beansie" Rosenthal came along. Beansie, a well-dressed Jewish businessman of thirty-eight years, set his sights on the Tenderloin District. Beansie had opened several small gambling houses on the Lower East Side and on Long Island in Rockaway, but they had all been shut down. Beansie wanted the brass ring and thought he'd found it in the Tenderloin District. A friend of Sullivan's, Beansie needed $1,500 to open a casino, chump change for someone like Becker. Sullivan directed Beansie to Becker for a loan. Knowing he needed to keep Sullivan's protection, Becker agreed to loan Beansie the money for the casino, but informed him of the silent rule in the district—the kickbacks to Becker—approximately 20 percent of his earnings. At the time, Beansie agreed and he launched his prized Hesper Club shortly thereafter.

However, Beansie quickly grew tired of having the New York Police Department as his partner. He had his own debts to pay and was doing so before handing one-fifth of his earnings to Becker. Finally, Beansie had enough. He wasn't going to pay Becker any more—a decision that proved to be fatal. For a short time, Beansie had Sullivan to protect him against Becker. Sullivan told Becker, "Just give him [Beansie], a little more time." Unfortunately for Beansie, Sullivan slowly started to grow insane from a severe case of syphilis and could no longer be counted on for protection. Becker soon upped the ante with an ultimatum—pay me or else.

For reasons unknown, Beansie arrogantly refused, either oblivious to the danger his decision presented or simply to taunt Becker. Even veteran gamblers saw what was coming to him as one clearly stated in the *Evening Post*: "The trouble with Herman (Beansie) is that he don't know the rules. The rules are pay your 'license' money . . . lay low, and play like gentlemen. When you get a hint, take it, and close down. It's when fighting among the brotherhood is too noisy that the powers step in."

A pivotal moment in the feud between Beansie and Becker came on the night of April 13, 1912, the same night two-thousand-plus people were enjoying their luxury cruise aboard the *Titanic* on the North Atlantic, unaware of their fate, which would be met less than two days later.

Becker decided he was no longer going to tolerate Beansie's opposition to "the system." Organizing his strong-arm unit, Becker oversaw a raid on Beansie's casino, a raid that completely destroyed everything and anything that Beansie owned. Becker had just violently closed him down for good, and Beansie was livid. Beansie not only owned the destroyed casino, but he also lived above it. He was further incensed when Becker permanently stationed two uniformed police officers in front of the business to keep watch both night and day.

Beansie cried foul repeatedly, but no one would listen. He asked for help from the mayor's office, the district attorney, and high-ranking police officials, but the walls of Tammany Hall were strong and Beansie no longer had Sullivan watching his back. Beansie eventually tried to tap into the city newspapers, but, again, no one would listen to the misgivings of a career gambler—except one person.

World reporter Herbert Bayard Swope listened to Beansie. He not only listened, but promised to out the widespread corruption in a front-page story. Swope was close friends with the district attorney, Charles Whitman, and had high hopes for his career in journalism. Beansie's story may have been just the jump start he needed.

Swope sat down with Beansie and laid out a complete and thorough affidavit of his dealings with Becker. Some of the charges were quite damaging. Beansie alleged that after the raid, Becker declared them "even." He said he would also make good on a promise not to indict one of Beansie's relatives, a promise that was not honored. He spoke of what transpired the weeks prior to, and after, the raid on his casino:

> Well, I went along for a few weeks when finally Lieutenant Becker met me by appointment and told me what a hard job he has got in stalling Waldo. That Waldo wanted him to "get me." I have told Waldo that I have got my men trying to get evidence. And by doing so, I kept stalling him. I met him three nights after that again. He told me that I must give him a raid. He said, "You can fix it up any way you like. Get an old roulette wheel and I'll make a bluff and smash the windows. That will satisfy Waldo, I suppose." I told him that I would not stand for it. That if he wanted to raid me he

would have to get the evidence. That I would not stand for a "frame-up." Well, he said, I'll do the best I can to stall him.

Two nights afterward, he called me on the wire at my home and he told me to go and see a certain party at half past ten in the evening at Fifty-ninth Street and Broadway, at a place called "Pabst's." When I reached Pabst's there was nobody there to meet me. Then I suspected something was wrong. So when I came back to my home I found the windows broken, the doors smashed, and the patrol wagon waiting outside. I wanted to go in when Policeman James White told me to get away, not to come. Everything is all right. It's Charlie making the raid and it's all right.

So I stood across the street and waited until everything was over and went into my home, when my wife told me that Charlie said he had to make this raid to save himself. That it is all right, not to worry. "And tell Herman to go down to the St. Paul Building tomorrow and get the papers from the lawyer. You tell him that I am standing the expenses of this raid, $1,500. You tell Herman that he and I are even, and I will see him tomorrow."

They arrested Jesse Fleming and Herbert Hull and charged them with being common gamblers. The next day in court, Charlie told me to waive examination, that he wanted to make the raid look natural and that he would turn it out in the Grand Jury room. I said, "Can I trust you?" He said, "Why it is all right. You can." So I had the case adjourned until the next day to think the matter over. So I waived examination the next day.

I next met Lieutenant Becker three or four nights later and hired a taxicab from Frawley's on Forty-fifth street and Sixth Avenue and met him by appointment at Forty-sixth street and Sixth Avenue. He jumped into the taxi with me. We rode downtown very slowly, talking over different things, and we finally had an argument. When we left, we were on very bad terms.

The last word I said to him that night, "You know your promise." "Well," he said, "we'll see." About a week later, the Grand Jury handed in an indictment against Jesse Fleming and Herbert Hull. I called Mr. Becker on the telephone that afternoon and I asked him what he meant by not living up to his promise. He told me, "Aw, you talk too much. I don't want to talk to you at all." I said, "You had better consider. You know what you are doing." "Aw," he said, "you can go to hell."

I have never spoken to him since. But I tried to right this wrong and sent some people to Commissioner Waldo to explain things to him without satisfaction. I went before District Attorney Charles Whitman and I laid the whole matter before him. It wasn't enough evidence for him to indict Becker. But he said, "I'll investigate this matter thoroughly."

I have repeatedly sent persons to Becker to ask him to take the policeman out of my home and he told them to tell me that as long as he was in the Police Department he would see that the copper was not taken. And he would also see that I would be driven from New York. I believe that the reason that Lieutenant Becker wants to drive me out of New York is because I have not hesitated to tell anybody the truth regarding my own experience with Lieutenant Becker, as representing the police."

He further agitated the matter when on Friday, July 12, 1912, he filed a lawsuit against all of the ranking police officials on the basis of cruel and unusual punishment for stationing uniformed officers in front of his illegal casino.

Beansie's story hit the front page of the *World* on Monday, July 15. Because Swope had publicly named Becker in the allegations, Commissioner Waldo and District Attorney Whitman were cutting trips out of town short to return to New York to investigate the matter. Neither was very happy about it. Whitman expressed his reservations in the article as well: "Rosenthal has told a story full of accusations and possibly full of truths, but as yet he has done nothing more than tell the story—he has not in any way substantiated it," Whitman told the reporter. "I have seen and am seeing to it that he is given the fullest chance to make good his charges, not because I am eager to see any scandal uncovered in the Police Department, but because his accusations are so serious as to call forth the utmost efforts of my office to determine their weight."

Beansie had gotten his wish and met with Whitman that same night, laying out precisely what he had said in his written affidavit for the newspaper. Whitman was receptive and made an appointment to meet with Beansie the following day for another interview. Walking down the courthouse steps into the warm summer night, Beansie felt vindicated after his meeting with Whitman. Flagging down a taxi on Pearl Street, he headed to the café at the bottom of the Metropole Hotel on Forty-third Street. Upon arrival at the packed café, Beansie took a seat toward the back of the establishment.

Shortly after midnight, as Beansie sat in the café boasting of his latest accomplishments, an anonymous phone call rang into the *World*'s pressroom.

"Has Rosenthal been killed yet?" the caller asked.

The reporter who took the call hadn't heard of anything involving Rosenthal that night.

"Watch out, you might hear of it at any moment," the caller warned.

Back at the Metropole, Beansie waited eagerly for the early editions of the newspaper to come out. Around 1:30 AM, the papers were delivered, headlines boasting "GAMBLER CHARGES POLICE LIEUTENANT WAS HIS PARTNER." Beansie bought seven copies and proceeded to pass them around, but he soon noticed the café had grown unusually quiet and people were leaving.

Around 1:40 AM, regular customer Bridgey Webber came into the café and stopped by Beansie's table. He essentially said, "hi" and left without purchasing anything. Beansie apparently didn't notice. Within ten minutes of Webber's exit, the streets outside the café were deserted. Cars were moved, people were pointed in the opposite direction, and taxis fled. At 2:00 AM, an unidentified man entered the café and asked Beansie to step outside, stating that someone wanted to speak with him. Utilizing little common sense, Beansie stepped out into the early morning silence of July 16, 1912.

Standing in wait were Gyp the Blood, Lefty Louie, Whitey Lewis, and Dago Frank. They opened fire on Herman "Beansie" Rosenthal, hitting him once in the nose, once in the neck, and twice in the side of his face. Furthering the gruesome hit, Lefty Louis stood over Beansie's body and said, "Hello, Herman," before firing a shot into Beansie's head that literally blew his skull into pieces. Afterward, Lefty said, "Goodbye, Herman."

The four hitmen jumped into an awaiting vehicle and fled the scene at the then breakneck speed of thirty-five miles per hour. It is the first documented case in history of a getaway car fleeing from a homicide.

The news of Beansie's murder quickly hit the news wire. As cops tried to determine exactly what happened, reporters flocked to the scene. The first story was printed only a few hours later, obviously lacking credible and reliable facts. The headline read, "GAMBLER ROSENTHAL SLAIN BY THREE MEN IN FRONT OF METROPOLE AT 2 A.M." As for Charles Becker, he was at home and sound asleep when he awoke to a telephone call that revealed the news.

In one of his more arrogant moves, Becker dressed and drove down to his precinct house where Whitman had taken over the captain's office to investigate the murder. Becker strode into the office offering his brilliant investigative services. Annoyed, Whitman told him, "You can leave. You are not needed here." Leaving the precinct house, Becker was barraged by a mob of reporters who had received word of his location. He took the opportunity to promote his innocence:

> Coming as this does at this psychological moment, it is most unfortunate. It ought to be needless for me to say—and I think I ought not to be asked to say—what you newspapermen know to be the fact that I know absolutely nothing about the crime— who perpetrated it, what the motive was, or what was to be gained by it. I want to say now that I have said this much—and perhaps I am violating a rule of the department by so saying— that it was to my best and only advantage that Rosenthal should have been permitted to live for many years. I bear this man no malice. He set himself up as my enemy. I have explained every move I made with this man to the satisfaction of my superiors.

Becker further added that he had hired attorney John Hart to file a libel suit against Beansie in the days prior to the murder.

The investigation into Beansie's murder moved quickly. A passerby had obtained the license plate of the getaway car and it was later found to have been rented by "Bald" Jack Rose— a key player in Jack Zelig's gang. Zelig, who knew of the hit, wanted no part of it because he was already facing another criminal charge. Rose and Zelig eventually became witnesses for the prosecution and testified against Charles Becker. The numerous men who Becker controlled for years were beginning to turn on him. Charles Becker was indicted for murder on July 29, 1912. He was arrested the very same day and transported to cell 112 inside the jailhouse known as "The Tombs."

Bridgey Webber, who later was identified as the "finger

man" in the murder, would also testify against Becker in exchange for immunity. It took authorities some time to find the four hitmen, but they were eventually located and charged with murder as well.

Charles Becker's murder trial began on October 7, 1912. Just two days before the trial was to begin, Big Jack Zelig was murdered while on a streetcar. Since he was killed by a local thug who claimed Zelig owed him money, prosecutors had little to no evidence as to whether or not his murder was put in motion to prevent his testimony against Becker.

Becker was represented by his civil attorney, John Hart, and famed New York defense attorney John F. McIntyre—a "dream team" back then. McIntyre, who had handled the most murder cases out of any attorney in the city, immediately asked the judge to separate Becker's trial from those of the four other men. This was granted.

Trials in this particular era had no time limits. Once the trial began in the morning, it was not uncommon for them to run into the late night or early morning hours. Overseen by Judge John Goff, known for his no-nonsense personality and lack of patience, the trial of Charles Becker was the hottest ticket in town. The courtroom was so packed that people were lining the stairwells above it just to listen in.

The prosecution's argument was simple and fared well with the judge and the jury. Charles Whitman addressed the jury:

> We are not going to claim, that in spite of the fact that Becker did not use the fatal weapons, notwithstanding the fact that he may not have been present at the scene of the crime, conceding, of course, that the others are guilty of the awful crime of feloniously taking human life, that the real murderer, the most desperate criminal of them all, was the cool, calculating, scheming, grafting police officer who used the very office

with which the people had entrusted him, the very power which was his for the enforcement of the law and order, to tempt and force others into the commission of crime, to extort, graft and blackmail from lawbreakers, and finally, for the protection of his infamous traffic in the purchase and sale of law enforcement, wantonly to sacrifice human life for the protection of which the very office which he held was created.

The defense took a predictable approach, claiming that the lack of evidence and testimony of known criminals couldn't be relied upon.

Regardless, the testimony of Bald Jack Rose proved most damaging. As he described the conversation with Becker discussing and planning Beansie's death, the jury was riveted: "Becker said, 'I don't want him beat up, I could do that myself. . . . No beating up will fix that fellow, a dog in the eyes of myself, you, and everybody else. Nothing for that man but taken off the earth,'" Rose testified, and further quoted Becker, "Have him murdered, cut his throat, dynamited, or anything."

Rose also testified how Becker would cover up the murder: "There is no danger to anybody that has any hand in the murder of Rosenthal," Becker told Rose. "There can't anything happen to anyone, and you know the sentiment over at police headquarters is so strong that the man or men that croak him would have a medal pinned on them."

"All right, Charlie," Rose testified to telling him. "I will help you. What is it you want?"

"Go visit Big Jack Zelig in the tombs. Ask him to issue an order from the Tombs to some of his gang to croak Rosenthal tonight, and tomorrow Zelig will be out on the street and relieved of any further worry about the [unrelated] charge against him," Becker reportedly ordered.

The testimony clearly influenced the jury. After 17 days, 98 witnesses, and 2,745 pages of transcripts, the jury took little time in coming to a verdict. Becker was found guilty on all counts. He was shocked, and showed himself to be human when he grabbed the railing to steady his balance. Helen Becker, now five months pregnant, fainted when she heard her husband's fate. Although sentencing was scheduled for October 30, it was only a matter of formality. The state of New York mandated an automatic death sentence for anyone convicted of first-degree murder. During the sentencing, Charles Becker was ordered to die by electrocution and was whisked immediately from the courtroom to his new home on death row at Sing Sing Prison.

His fate clearly rattled the other four men awaiting trial. It was justifiable emotion since they, like Becker, were all found guilty of murder and sentenced to death as well. McIntyre filed an appeal the day after Becker's death sentence, a move that only prolonged the inevitable.

On February 24, 1914, Becker's conviction was overturned based on judicial misconduct. He was thrilled, confident that the state would not retry the case. Whitman was no longer the district attorney; Becker's conviction had catapulted his status and he was elected governor shortly after. It had been a long two years for Becker and his wife. The baby she had been carrying during the trial—a girl—died the day after it was born, and Becker had not seen his son from his second marriage in many years.

The four hitmen were not as fortunate, or unfortunate, depending on how one looks at it. Their execution was set for April 13, 1914, and all of their appeals had been exhausted. At sunrise, the men were led one by one to the death chamber for execution by the electric chair. The executioner for the four men, and subsequently Becker, was none other than the actual inventor of the electric chair—Edwin R. Davis. The men went in order based on who was the most emotional. The prison felt that to make the one who was most upset wait through the other three executions was cruel and unusual. Dago Frank went first. Lefty Louie went last, and endured four jolts before he was finally pronounced dead. It took a total of thirty-nine minutes to execute the four hitmen.

Becker was entirely too confident in his appeal. Whitmore, although no longer the district attorney, was adamant that the state retry him. Becker's retrial began on May 29, 1914, to a crowd similar to that of his first trial. And, like in the first trial, Becker was found guilty and sentenced to death.

With no more appeals left, the morning of July 30, 1915, proved to be the end for Charles Becker. Escorted by two priests to the death chamber, Becker uttered his last words—the priests helping him walk due to sheer emotional distress. "Jesus, Mary, and Joseph, I give you my heart and soul," he whispered.

Becker's life ended controversially, much like it had been lived. The guards didn't apply the straps that restrained Becker to the electric chair correctly, and as the executioner flipped the switch, a large flame burst out of the side of Becker's right temple. Quickly checking the prisoner's heartbeat, the doctor determined that Becker was still alive. It took another jolt and some more readjustment to finally end the life of Charles Becker. It had taken nine minutes to electrocute him to death. Some observers became sick while others fainted at the debacle. Nonetheless, Becker's corruption of New York had come to an end. For Helen Becker, she believed in her husband even after death, having a steel inscription placed on his casket. It read:

CHARLES BECKER
Murdered July 30, 1915
by
GOVERNOR WHITMAN

The district attorney, Francis Martin, ordered law enforcement to remove the plate as it violated libel laws.

CHAPTER 18

THE WORST FOR LAST

GERARD SCHAEFER
DEPUTY SHERIFF, MARTIN COUNTY, FLORIDA

In addition to being heralded as the foremost killer of women in this century, I am also known as "The Sex Beast." The media has reported that I hang women, have sexual experiences with their rotting corpses, and then hack them into pieces with a machete.

Amind-numbing declaration from Gerard Schaefer this appeared in a letter he wrote to FBI agent and famed criminal profiler Roy Hazelwood. What intensifies this story about one of the worst serial killers on record was that he was a police officer and deputy sheriff when he committed several murders. He was only convicted of two murders but was tied to nine and suspected of at least thirty-four—one murder more than Ted Bundy, a fact that Schaefer was proud of and actually debated with Bundy while they were incarcerated together in Starke, Florida.

Without a doubt the most vicious and heinous murderer to appear in the pages of this book, Schaefer would most likely laugh at the other officers who are included with him here. In his eyes, they would be weak, ignorant, and couldn't *possibly* compare to him. In fact, to hear him speak of his crimes, one would think that he truly believed he was doing society a favor. He considered himself something like an angel of God, a self-proclaimed messiah put upon the earth to rid the world of all whores, sinners, and disobedient women. However, this type of psychotic justification loses all semblance of "righteousness" when it comes to the case of two girls, ages eight and nine, considered as two of his many innocent victims.

If Satan himself were to rise from the depths of hell and become a police officer, he would have certainly done it in the form of Gerard Schaefer. What's most interesting about Schaefer is there is no indication of any traumatic event in his life that would lead him down this path, no one particular time or circumstance that rattled his compassion for humanity or religious morals. Schaefer was simply a man who was pure evil from the minute he was born. His unusual behavior was documented to have started at age twelve, but it undoubtedly began before that.

Born March 25, 1946, as Gerard John Schaefer, he was the firstborn son to parents Gerard Sr. and Doris. He was the oldest of three children, including a sister, Sara, and their youngest brother, Gary. Although he was born in Wisconsin, when Gerard was just a young boy the senior Schaefer, a traveling salesman, transferred his family to Chamblee, Georgia. The Schaefers were a strong Catholic couple with deep religious roots and immediately enrolled their children in a parochial school upon their arrival in the Atlanta suburb.

In her book about Schaefer, *Silent Screams*, author Yvonne Mason describes one of Schaefer's ongoing problems—his relationship with his father. Gerard felt that his father didn't love him enough and that he favored Sara more. A common feeling among children with siblings, this normal occurrence hardly seems traumatic enough to tempt one to, as an adult, scour the earth and slaughter countless women. Schaefer added to his own anguish by convincing himself that his father took a job as a salesman for the sole purpose of having extramarital affairs. Again, there was never any indication this occurred, nor was there any plausible reason that Schaefer felt this way. Regardless, Schaefer acted as any young boy would, playing sports and hanging out with friends.

By the age of twelve, however, Schaefer's apparently normal behavior took a significantly sharp turn toward deviancy. This was the age when Schaefer discovered he was sexually aroused by his sister's underwear. This alone would not be entirely disastrous for a young boy approaching puberty; however, it was his actions involving the underwear that would make any prudent person take pause.

Schaefer somehow discovered the disturbing act of autoerotic asphyxiation. In the late 1950s this practice was almost unheard of, let alone the notion of a twelve-year-old boy engaging in it. It was during that age that Schaefer, wearing his sister's underwear, would stroll into the nearby woods—carrying a hangman's noose. Finding a suitable location, Schaefer would hang himself while masturbating, learning that his climax became much more intense when he was on the verge of unconsciousness. Schaefer's obsession with nooses was forever a key theme in his future atrocities. And, during this time of discovering the crude sex act, when Schaefer played games with his friends, he insisted that he play a role in which he was killed. Unfortunately, throughout this period, his alarming behavior went unnoticed by his family, friends, and teachers.

In 1960, the Schaefer family moved to Ft. Lauderdale,

Florida. Gerard had just turned fourteen, and began attending St. Thomas Aquinas Catholic High School. For Schaefer, this was where his compatibility with the rest of society seemed to wane. His classmates described him as "weird" or a "loner." Several unusual incidents that occurred while he attended there could be seen as prophetic indications of what lay ahead. In one incident, while discussing the Virgin Mary, Schaefer engaged in a heated debate with the teaching nun over whether or not Mary was actually a virgin at the time of conception. In Schaefer's eyes, she was just another whore who got knocked up out of wedlock and was covering it by proclaiming that it was an "immaculate" conception. His take on the matter no doubt horrified the devoutly religious teacher.

During this period, Schaefer kept to himself, finding a peaceful reprieve in the Everglades. Schaefer would spend hours there daily, learning the terrain and hunting for animals that were completely inedible.

In the spring of 1964, Schaefer found himself in the unusual position of having a girlfriend. Sondra Stewart, a classmate, would later become a pivotal character in the crimes of Schaefer when she outwardly admitted that he would express his urges to kill women while they dated in high school. Specifically, Schaefer would talk to Stewart about his neighbor, Leigh Hainline, and another woman who would sunbathe in the nude—he obsessed about it. He claimed Leigh didn't have the morals that good Catholic girls have and that he was appalled by her actions. However, Stewart stayed mum—for a while. She and Schaefer ended their relationship in the fall, as both were to begin attending Broward Community College. To compensate for the breakup, Schaefer began spending more time in the Everglades and obsessing over Leigh Hainline's moral failures.

Consumed with the young neighbor's activities, Schaefer

reportedly told people that she was "asking for it for being so loose" and that he was going to "give it to her." Clearly, he wasn't quite as appalled by Hainline's actions as he led others to believe, since he would frequently walk next door and stand below her window to watch her undress.

On September 8, 1969, Schaefer decidedly had enough of Hainline's promiscuity. He told an interviewer that he went to her house and knocked on the door. This time, he claimed, he told her she was asking for it and now he would oblige her. Schaefer didn't elaborate, but Leigh Hainline disappeared that day. Only her skull would later be found at a new construction site in 1978. The identification of the skull didn't occur until 2004, nine years after Schaefer's death. The skull was positively identified as Leigh Hainline. A locket belonging to Hainline was found, with the belongings of other victims, during a search warrant served at Schaefer's mother's house in 1973. But since there was no body or other evidence, Schaefer was never charged with Hainline's disappearance.

Prior to Hainline's murder, Schaefer was so inspired by his own moral values and his determination to rid society of its unsightly whores that he had a change of heart about enrolling in college and decided to enroll in the seminary instead—he wanted to be a priest. Laughable at best, horrific at worst, Schaefer applied to St. John's Seminary in West Coral Gables, Florida, and was immediately denied. The seminary determined that Schaefer was simply not dedicated enough, nor did he have the right mind-set to be a priest. Perhaps the future police departments that employed Schaefer should have taken a hint from the seminary. Regardless, Schaefer was livid over the rejection and turned his back on the church completely.

He enrolled at Broward Community College and took a creative writing class. He wasn't there long before he confessed his homicidal tendencies to his writing teacher. The teacher referred him to the campus counselor to whom Schaefer made some stunning confessions of what went on inside his head.

Schaefer informed the counselor that he wanted to join the army just for the chance to kill—he liked the thought of it. Furthermore, he added how he had fantasies of killing live-stock, mutilating them, and raping their carcasses. The counselor thought this either to be normal or most likely didn't believe him, because Schaefer continued his education there, eventually graduating with an associate's degree in business administration. In January 1968, he enrolled in Florida Atlantic University to pursue his bachelor's degree—now he wanted to be a teacher. However, his failing grades caused him to receive a draft notice in April.

Schaefer left the area and went into hiding, missing his opportunity to enter the military and kill things—as he previously claimed was his desire. He was found wearing women's underwear and was immediately ordered to undergo a psychiatric evaluation. Schaefer claimed he was unstable and suicidal, a claim that he was sure would keep him out of the military. He was right. Deemed unfit to serve, Schaefer breathed a sigh of relief. In May, Schaefer was faced with his parents' divorce after his father lost his job. By July, he decided to take a break and left for Michigan, returning several months later with a new girl-friend, Martha Fogg, who he would marry that December.

Schaefer enrolled again at Florida Atlantic University to pursue his short-lived dream of becoming a teacher. He was given several student teaching positions at area high schools, none of which lasted more than a few weeks. He had been dis-missed—and told never to return—from the positions for a variety of reasons, including inappropriate behavior. Schaefer dropped out of school for a few months but returned in Sep-tember—just after the disappearance of Leigh Hainline. In May 1970 Martha Fogg Schaefer filed for divorce from

Gerard, causing him to flee the country for parts unknown. It was confirmed that he had briefly been in Europe and Africa, but his actions there can only be related from his future writings, in which he described committing murders while abroad. Upon his return to the United States, he took a job as a security guard and met his second wife, Teresa Dean. By August 1970 he graduated with a bachelor's degree in geography.

The degree no longer suited Schaefer. Perhaps the power he felt while wearing the uniform of a security guard turned him on to the exciting career of law enforcement. On September 3, 1970, after undergoing no psychological tests or background checks, Gerard Schaefer was sworn into the Wilton Manors Police Department as a police officer. Wilson Manors officially earned the title of the first police department on record to hire an active serial killer to enforce the law. Now, Gerard Schaefer had a badge, a gun, and most important—power.

However, Schaefer did enforce the law to some extent—a rather contradictory statement, considering how many murders he most likely committed during this period. In fact, he received an award in March 1972 for a drug arrest. Despite this, his erratic behavior continued to get the best of him. After getting into a heated altercation with the police chief, Schaefer knew that he was going to be fired and quickly applied to the Broward County Sheriff's Department. Failing his psychological test, Schaefer was rejected and immediately applied as a deputy in nearby Martin County. He was officially terminated from Wilton Manors when word spread that he had applied elsewhere. Regardless, armed with a forged letter of recommendation from the very chief who fired him, Schaefer was hired as a deputy sheriff by Martin County.

Schaefer undoubtedly carried his wrath and his ego into his new job. Being so accustomed to not being caught, and feeling that he was such an expert in the area of brutal murders,

Schaefer slipped and made a costly error less than one month after he began working for Martin County.

On July 21, 1972, Nancy Ellen Trotter, eighteen, and Pamela Sue Wells, nineteen, were hitchhiking along a road in Stuart, Florida, on their way to the beach. Schaefer, in his marked patrol car, stopped and asked the girls if he could offer them a ride; they were happy to accept. Dropping them off at their destination, he further surprised the young women when he offered to return the following day to drive them wherever they needed to go. Unquestionably amazed by the over-whelming kindness of the man in uniform, they again agreed.

Saturday, July 22, 1972, began like any other day for the two young women from Michigan. Unfortunately, it would prove to be the most traumatic day of their lives. Eager to head back to the beach, both women jumped into Schaefer's vehicle without hesitation. Unbeknownst to both, they were about to be taken on an abrupt detour. Yes, Schaefer would eventually drive them to the beach, but he first wanted to show them some historical old Spanish forts, which were prevalent throughout Martin County. As Schaefer drove the women to a remote area, he lectured them on the dangers of hitchhiking. Arriving not at a historical site, but an old abandoned barn on Hutchinson Island, Schaefer ordered both women out of the car before handcuffing them.

While Pamela watched helplessly, Schaefer hung a noose from a tree, placed it around Nancy's neck, gagged her, tight-ened the noose, and forced her to maintain her balance on a large root below. He then tied Pamela to another tree by his beloved noose. For reasons unknown, Schaefer told both women he would return and then fled the scene. In *Silent Screams*, author Yvonne Mason asked the then and current Martin County sheriff, Robert Crowder, why he believes Schaefer left the scene. Sheriff Crowder believes that Schaefer may have forgotten an important tool or such necessary to carry out the crime. At the time of the incident, Crowder was just twenty-six years old and a newly elected sheriff.

During Schaefer's absence, Nancy Trotter managed to escape from the noose. Still bound by handcuffs, she made her way through the thick wooded area to a nearby road before flagging down a car. By the time Schaefer came back, both girls were gone, and he was left in an intense panic. In an unusual response to a predicament where one is faced with the potential of years in jail, Schaefer quickly drove home and called Sheriff Crowder, and explained what he had done. However, Schaefer added his own twist—his justification for kidnapping and assaulting two innocent women. Schaefer claimed that he had previously lectured the women on the dangers of hitchhiking and they laughed at him. Therefore, he felt they needed to be taught a lesson. He informed the sheriff that he was simply trying to scare the girls for their own good, and in the process may have gone a bit overboard.

Incredulous and astonished at his deputy's confession, the sheriff quickly became enraged and ordered Schaefer to immediately report to the desk sergeant. Sheriff Crowder then took it upon himself to drive to Hutchinson Island in an attempt to find the two women. It wasn't difficult. He was flagged down quickly by the car that had stopped for Nancy. Both women, who were understandably distraught, were transported to the sheriff's department to give their statements.

Gerard Schaefer was fired and charged with two counts of aggravated assault and false imprisonment. He was put in jail, but only stayed a little over two months before he was released on a personal recognizance bond in September 1972—a grave mistake on the part of law enforcement.

On September 27, 1972, after Schaefer had been out of jail less than two weeks, Susan Place, seventeen, and Georgia

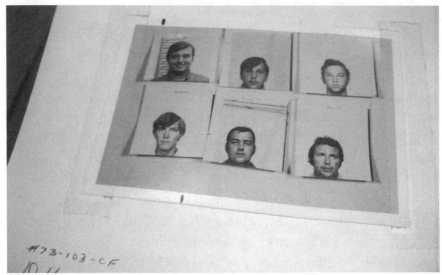

H73-103-CF

This was a lineup showing Schaefer. Courtesy of the Clerk of Courts of St. Lucie County, Florida.

Jessup, sixteen, were last seen leaving with a man named Jerry Shepherd by Susan's mother. The two teens had befriended the man and had plans that day to go to the beach. Susan's mother, Lucille, felt her maternal instincts kick in almost immediately. She didn't like Jerry and warned her daughter against him. Lucille even went so far as to go outside and write down the license plate number of the car Jerry was driving. Nonetheless, like a shepherd leading his flock, Schaefer drove away with the two teens and they were never seen again—at least, not alive. Lucille reported the teens officially missing on October 1, 1972. But the two girls had spotty records for drug use and other delinquencies, and they were simply written off as runaways.

On October 23, 1972, Mary Briscolina and Elsie Farmer, both fourteen, disappeared while hitchhiking to a nearby store. Elsie's skeletal remains were found near a local high school on January 17, 1973, and a piece of her jewelry was

Gerard Schaefer's Datsun. Courtesy of the Clerk of Courts of St. Lucie County, Florida.

found at Doris Schaefer's home. Mary's remains have never been located, nor was Schaefer officially charged in their murders, although he gave a halfhearted confession several years later.

In December 1972, prior to any remains being found, Schaefer was sentenced for his crimes against Nancy Trotter and Pamela Wells. Shockingly, all of the charges were dropped by the state's attorney and the judge found him guilty of only one count of assault. The judge sentenced Schaefer to six months in jail, but allowed him to have some time to move his wife and get his affairs in order. He could then report for jail in mid-January. Although he was clearly given preferential treatment because of his position in law enforcement, Schaefer tried the judge's patience when he begged for straight probation. He also continued to plead his case that he was merely trying to show the women how dangerous the world was. In an almost humorous outburst, the judge unloaded:

> It is beyond this court's imagination to conceive how you were such a foolish and astronomic jackass as you were in this case. If I were to let you off scot-free before I walked in court this morning I may as well have let all these people go. We have unanimous opinions that you acted foolishly. I can't understand how a man of your background could do such a foolish thing. You can't be a fool as far as the court is concerned. The State Attorneys went the last mile in dropping the other charges. I am going the last mile in trying to put you on the work release program. I could have sent you to the State prison!

On January 8, 1973, just days before Schaefer was scheduled to report to jail, Colette Goodenough and Barbara Wilcox, both nineteen, disappeared as they hitchhiked from Sioux City, Iowa, to Florida. Several of Colette's teeth and numerous personal items of both women including driver's licenses, a diary, and passports were found in Doris Schaefer's home. Their partial remains would not be found for four more years.

As Schaefer sat in jail, he was interviewed by two Oakland police detectives in their investigation of the murders of Elsie Farmer and Mary Briscolina. During the interview, Schaefer mocked the seasoned investigators, shouted at them, and acted rudely. The detectives were infuriated and vowed to nail Schaefer. Unfortunately, he was never charged with either murder.

In April 1973, a father and son were collecting aluminum cans on Hutchinson Island in an area known as Blind Creek, not far from where Nancy Trotter and Pamela Wells were tormented. The father and son found several body parts and quickly notified the sheriff's department. As law enforcement descended upon the area, numerous other body parts were found, some near a hole that had been dug into the ground. Clothing, along with two upper torsos, parts of a pelvis and leg, a lower half of a body, teeth, and scalps containing brown and blonde hair were also located. A skull was found at the site days later. Based on the clothing, hair colors, and other items found, investigators were certain they had found the remains of Susan Place and Georgia Jessup.

Authorities closed in on Gerard Schaefer. Even more damning, Schaefer had taken Georgia Jessup's purse and given it to his wife, Teresa. Teresa, in turn, gave the purse to her brother, Henry Dean, who was a police officer. Henry discovered a paper bag containing a .22-caliber handgun, catridges, and spent casings, which he promptly turned over to the investigating agency.

A search warrant served at Schaefer's residence yielded nothing. However, a second search warrant executed at his mother's home resulted in dark and damning evidence. Inside the room that by Doris Schaefer's own admission was Gerard's, investigators found Schaefer's trophy chest. It was a large trunk that held human bones, several teeth, photographs of dead and mutilated women, a photograph of a nude male body, jewelry, purses, driver's licenses, passports, a diary, and perhaps the most compelling piece of evidence—Schaefer's manuscripts that were his own fictionalized versions of the very murders he had committed.

Sensing an impending indictment, Schaefer launched into a series of events that he hoped would lay the groundwork for an insanity defense. With the aid of his wife and mother, he was voluntarily committed into the state psychiatric hospital prior to an official hearing that would determine his competency. Schaefer assumed he would be indicted and immediately transferred to another hospital by the state. However, after a secret grand jury returned first-degree murder indict-

Drawings found during a search at Doris Schaefer's home. Gerard Schaefer drew this picture. Courtesy of the Clerk of Courts of St. Lucie County, Florida.

ments for the Place and Jessup murders, Schaefer was taken directly to jail. Numerous motions and appeals were filed by the state and the defense.

On May 21, 1973, Schaefer was officially court-ordered into a thirty-day psychiatric evaluation. What he considered a coup on his part came to a crashing halt when the judge refused to extend Schaefer's stay in June. Schaefer thought for sure that he had been convincing enough during his stay, and that the judge would have no other option but to keep him there. Consequently, after the judge's ruling, Schaefer lit up the courtroom with his rage. Shaking his fists, he began shouting at the prosecutors before he was led away. His wife and mother, who were there to support him, remained silent.

One of the larger hurdles faced by prosecutors at that moment was to determine whether or not Place and Jessup were murdered prior to December 4, 1972. If so, the death penalty wouldn't apply. Moreover, the question of his sanity again came into play and another hearing was set to discuss the matter for July. For unknown reasons, Schaefer changed both his mind and his plea. Withdrawing his insanity plea for one of not guilty, Schaefer would stand trial for the murders of Susan Place and Georgia Jessup beginning on September 17, 1973.

Before a six-member and one alternate jury, prosecutors opened the trial with their belief that the jury would have no doubt of Schaefer's guilt once they were finished. They spoke of the license plate and identification provided by Lucille Place, and how horribly the victims were tortured and mutilated. They also spoke of Georgia Jessup's purse and what an important role it would play. During their opening, prosecutors brought in the actual tree limbs the victims were hanged from that still had the markings from the noose. They also displayed the large roots that had been cut from the scene to display how the victims were forced to balance themselves. The visual aids from the crime scene were extremely upsetting to the jury; several appeared visibly shaken and pale. During the exhibit, Schaefer merely shrugged his shoulders.

After several witnesses, including the responding officers and the man who found the remains, Lucille Place was called to the witness stand. After being shown a photograph of her daughter, she began to sob. Prosecutors asked Lucille in the presence of the jury if she could identify the man Susan Place was last seen with. Lucille pointed directly at Schaefer and reiterated her "bad feeling" the day Susan left with him, and how she wrote down the license plate that was registered to Schaefer. During cross-examination, the defense focused on Susan's previous delinquency and drug use, a failed attempt to open the door to numerous other suspects.

As prosecutors described how several pillowcases were found at the murder scene, they referred to Schaefer's manuscript that described similar circumstances. When Georgia Jessup's father,

George, took the stand, he gave an astonishing account of how Schaefer returned to their home, after the girls were missing, and claimed he needed to see Georgia—it was important.

The defense objected when Teresa Schaefer was called to the stand to testify regarding the purse. With the objection sustained, her brother, Henry Dean, was called in her place to describe finding the gun and ammunition inside the purse that belonged to Georgia Jessup. He said that Teresa gave him the purse to take to Schaefer's mother, Doris. Instead, he turned it over to police: "I took the items, and told Teresa I was taking them to Ft. Lauderdale to Lt. David Yurchuck. I knew Dave was connected to this case and he was an old friend of mine," Dean testified. "I thought maybe if I gave this purse to Dave it could clear up matters."

Dean further added that Schaefer told him during a jail visit that he was offered money for his story and was considering the offer for Teresa's financial well-being.

The county medical examiner then explained to the jury that the remains of the victims were so decomposed and mutilated it was hard to tell them apart. He graphically described the detailed cuts on the bones, and how the cuts told him where the women's body parts had been separated with a large knife. There were no gunshot wounds or blunt instruments used as far as he could tell.

The jury's attention was significantly held during the riveting testimony of Nancy Trotter and Pamela Wells when they testified to their traumatic encounter with Gerard Schaefer. As if their words weren't enough to pack a punch to the jurors, the prosecutors showed them a video, a reenactment using Trotter and Wells that depicted their ordeal blow by blow. No words or testimony could possibly impact the jury like a visual aid that showed actual victims hanging by nooses from trees— a novel courtroom tactic then, but a common one now. And, while the prosecutors still had the jury in a state of shock from the video, they drove the last nail into Gerard Schaefer's coffin; they presented his manuscripts.

The jury received a copy, titled "How to Go Un-Apprehended in the Perpetration of an Execution Style Murder," of which an excerpt is included here—including Schaefer's grammatical errors:

> In order to remain un-apprehended the perpetrator of an execution style murder such as I have planned must take precautions. One must think out, well in advance a crime of this nature in order for it to work. We will need an isolated area assessable by car and a short hike away from any police patrols or parking lovers. The execution site must be carefully arranged for a speedy execution once the victim has arrived.... "Ideally would be two sawhorses with a 2X4 between them. A noose attached to the overhanging limb of a tree and another rope to pull away the 2X4 preferably by car. A grave away from the place of execution. The victim could be anyone of the many women who flock to Miami and Ft. Lauderdale during the winter months. Even two victims would not be difficult to dispose of since women are less wary when traveling in pairs. In case, it may be more preferable to bind and gag the victims before transporting them to the place of execution. Then again, depending on what torture or defilement is planned for them, other items may be used.... After death has occurred the corpse should be violated, if not violated already. The body should then be mutilated and carried to the grave and buried. All identity papers should be destroyed.

Following a weak defense by Schaefer's attorney, Elton Schwarz, the jury was given its opportunity to deliberate. It was September 27, 1973, the one-year anniversary that marked the day Susan Place and Georgia Jessup disappeared. After a few hours of deliberating, a bomb threat directed at the courthouse was called into the sheriff's department, causing an immediate evacuation. Once the building was cleared, and the jurors reconvened, they were subjected to numerous anonymously called-in death threats should they find Schaefer not guilty. At 11:06 PM, they had reached a verdict.

As the spectators entered the courtroom, and before the verdict was read, the judge issued a heavy warning to all present: "This has been a long trial and it is an emotional situation, but let me warn you that if there is a person in the courtroom now who can't handle the emotional impact of the verdicts, I suggest you leave the courtroom at this time."

George Jessup left the courtroom and the verdict was announced: guilty on all counts of first-degree murder. Upon hearing the verdict, Schaefer sat terse and emotionless, stating, "They didn't prove it." The victim's families were thrilled with the verdict despite their heavy hearts.

Speaking with reporters after the trial, Schaefer boldly declared, "I'm not convicted. They didn't prove I did it."

The state's attorney, Robert Stone, had a different take on the matter: "He is still connected to seven to nine murders, and possibly twenty-eight. I said it before, and I'll stand by that statement."

On October 4, 1973, Gerard Schaefer was sentenced to life in prison. However secure the prison was, Schaefer's wrath continued to rain down on law enforcement.

His tenure in prison certainly didn't begin well. A short time after her husband's conviction, Teresa Schaefer made her first, and last, visit to her Gerard. Serving him with divorce papers, she made the astonishing announcement that she was romantically involved with Schaefer's own attorney, Elton Schwarz. They were married precisely six weeks after Schaefer was found guilty.

For the next several years, Schaefer conducted a campaign

of sheer annoyance, repeatedly suing and threatening everyone involved in the case. In 1979, he married a Filipina mail-order bride with whom he was allotted several conjugal visits. The marriage didn't last long, and the bride filed for divorce once she obtained her green card.

The decade that followed Schaefer's imprisonment proved to be overwhelming for numerous law enforcement agencies. They were left to pick up the pieces of his terror spree—literally. Assorted bones, a full skeleton, and a lone skull were discovered in various locations throughout the years that followed; these remains were identified as missing women who had most likely fallen prey to Schaefer. However, there was no physical or direct evidence linking him to the women, and he was never charged with their murders.

In 1983, Schaefer wrote a letter to the Lake County Sheriff's Department regarding two women who had been missing for well over a decade. Schaefer arrogantly offered his assistance and said he could lead officials to over thirty-four bodies and burial sites within the state of Florida. He further added that his killing spree had begun in 1963, when he was just seventeen.

During his incarceration, Schaefer was housed with a virtual "Who's Who" of serial killers. When Ted Bundy was sent to Starke Prison, he and Schaefer bonded instantly. They frequently discussed their crimes and debated inconveniences that occurred during murders, such as problems with maggots, and how to thoroughly clean the inside of their cars after dying victims urinated inside them. Schaefer claimed that Bundy idolized him because his murder victims totaled one more than Bundy's, and also because of Schaefer's "doubles theory." Schaefer claimed he always killed two women at a time so one could watch while the other was tortured and mutilated, knowing it would be happening to her soon—psychological torture in epic proportions.

Schaefer was also housed with Ottis Toole, the convicted serial killer who at one point terrorized half the country with his sidekick, Henry Lee Lucas. Toole was also a main suspect in the murder of Adam Walsh, something he confessed to Schaefer and others but would deny to law enforcement. Not one to miss an opportunity to cause pain and anguish to others, Schaefer wrote a letter to the murdered boy's father, John Walsh. Claiming to be Ottis Toole, Schaefer demanded $50,000 from Walsh in exchange for the rest of Adam's remains; to date only his head had been located. The letter was ignored by John Walsh.

Subsequently, the case of Adam Walsh was officially closed in December 2008. The Hollywood, Florida, Police Department stated that Toole was their main suspect, and had he still been alive today, he would be formally charged with the boy's murder. There are those, including some law enforcement officials, who scoff at the notion Toole was the true murderer. Serial killer Jeffrey Dahmer also happened to be in the state when Adam Walsh was abducted, a fact that hasn't been made well known to the public. Although unlikely, it certainly raises some questions. Had Gerard Schaefer not been sitting behind bars at the time Adam Walsh disappeared, law enforcement would have undoubtedly been looking his way as well. Regardless, Ottis Toole's connection to the murder of Adam Walsh allegedly played an integral part in Schaefer's own death.

Schaefer suffered somewhat of a personal loss on January 24, 1989. His close confidant and prison brother, Theodore Robert Bundy, was executed by the electric chair for his own heinous crimes. However, things began to pick up for Schaefer in late 1989 when his high school sweetheart, Sondra Stewart, now Sondra London, contacted him.

No less than an "Ann Rule wannabe," London began a romantic relationship with Schaefer for the sole purpose of publishing his graphic and disturbing manuscripts. Schaefer's first manuscript, *Killer Fiction*, was released in June 1989. With fifteen stories written in the first person, the narrator engages in the sex acts, murder, and subsequent mutilation of prostitutes. The book was deemed utterly revolting by most—a fact Schaefer reveled in. "The stories were meant to make people throw up," Schaefer claimed.

London quickly put out Schaefer's second book, *Beyond Killer Fiction*, about a rogue cop who slaughters prostitutes. This book garnered a similar response. With her already non-existent career slowly sinking, London became engaged to Schaefer. However, for unknown reasons, he sent her a scathing letter that essentially blamed her for all of his problems: "I will tell you here and now that plenty of your women died because you couldn't help me solve my various crises in 1965. I tried to tell you about it but you couldn't deal with it. You bolted, you abandoned me; that's when it started."

So enamored by his letter, London appeared on a television interview and basically defended him. In a bizarre declaration, London stated, "He was normal, except he had a compulsion to kill." Her statement undoubtedly had psychiatrists world-wide scratching their heads.

London decided to better her life. This was akin to moving on from an urban sewage treatment plant to a rotten manure field. Ending her relationship with Schaefer, London moved on to bigger and better things. One of these things happened to include a new relationship, and subsequent engagement, to the serial-killer-of-the-month, Danny Rollings. Rollings was on Florida's death row for the murders of eight University of Florida co-eds. Obviously, Schaefer was enraged, livid at the thought of being replaced by someone who had so many fewer victims than he did. After launching into a tirade of threatening letters and lawsuits, he eventually got over it.

In fact, Schaefer seemed to have a slight change of heart

and began attempting to help the families of his victims. In true Gerard Schaefer fashion, he wrote a letter to a missing persons agency promising his help and expertise:

Dear Sirs,

I've heard your company concerns itself with missing persons. I'm enclosing a *Time* magazine story about my case. I'm also written up in many other magazines and books. Since 1973 I've been linked to 170 dead and missing women on 3 continents. The links include 105 photographs of female victims taken either before or after death and 170 pairs of panties stripped from victims. Depending on what book you read I am *credited* with as few as 34 kills and as high as 170. All sources agree that I am unquestionably the most prolific killer of women between the years 1963 and 1973.

The years went past and only 6 of the 170 victim's corpses were recovered. Very few of the victims were ever identified by some. There were 3 continents involved, over the 40 states and 20 from countries over a period of ten years. I've never talked to the cops. Still don't.

Last year I had a letter from an old woman who read a crime tabloid story about how I'd killed roadside hookers by driving them out to a rented warehouse where they were murdered by hanging. The old lady wrote and wanted to know if I'd gotten her hooker daughter. As it turned out I had hanged the whoredaughter. The old lady was glad to know the kid wasn't walking around with amnesia.

It's now 1991. I'm still not talking to cops but I suppose there are people who wonder about happened to hippie daughter who hit the road and never returned. If your company searches for females missing since the 1963–1973 time period it may be useful to be able to have me ready to take a look and let someone know if I got the person they're looking for. This would necessarily be a private sort of thing since I never talk to cops. Just a thing to set a parent's mind at ease about what happened.

I am completely infamous as a killer of young women but that was long, and if I can help a parent privately without police meddling. I will do so.

Please advise if you are interested
Sincerely, GJ Schaefer

Schaefer must have sensed his days were numbered. Fed up with his arrogance and suspicious behavior, his fellow inmates began to engage in vicious behavior and torments that included physical attacks, pelting him with urine and feces, and setting his cell on fire. The motive for his death remains a mystery. Some believe he was murdered over the simple task of getting an extra cup of hot water, while others, like his sister Sara, truly believe he was murdered to prevent him from gathering information from Ottis Toole on the Adam Walsh murder. They were afraid he would turn the information over to law enforcement.

No one knows for sure as to why, but on December 3, 1995, convicted double-murderer Vincent Rivera entered Schaefer's cell and proceeded to stab him upward of forty times with a homemade shank. The stabbing vicious, Rivera slit Schaefer's throat and gouged his eyes out. Gerard John Schaefer, forty-nine, vicious murderer of countless women, was dead.

Victimized families and law enforcement rejoiced, but Schaefer's memory wouldn't dissipate so quickly. Remains of some of the unknown victims of Schaefer surfaced as recently as 2005, forty-one years after two young women went missing in the Ocala National Forest. For those who knew Schaefer, those dark days will forever linger. The prosecutor who convicted him, Robert Stone, saw his dark side and will never forget: "He was the most sexually deviant person I have ever known. . . . He made Ted Bundy look like a Boy Scout. . . . Schaefer's IQ was well over 130 and he was more dangerous than all the other notorious serial killers and had every possible sexual hang-up that existed."

For the victims' families, and those who continue to wait and wonder if their loved ones who had fallen into the hands of Gerard Schaefer will ever be found, Lucille Place's comments to the press will be forever embedded in their minds: "Don't ever believe it can't happen to you. Don't ever allow yourself to believe it can't happen—it can."

It was later learned that during the course of his law enforcement career Schaefer stopped five times more women than any other officer, often obtaining phone numbers and addresses. To this day, residents in the area undoubtedly whisper, and wonder, if, and when, another victim will turn up. According to a local reporter, Schaefer's tirade permanently placed a stigma on the sleepy community.

"The city of Stuart is no longer known as the Sailfish capital . . . it's now known as the town of a cop serial killer."

REFERENCE LIST

CHAPTER 1: DREW PETERSON

Associated Press. "Drew Peterson Talks about His Life in the Spot-light," March 24, 2008.

———. "Friends, Police Recount the Day Stacy Peterson Disappeared in Illinois," December 25, 2007.

———. "Search Resume's for Peterson's Wife," March 30, 2008.

Chicago Sun-Times. "Autopsy: Kathleen Was Murdered," February 22, 2008.

———. "Feds Digging into Savio's Death, Probe; New Autopsy Results Still Awaited in Drowning of Drew's 3rd Wife," December 15, 2007.

———. "Inside the Cops' Search for Stacy; Four Search Warrants Illustrate Depth of Investigation into Bolingbrook Woman's Disappearance—and Whether Her Cop Husband Involved," December 7, 2007.

———. "Peterson Is Now Clearly a Suspect; Stacy a 'Potential Homicide'; 3rd Wife Murdered?" November 10, 2007.

Chicago Tribune. "Drew Peterson Must Wait Longer to Learn Fate of His 11 Guns; Hearing on His Property Postponed until April 17," March 24, 2008.

———. "Drew Peterson's Ex-Friend Tells Grand Jury about Following Kathleen Savio," January 24, 2008.

———. "Drew Peterson's Lawyer Says Bolingbrook Neighbors Harassing Ex-Cop," March 19, 2008.

———. "Family Eager to Resume Search for Stacy Peterson," March 26, 2008.

———. "Savio Pathologist Appears at Grand Jury," March 28, 2008.

Evans-Donaldson, Catherine. "Drew Peterson Failed Half a Polygraph Test on Missing Wife Stacy." FoxNews.com, October 9, 2008. http://www.foxnews.com/printer_friendly_story/0,3566,434441,00.html (accessed 12/7/2008).

FoxNews. "Drew Peterson Talks about Wife's Disappearance, Grief on FOX," January 25, 2008. http://www.foxnews.com/printer_friendly_story/0,3566,325685,00.html (accessed July 7, 2008).

Joliet Herald News. "Pastor: Stacy Was Fearful," November 30, 2007.

———. "Peterson Defends On-Camera Actions," March 25, 2008.

———. "Peterson's Exes Testify before Grand Jury in Joliet," April 4, 2008.

———. "Sons Won't Appear before Grand Jury," March 5, 2008.

Underwood, Melissa. "Police Investigating Letter Claiming a Sighting of Missing Stacy Peterson." *FoxNews*, January 9, 2008. http://www.foxnews.com/printer_friendly_story/0,3566,321328,00.html (accessed December 7, 2008).

CHAPTER 2: BOBBY CUTTS JR.

Achladis, Ted. "Juror: Cutts Trial Could Have Ended in Hung Jury." MyFoxCleveland. February 28, 2008. http://www.myfoxcleveland.com/myfox/pages/Home/Detail?contentId=5905063&version=.... (accessed July 7, 2008).

———. "Trial Ends, Pain Does Not." MyFoxCleveland, February 27, 2008. http://www.community.myfoxcleveland.com/blogs/CuttsTrial (accessed July 7, 2008).

America's Most Wanted. "Jessie Marie Davis: Recovered." http://www.amw.com/missing_persons/case.cfm?id=45920 (accessed July 23, 2008).

Associated Press. "Friend: Former Police Officer Haunted by Slain Woman's Last Words." *AOL News*, March 1, 2008. http://news.aol.com/story/_a/friend-former-police-officer-haunted-by/n20080301183209990002 (accessed 3/6/2008).

Canton Repository. "Day 4: FBI Agent Recalls Searching Cutts' Home, Truck," February 7, 2008. http://www.cantonrep.com/printable.php?ID=398457 (accessed July 22, 2008).

———. "Prosecutor Grills Cutts," February 11, 2008. http://www.cantonrep.com/printable.php?ID=399030 (accessed July 22, 2008).

———. "Stark County Prosecutor Describes Events of June 14," February 4, 2008. http://www.cantonrep.com/printable.php?ID=398021 (accessed July 22, 2008).

———. "Third Day of Cutts' Trial Begins with Football Coach," February 6, 2008. http://www.cantonrep.com/printable.php?ID=398302 (accessed July 22, 2008).

CBS News, "Ex-Cop on Trial for Killing Pregnant Woman," February 4, 2008. http://www.cbsnews.com/stories/2008/02/04/national/printable3787363.shtml (accessed March 8, 2008).

CNN. "Ex-Cop: 'I Didn't Mean to Hurt Her," February 11, 2008. www.cnn.com/ (accessed March 8, 2008).

———. "Ex-Police Officer Indicted in Pregnant Woman's Death." www.cnn.com/ (accessed March 8, 2008).

———. "'Sorry' Killer's Life in the Jury's Hands," February 14, 2008. www.cnn.com/ (accessed July 7, 2008).

Duer, Benjamin. "Cutts' 'Partners' Testify on his Behalf." *Canton Repository*, February 25, 2008. http://www.cantonrep.com/printable.php?ID=400946 (accessed July 22, 2008).

———. "Ex-Lovers Take Stand at Cutts Trial." *Canton Repository*, February 5, 2008. http://www.cantonrep.com/printable.php?ID=398206 (accessed July 22, 2008).

———. "Cutts Would Owe Lots of Child Support." *Canton Reposi-*

tory, February 8, 2008. http://www.cantonrep.com/printable.php?ID=398593 (accessed July 22, 2008).

Hoover, Shane. "Cutts' DNA on Rug Is Only Link to Davis." *Canton Repository*, February 7, 2008. http://www.canton rep.com/printable.php?ID=398592 (accessed July 22, 2008).

———. "Jury Heard Only Part of Myisha L. Ferrell's Story." *Canton Repository*, February 14, 2008. http://www.canton rep.com/printable.php?ID=401679 (accessed July 22, 2008).

———. "Threats Revealed at Cutts Trial." *Canton Repository*, February 6, 2008. http://www.cantonrep.com/printable.php?ID =398405 (accessed July 22, 2008).

Kenworthy, Pete. "Cutts Trial Blog: Day One Ends." *NewsNet5*, February 4, 2008. http://www.newsnet5.com/print/15184484/detail.html (accessed March 6, 2008).

———. "Cutts Trial Blog Day 2: Friend Says She Saw Cutts Dump Body." *NewsNet5*, February 5, 2008. http://www.newsnet5.com/print/15217700/detail.html (accessed March 6, 2008).

———. "Cutts Trial Blog Day 3: "I'm Going to Kill that B—." *NewsNet5*, February 6, 2008. http://www.newsnet5.com/print/15231407/detail.html (accessed March 6, 2008).

———. "Cutts Trial Blog Day 5: Jessie's Body Partially Skeletonized, Medical Examiner Says." *NewsNet5*, February 8, 2008. http://www.newsnet5.com/print/15251106/detail.html (accessed March 6, 2008).

———. "Cutts Trial Blog Day 6: Bobby Cutts Jr.—'I Didn't Mean to Hurt Her.'" *NewsNet5*, February 11, 2008. http://www.news net5.com/print/15268368/detail.html (accessed March 6, 2008).

———. "Cutts Trial Blog Day 6: No Blood Found in Jessie's Home." *NewsNet5*, February 11, 2008. http://www.news net5.com/print/15238807/detail.html (accessed March 6, 2008).

———. "Cutts Trial Blog Day 7: Closing Arguments." *NewsNet5*, February 12, 2008. http://www.newsnet5.com/print/15278401/detail.html (accessed March 6, 2008).

Post Chronicle. "Bobby Cutts Jr. Arrested: Charge After Jessie Davis's Body Found." *Fox*, June 23, 2007.

Sheeran, Thomas. "Ex-Cop Spared Death in Pregnant Killing." FOX, February 28, 2008. http://www.foxnews.com/printer _friendly_wires/2008Feb28/0,4675,PregnantWomanDead,00.ht ml (accessed March 8, 2008).

Tye, Chris. "Cutts Trial Day 3: Witness Testifies Cutts Threatened to Kill Jessie Davis." NBC, February 6, 2008. http://www.wkyc .com/news/news_article.aspx?storyid=82769&provider=top (accessed July 23, 2008).

CHAPTER 3: CHARLES OSWALT

Mansfield, Ohio, Police Department. Case File No. 88-1657. Complaint No. C-020-88. Victim: Marjorie Coffey, Offense: Homicide. March 28, 1988.

Included in Case File:

Alberts, Bernard L. Ohio Bureau of Criminal Investigation Lab Report. Mansfield Police Department Case No. 88-1657. February 4, 1988.

Brunk, Chris. "MPD Supplemental Report No. 88-48, Vehicle Towed." Mansfield, OH, Police Department. January 22, 1988.

Cairns, W. L., Capt. Report No. 88-020, "Confidential Supplement Meeting with Prosecutor/Sheriff." Mansfield, OH, Police Department. February 1, 1988.

Civil Deposition Case No. 86D-1077: Marjorie Coffey v. Charles Oswalt—Transcripts. Richland County Common Pleas Court (Juvenile & Domestic Relations). November 12, 1987.

Couch, Bambi Susan. Richland County Sheriff's Department Statement No. 9-88. January 27, 1988.

Daugherty, Joe, Capt. Case No. 88E057. Richland County Sheriff's Department Evidence Report. Re: Homicide Victim: Marjorie Coffey. January 30, 1988.

Erre, Tim Sgt. Mansfield Police Department Laboratory Report No.26962 L-060-88. Mansfield, OH, Police Department. January 22, 1988.

Flow Chart of events for Lt. Charles Oswalt's Activities on 1/20/88. Mansfield Police Department Case no. 88-1657.

Hamilton County Coroner's Office Autopsy Report OC-14-88. Pathologic Diagnoses of the Body of Margie Coffey. Mansfield Police Report Case No. 88-1657.

Hassinger, Harold. Mansfield Police Department Statement No.WS-096-88. February 1, 1988.

———. Richland County Sheriff's Department Statement No.18-88. February 1, 1988.

———. Richland County Sheriff's Department Statement No. 24-88. February 1, 2008.

Hoffer, J. A., Chief. "Confidential Supplement Assist Robert Lemon." Lexington, OH, Police Department. Report No. CF-005.

Howard, William. Mansfield Police Department Statement No. WS-068-88. February 21, 1988.

Johnson, Richard. Richland County Sheriff's Department Statement No.17-88. January 31, 1988.

Lab Specimen Results Reference Mansfield Police Department Case No. 88-1657. Federal Bureau of Investigation. February 24, 1988.

Lemon, Robert. Mansfield Police Department Statement No. WS-067-88. January 23, 1988.

———. Richland County Sheriff's Department Deposition, Case No. 88-E-057. December 9, 1987.

———. Richland County Sheriff's Department Statement No.15-88. January 29, 1988.

———. Richland County Sheriff's Department Statement No. 3-88. January, 23, 1988.

Messmore, Dave, Lt. "Follow-Up Missing Person." Report No. 88-050. Mansfield, OH, Police Department. January 25, 1988.

MPD Evidence Receipt No. 26962, Re: Letters/Case Submitted to Lab. Mansfield, OH, Police Department. January 24, 1988.

MPD Evidence Receipt No. 27053, Re: Logging Tape Submitted to Lab. Mansfield, OH, Police Department. February 4, 1988.

MPD Evidence Receipt No. 27220, Re: Oswalt Intelligence Report Submitted to Lab. Mansfield, OH, Police Department. March 4, 1988.

Oswalt, Charles. Richland County Sheriff's Department Statement No.14-88. January 29, 1988.

———. Richland County Sheriff's Department Statement No. 29-88. February 2, 1988.

RCSO Evidence Receipts Case No. 88-E-057. Richland County Sheriff's Department. Evidence from Marjorie Coffey's Vehicle. January 22, 1988.

RCSO Evidence Receipts Case No. 88-E-057. Richland County Sheriff's Department. Evidence from Robert Lemon's Body. January 30, 1988.

RCSO Evidence Receipts Case No. 88-E-057. Richland County Sheriff's Department. Evidence from Robert Lemon's Van. February 1, 1988.

RCSO Evidence Receipts Case No. 88-E-057. Richland County Sheriff's Department. Evidence from MPD Cruiser No. 306. February 1, 1988.

RCSO Evidence Receipts Case No. 88-E-057. Richland County Sheriff's Department. Evidence from Charles Oswalt's Body. February 4, 1988.

RCSO Evidence Receipts Case No. 88-E-057. Richland County Sheriff's Department. Evidence from MPD Surveillance Van. March 7, 1988.

RCSO Evidence Receipts Case No. 88-E-057. Richland County Sheriff's Department. Evidence from Rear Floor of MPD Cruiser No. 306. March 10, 1988.

Remy, Tim. Richland County Sheriff's Department Statement No. 4-88. January 23, 1988.

———. Richland County Sheriff's Department Statement No. 4-88. January 23, 1988.

Search Warrant on Charles Oswalt's Lockers at MPD. Mansfield Police Department Case No. 88-1657.

Smallstey, Don, Sgt. "Follow-Up Missing Person." Report No. 88-180. Mansfield, OH, Police Department. March 3, 1988.

Spognardi, William. Richland County Sheriff's Department Statement No. 34-88. February 6, 1988.

Spognardi, William, and James Stierhoff. Phone Conversation, No. 28-88. February 2, 1988. Richland County Sheriff's Department.

Stipulation, Oswalt vs. City of Mansfield, Ohio. Richland County Common Pleas Court. January 20, 1988.

Waiver to Search Charles Oswalt's Body Fluids, Blood, Hair. Mansfield Police Department Case No. 88-1657.

Waiver to Search Charles Oswalt's Private Vehicle. Mansfield Police Department Case No. 88-1657.

Waiver to Search Harold Marshall's Body Fluids, Blood, Hair. Mansfield Police Department Case No. 88-1657.

Wendling, Gordon. "MPD General Offense Report No. 88-1657, Missing Person." Mansfield, OH, Police Department. January 21, 1988.

———. "MPD Supplemental Report No. 88-47, Missing Person."Mansfield, OH, Police Department. January 21, 1988.

Wendling, John. Transcript of Closed Court Proceedings. Richland County Common Pleas Court. Re: Mansfield Police Case No. 88-1657, Marjorie Coffey Homicide. February 5, 1988.

Hudak, Stephen. "Case from Opposite Corners." *Mansfield News Journal*, June 25, 1988.

———. "Coffey's Paternity Lawyer Testifies: Experts 99.66% Certain Oswalt the Dad, Jury Told." *Mansfield News Journal*, June 9, 1988.

———. "Hassinger Denies Dumping Corpse." *Mansfield News Journal*, June 21, 1988.

———. "Judge Reduces Charge Against Oswalt." *Mansfield News Journal*, June 22, 1988.

———. "Margie Coffey: Murder Victim's Tragic Past." *Mansfield News Journal*, February 14, 1988.

———. "Officer Tells of Sighting Oswalt in Off-Duty Jacket." *Mansfield News Journal*, June 14, 1988.

———. "Oswalt Jury Hears Closing Arguments." *Mansfield News Journal*, June 25, 1988.

———. "Police Dispatcher Suspended with Pay." *Mansfield News Journal*, July 12, 1988.

————. "Police Veterans Quizzed in Death." *Mansfield News Journal*, February 4, 1988.

Mansfield News Journal. "Obituary: Marjorie E. Coffey," February 3, 1988.

————. "Sheriff Awaits Autopsy Results in Murder Probe," February 2, 1988.

Rowland, Darrel. "Police Start Yet Another Inside Probe." *Mansfield News Journal*, June 21, 1988.

Simon, Ron. "Woman's Body Found in Possum Run." *Mansfield News Journal*, February 2, 1988.

CHAPTER 4: KEN DeKLEINE

Behind the Blue Wall Crime Blog. "Lori DeKleine." http://behindtheblue wall.blogspot.com/search?q=lori+dekleine (accessed November 17, 2008).

Fleszar, Chris, and John Bumgardner. "Neighbors Say Officer Charged with Killing His Wife Had Restraining Order against Him." *WZZM 13 News.* http://www.wzzm13.com/print.aspx ?storyid=86142 (accessed November 17, 2008).

Grand Rapids Press. "Chief Says Cop Charged in Slaying Seemed Stable," January 14, 2008. http://blog.mlive.com/grpress/2008/01/ chief_says_cop_charged_in_slay/print.html (accessed November 17, 2008).

————. "Church Grieves Slain Member; Cop to Be Arraigned," January 14, 2008. http://blog.mlive.com/grpress/2008/01/church _grieves_slain_member_co/print.html (accessed November 17, 2008).

————. "Defense in DeKleine Case Rests without Calling Witnesses," July 10, 2008. http://blog.mlive.com/grpress/2008/07/ defense_in_dekleine_case_rests/print.html (accessed November 17, 2008).

————. "DeKleine's Brother Testifies That Former Holland Cop Admitted Killing Wife," July 10, 2008. http://blog.mlive.com/

grpress/2008/07/dekleins_brother_testifies_tha/print.html (accessed November 17, 2008).

———. "DeKleine's Friend: Murder Suspect Obsessed with Role of Wife's Therapist," July 9, 2008. http://blog.mlive.com/ grpress/2008/07/dekleines_friend_murder_suspec/print.html (accessed November 17, 2008).

———. "Detective: Cop Hid in Attic before Murder," January 25, 2008. http://www.mlive.com/news/index.ssf/2008/01/detective _officer_confessed_to.html (accessed November 17, 2008).

———. "Examiner Testifies in Murder Trial That Holland Victim Suffered Numerous Injuries," July 9, 2008. http://blog.mlive .com/grpress/2008/07/examiner_testifies_in_murder_t/print.html (accessed November 17, 2008).

———. "Families Wome Together after Former Holland Cop Ken DeKleine Found Guilty of Murder," July 11, 2008. http://blog.mlive.com/grpress/2008/07/families_come_together_ after_f/print.html (accessed November 17, 2008).

———. "Former Holland Police Officer Ken DeKleine Found Guilty," July 11, 2008. http://blog.mlive.com/grpress/2008/07/ defense _suggests_reduced_charg/print.html (accessed November 17, 2008).

———. "Friend: Slain Woman Feared Husband," January 12, 2008. http://blog.mlive.com/grpress/2008/01/friend_slain_woman_fear ed_husb/print.html (accessed November 17, 2008).

———. "Hidden Evidence Revealed in Ken DeKleine Murder Trial," July 8, 2008. http://blog.mlive.com/grpress/2008/07/ hidden_evidence_revealed_in_ke/print.html (accessed November 17, 2008).

———. "Holland Cop Arrested for Wife's Murder," January 11, 2008. http://blog.mlive.com/grpress/2008/01/holland_cop_arrested _for_wifes/print.html (accessed November 17, 2008).

———. "Holland Police Officers Testify to Ken DeKleine's Unhappy Marriage," July 9, 2008. http://blog.mlive.com/ grpress/2008/07/holland_police_officers_testif/print.html (accessed November 17, 2008).

————. "Hope College Charity Basketball Game Raises $5,000 for Kids of Holland Police Officer Accused of Killing Wife," April 23, 2008. http://blog.mlive.com/grpress/2008/04/hope_college _charity_basketbal/print.html (accessed November 17, 2008).

————. "In Taped Confession, DeKleine Details Why He Killed His Wife," July 10, 2008. http://blog.mlive.com/grpress/2008/07/in _taped_confession_dekleine_d/print.html (accessed November 17, 2008).

————. "Juror, Colleagues React to Ken DeKleine Trial," July 11, 2008. http://blog.mlive.com/grpress/2008/07/juror_colleagues _react_to_ken/print.html (accessed November 17, 2008).

————. "Muziekparade Will Give Cop's Family a Lift," January 11, 2008. http://blog.mlive.com/grpress/2008/01/muziekparade _will_give_cops_fa/print.html (accessed November 17, 2008).

————. "Officer Testifies That DeKleine Put Tape Recorder in Wife's Backpack," July 9, 2008. http://blog.mlive.com/grpress/ 2008/07/officer_testifies_that_deklein/print.html (accessed November 17, 2008).

————. "Police: Cop Confesses to Killing," January 14, 2008. http://blog.mlive.com/grpress/2008/01/affidavit_cop_ambushed _wife_th/print.html (accessed November 17, 2008).

————. "Prosecutor in Ken DeKleine Trial May Call 40 Witnesses," July 8, 2008. http://blog.mlive.com/grpress/2008/07/prosecutor _in_ken_dekleine_tri/print.html (accessed November 17, 2008).

————. "Psychologist Suspended; Testimony Shows He Had Affair with Murdered Lori DeKleine," July 11, 2008. http://blog.mlive .com/grpress/2008/07/psychologists_license_suspende/print.html (accessed November 17, 2008).

————. "Records: Slain Wife Said Husband Always a "Bully," January 14, 2008. http://blog.mlive.com/grpress/2008/01/records _slain_wife_said_husban/print.html (accessed November 17, 2008).

————. "Slain Wife Warned Friends of Her Fears," January 15, 2008. http://blog.mlive.com/grpress/2008/01/slain_wife_warned _friends_of_h/print.html (accessed November 17, 2008).

————. "Son Testifies about Finding Mother's Body in DeKleine

Murder Trial," July 8, 2008. http://blog.mlive.com/grpress/2008/07/dekleine_murder_trial_begins_i/print.html (accessed November 17, 2008).

———. "Son Who Found Body Expected to Testify in DeKleine Murder Trial," July 8, 2008. http://blog.mlive.com/grpress/2008/07/son_who_found_body_expected_to/print.html (accessed November 17, 2008).

———. "Transcript Released for DeKleine Arrest Warrant," January 14, 2008. http://blog.mlive.com/grpress/2008/01/transcript_released_for_deklei.html (accessed November 17, 2008).

———. "Woman Testifies She Had Secret Affair with Cop Accused of Murder," July 9, 2008. http://blog.mlive.com/grpress/2008/07/woman_testifies_she_had_secret/print.html (accessed November 17, 2008).

LaFurgey, Joe. "Wife to Holland Cop: 'Think about the Kids.'" *Wood TV News*, January 25, 2008. http://www.woodtv.com/Global/story.asp?S=7773517&nav=0RceNb6X (accessed November 17, 2008).

Schmidt, Megan. "DeKleine Pleads Not Guilty; Trial of Police Officer Accused of Killing His Wife at Home Is Scheduled for June." *Holland Sentinel*, February 2, 2008. http://www .hollandsentinel.com/stories/020208/local_20080202005.shtml (accessed November 17, 2008).

———. "DeKleine Sentenced to Life for Killing Wife." *Holland Sentinel*, August 25, 2008. http://www.hollandsentinel.com/news/x1311851501/DeKleine-sentenced-to-life-for-killing-wife.html (accessed November 17, 2008).

Tunison, John. "Cop: DeKleine Had Milkshake after Killing." *Grand Rapids Press*, January 25, 2008. http://blog.mlive.com/grpress/2008/01/dekleine_had_a_milk_shake_afte.html (accessed November 17, 2008).

Wood TV News. "Holland Police Officer Bound over for Trial in Wife's Death," January 25, 2008. http://www.woodtv.com/Global/story.asp?S=7774143&nav=menu44_2 (accessed November 17, 2008).

WWMT News Channel 3. "Officer Arraigned for Wife's Murder," January 14, 2008. http://www.wwmt.com/news/holland -1346237-officer-ken.html (accessed November 17, 2008).

CHAPTER 5: ROY KIPP JR.

Borges, Manfred, Jr., M. D. "CourtTV.com: Florida v. Kipp— Autopsy Report of Jeffrey Klein." CourtTVNews.com. Autopsy Report No. 2000-138. May 22, 2000. http://www.courttv.com/ archive/trials/kipp/docs/kleinautopsy1.html (accessed September 16, 2008).
———. "CourtTV.com: Florida v. Kipp—Autopsy Report of Sandra Kipp." CourtTVNews.com. Autopsy Report# 2000-137. May 22, 2008. http://www.courttv.com/archive/trials/kipp/ docs/kippautopsy1.html (accessed July 8, 2008).
———. "CourtTV.com: Florida v. Kipp—Crime Scene Report." CourtTVNews.com. Autopsy Report# 2000-138. May 21, 2000. http://www.courttv.com/archive/trials/kipp/docs/scene1.html (accessed September 16, 2008).
Collier County Sheriff's Office. "Collier County: Domestic Violence Unit." http://www.colliersheriff.org/Index.aspx?page=1944 (accessed September 28, 2008).
———. "Collier County: History." http://www.colliersheriff.org/ index .aspx?page=1934 (accessed September 28, 2008).
———. "Collier County: Population and Tourism." http://www .colliersheriff.org/Index.aspx?page=1930 (accessed September 28, 2008).
Cossack, Roger. "CourtTV.com: Florida v. Kipp—Transcripts." CourtTVNews.com. http://www.courttv.com/talk/chat_transcripts/ 2002/0304kipp-cossack.html (accessed September 16, 2008).
CourtTVNews.com. "CourtTV.com: Florida v. Kipp—Florida State Statutes." http://www.courttv.com/archive/trials/kipp/law.html (accessed September 16, 2008).
———. "CourtTV.com: Florida v. Kipp—Profiles of Key Players."

http://www.courttv.com/archive/trials/kipp/keyplayers.html (accessed September 16, 2008).

———. "CourtTV.com: Florida v. Kipp—Witnesses for the Defense." http://www.courttv.com/archive/trials/kipp/witnesses-def.html (accessed September 16, 2008).

———. "CourtTV.com: State of Florida v. Kipp—Witnesses for the State." http://www.courttv.com/archive/trials/kipp/witnesses-sta.html (accessed September 16, 2008).

———. "CourtTV.com: State of Florida vs. Royle John Kipp Jr. Indictment." Case No. 00-1216-CFA. May 31, 2000. http://www.courttv.com/archive/trials/kipp/docs/indictment1.ht ml (accessed July 8, 2008).

Kelly, J., Det. "CourtTV.com: Florida v. Kipp—Prosecution Report." CourtTVNews.com. CCSO Case No. 16564-00. May 21, 2000. http://www.courttv.com/archive/trials/kipp/docs/report1.html (accessed September 16, 2008).

Naples, Florida. "History of Naples." http://www.naples-florida.com/ hiscul.htm (accessed September 28, 2008).

Ryan, Harriet. "Ex-Cop Faces Death Penalty," CourtTVNews.com. http://www.courttv.com/archive/trials/kipp/ (accessed April 19, 2008).

———. "Ex-Cop Faces the Death Penalty for Slaying of Wife, Her Lover." CourtTVNews.com. http://www.courttv.com/archive/ trials/kipp/ backgrounder.html (accessed July 8, 2008).

Suddeth, Melissa. "CourtTV.com: Florida v. Kipp—DNA Report." CourtTVNews.com. FDLE Number: 2000-0603465. September 12, 2000. http://www.courttv.com/archive/trials/kipp/docs/ dna1.html (accessed September 16, 2008).

CHAPTER 6: DAVID CAMM

Glatt, John. *One Deadly Night: A State Trooper, Triple Homicide, and a Search for Justice.* New York: St. Martin's Press, 2005.

Schlesinger, Richard. "48 Hours: The Alibi, Disturbing the Peace."

CBS, January 22, 2005. http://truthinjustice.org/David
-Camm.htm (accessed April 19, 2008).

WLKY. "Boney Trial Begins; So Does Camm Jury Selection," January 8, 2006. http://www.wlky.com/print/5931379/detail.html
(accessed July 22, 2008).

————. "Jury Foreman Believes 'Camm Pulled the Trigger," March 7, 2006. http://www.wlky.com/print/7786332/detail.html
(accessed July 22, 2008).

————. "Tape of Frantic 911 Call Played at Camm Trial," January 16, 2006. http://www.wlky.com/print/6158636/detail.html
(accessed July 22, 2008).

CHAPTER 7: KENT McGOWEN

Casey, Kathryn. *A Warrant to Kill: True Stories of Obsession, Lies and a Killer Cop.* New York: Avon True Crime, 2000.

Cop Crimes. "Ex-Deputy Convicted of Murder Free on Bond," March 12, 1994. http://www.civiliansdown.com/copcrimes
%20Page%202.htm (accessed January 11, 2009).

Crime and Investigation Network. "Crime and Punishment: A Warrant to Kill."http://www.crimeandinvestigation.co.uk/tv_programme/
1376/Crime_and_Punishment_A_Warrant_to_Kill.htm (accessed January 11, 2009).

Draughn, Joe L. "*Joseph Kenton McGowen, Appellant vs. The State of Texas, Appellee.*" Fourteenth Court of Appeals. No.14-94-00246-CR. February 3, 2000. http://www.14thcoa.courts.state
.tx.us/Case/Opinions/020300/940246rf.PDF (accessed January 11, 2009).

McVicker, Steve. "Killer behind the Badge." *Houston Press*, January 12, 1995. http://www.houstonpress.com/content/print Version/216750 (accessed January 11, 2009).

————. "Price of Justice." *Houston Press*, October 3, 1996. http://www.houstonpress.com/1996-10-03/news/price-of-justice/
(accessed January 11, 2009).

CHAPTER 8: LAWRENCIA BEMBENEK

Barton, Gina. "Bembenek Seeks DNA Testing." *Milwaukee Journal Sentinel*, JS Online, August 25, 2002. http://www.truthinjustice .org/bambi1.htm (accessed April 19, 2008).

Kunen, James S. "Ex-Cop Lawrencia Bembenek Claims She Was Wrongly Convicted of Murder in the Case of the Unsmoking Gun." *People Magazine* 28 no. 23, December 7, 1987. http://www.people.com/people/archive/article/0,,20097771,00.h tml (accessed April 19, 2008).

Radish, Kris. *Run, Bambi, Run: The Beautiful Ex-Cop and Convicted Murderer Who Escaped to Freedom and Won America's Heart*. New York: Carol, 1992.

TruTV Crime Library. "Bambi Bembenek." http://www.trutv.com/ library/crime/notorious_murders/women/bembenek/1.html (accessed April 19, 2008).

CHAPTER 9: ANTOINETTE FRANK

Hustmyre, Chuck. "Blue on Blue: Murder, Madness and Betrayal in the NOPD."

TruTV Crime Library. http://www.trutv.com/library/crime/gangsters _outlaws/cops_others/antoinette_frank/index.htm (accessed October 22, 2008).

———. *Killer with a Badge*. New York: Berkley True Crime, 2004.

CHAPTER 10: STEVEN RIOS

Breckenridge, Patricia. Opinion—Missouri Court of Appeals Western District *State of Missouri. Respondent v. Steven Arthur Rios, Appellant*. Case No. WD65708. April 27, 2007. http://www.courts.mo.gov/page.asp?id=12087&search=WD657 08&dist=Opinions%20Western&n=0 (accessed July 7, 2008).

Columbia Daily Tribune. "AG Asks for Review of Ruling in Rios Case," July 12, 2007. http://archive.columbiatribune.com/ 2007/jul/20070712news002.asp (accessed July 7, 2008).

———. "Grissom: 'I Believe in Steven Rios' Innocence.'" Police Scanner, February 29, 2008. http://blogs.columbiatribune .com/crime/2008/02/grissom_i_believe_in_steven_ri.html (accessed July 7, 2008).

———. "Rios' Attorney's Acting Credentials." Police Scanner, February 19, 2008. http://blogs.columbiatribune.com/crime/ 2008/ 02/rios_attorneys_acting_credenti.html (accessed July 7, 2008).

———. "Police Investigating East Campus Death," June 6, 2004. http://archive.columbiatribune.com/2004/jun/20040606news00 8.asp (accessed July 7, 2008).

———. "Trail to a Suspect," July 1, 2004. http://archive.columbia tri-bune.com/2004/jul/20040701news005.asp (accessed July 7, 2008).

Kravitz, Derek, "Rios Aims for Private-Practice Lawyers in Retrial of Murder Case." *Columbia Daily Tribune*, February 19, 2008. http://www.showmenews.com/2008/Feb/20080219news054.asp (accessed July 7, 2008).

Meyer, Joe. "Court Won't Reconsider Ruling in Rios Case." *Columbia Daily Tribune*, June 27, 2007. http://archive.columbiatribune .com/2007/jun/20070627news003.asp (accessed July 7, 2008).

———. "Ex-Cop Gets New Murder Trial." *Columbia Daily Tribune*, October 31, 2007. http://www.columbiatribune.com/2007/ oct/20071031news002.asp (accessed July 7, 2008).

———. "State Supreme Court Sets Stage for New Rios Trial." *Columbia Daily Tribune*, October 30, 2007, http://www .columbiatribune.com/2007/oct/20071030news027.asp (accessed July 7, 2008).

———. "Steven Rios Case Boils down to Hearsay Evidence." *Columbia Daily Tribune*, October 31, 2007. http://showmen ews.com/2007/oct/20071031news007.asp (accessed July 7, 2008).

———. "Valencia Mom Shocked by Ruling." *Columbia Daily Tribune*, June 24, 2007. http://archive.columbiatribune.com/ 2007/jun/20070624news006.asp (accessed July 7, 2008).

Pullega, John. "Steven Rios Granted Retrial in Columbia." *Maneater*, November 9, 2007. http://www.themaneater.com/stories/2007/11/9/steven-rios-granted-retrial-columbia/ (accessed July 7, 2008).

Randles, Jonathan, and Sean Sposito. "Moberly Attorney and Former KMIZ Anchor to Represent Rios in Retrial." *Columbia Missourian*, February 19, 2008. http://www.columbiamissourian.com/ (accessed July 7, 2008).

Ryan, Harriet. "Despite DNA, Colleague Testimony Might Be Key in Gay Officer's Murder Trial." CourtTV.com. May 20, 2005. http://www.courttv.com/scripts/features/fea_printpage.asp?thisfile=/trials/rios/051905_ctv (accessed July 7, 2008).

———. "Gay Affair between Cop and Student Led to Murder, Prosecutors Say." CourtTV.com. May 20, 2005. http://www.courttv.com/scripts/features/fea_printpage.asp?thisfile=/trials/rios/051805_bac (accessed July 7, 2008).

———. "Married Police Officers Tells Jurors He Didn't Kill His Gay Lover." CourtTV.com. May 20, 2005. http://www.courttv.com/scripts/features/fea_printpage.asp?thisfile=/trials/rios/052005_ctv (accessed July 7, 2008).

———. "Police Officer Convicted of Killing His Gay Lover." CourtTV.com. May 23, 2005. http://www.courttv.com/scripts/features/fea_printpage.asp?thisfile=/trials/rios/052105_ver (accessed April 19, 2008).

Sullivan, John. "Officer Threatens to Leap from Ledge." *Columbia Daily Tribune*, June 12, 2004. http://archive.columbiatribune.com/2004/jun/20040612news008.asp (accessed July 7, 2008).

Wells, Mike. "City's Detective Unit Stretches Resources with Valencia Case." *Columbia Daily Tribune*, June 20, 2004. http://archive.columbiatribune.com/2004/jun/20040620news004.asp (accessed July 7, 2008).

———. "Ex-Officer Charged with Murder." *Columbia Daily Tribune*, July 1, 2004. http://archive.columbiatribune.com/2004/jul/2004070news009.asp (accessed July 7, 2008).

———. "Ex-Officer Convicted." *Columbia Daily Tribune*, May 22, 2005. http://archive.columbiatribune.com/2005/May/20050522news002.asp (accessed July 7, 2008).

———. "Jurors Didn't Believe Rios, Panelist Says." *Columbia Daily Tribune*, May 23, 2005. http://archive.columbiatribune .com/2005/may/20050523news009.asp (accessed July 7, 2008).

———. "Officer in Protective Custody." *Columbia Daily Tribune*, June 11, 2004. http://archive.columbiatribune.com/2004/jun/ 20040611news008.asp (accessed July 7, 2008).

———. "Officer Not a Suspect in Valencia Slaying." *Columbia Daily Tribune,* June 14, 2004. http://archive.columbiatribune .com/2004/jun/400406news006.asp (accessed July 7, 2008).

———. "Outsider Assigned to Case." *Columbia Daily Tribune*, June 23, 2004. http://archive.columbiatribune.com/2004/ jun/20040623news003.asp (accessed July 7, 2008).

———. "Police Department Seeks Dismissal from Rios Suit." *Columbia Daily Tribune*, September 2, 2004. http://archive .columbiatribune.com/2004/sep/20040902news005.asp (accessed July 7, 2008).

———. "Police Inquiry Remains Internal." *Columbia Daily Tribune*, June 10, 2004. http://archive.columbiatribune.com/2004/ Jun/20040610News007.asp (accessed July 7, 2008).

———. "Police Seek Clues in Student's Death." *Columbia Daily Tribune*, June 8, 2004. http://archive.columbiatribune .com/2004/ jun/20040608news007.asp (accessed July 7, 2008).

———. "Police Seek Evidence in Rios' House." *Columbia Daily Tribune*, June 16, 2004. http://archive.columbiatribune .com/2004/jun/20040616news003.asp (accessed July 7, 2008).

———. "Rios Has Quit Post, Chief Says." *Columbia Daily Tribune*, June 17, 2004. http://archive.columbiatribune.com/2004/ jun/20040617news004.asp (accessed July 7, 2008).

———. "Rios Sees Freedom in Future." *Columbia Daily Tribune*, August 3, 2004. http://archive.columbiatribune.com/2004/ aug/20040803news001.asp (accessed July 7, 2008).

———. "Rios, Wife Testify in Trial." *Columbia Daily Tribune*, May 20, 2005. http://archive.columbiatribune.com/2005/ may/20050520news010.asp (accessed July 7, 2008).

———. "Tears Flow on Steps of Courthouse." *Columbia Daily Tri-*

bune, May 22, 2005. http://archive.columbiatribune.com/2005/
may/20050522news008.asp (accessed July 7, 2008).

———. "Testimony Draws Time Line." *Columbia Daily Tribune*,
May 18, 2005. http://archive.columbiatribune.com/2005/
may/20050518news007.asp (accessed July 7, 2008).

———. "Testimony Links Rios, Victim." *Columbia Daily Tribune*,
May 19, 2005. http://archive.columbiatribune.com/2005/may/
20050519news003.asp (accessed July 7, 2008).

———. "Throat Wound Killed Victim, Autopsy Finds." *Columbia
Daily Tribune*, June 7, 2004. http://archive.columbiatribune
.com/2004/jun/20040607news003.asp (accessed July 7, 2008).

———. "Valencia's Mom Faces Rios' Smile." *Columbia Daily Tribune*, August 20, 2004. http://archive.columbiatribune.com/
2004/aug/20040820news001.asp (accessed July 7, 2008).

CHAPTER 11: LEN DAVIS

Evans, C. "Len Davis Trial 1996: Defense Fights Back." Law
Library—American Law and Legal Information. http://law
.jrank.org/ (accessed July 13, 2008).

———. "Len Davis Trial 1996: Undercover Tapes! Defense Fights
Back." Law Library—American Law and Legal Information.
http://law.jrank.org/ (accessed July 13, 2008).

Sayre, Alan. "Len Davis, Ex-Cop Convicted of Murder Wants to
Represent Himself." *Louisiana Weekly*, August 27, 2001.
http://louisianaweekly.com/weekly/news/articlegate.pl?2001082
7i (accessed April 19, 2008).

Shapiro, Dean. "Len Davis: The Desire Terrorist." *TruTV* Crime
Library. http://www.trutv.com/library/crime/gangsters_outlaws/
cops_others/ len_davis/index.html (accessed July 13, 2008).

United States Department of Justice. "Former New Orleans Police
Officer and Local Hit Man Sentenced to Death." May 1, 1996.
http://www.usdoj.gov/opa/pr/1996/may96/202.cr.htm (accessed
July 13, 2008).

CHAPTER 12: RICHARD DiGUGLIELMO

Blassberg, Richard. "Eyewitness Who Refused to Lie under Pressure Exposes District Attorney and Dobbs Ferry Police." *Westchester Guardian*, December 13, 2007.

———. "Richard DiGuglielmo: Setting the Facts Straight." *Westchester Guardian*, January 10, 2008.

———. "When Truth and Justice Are Overwhelmed by Celebrity Worship." *Westchester Guardian*, January 17, 2008.

County Court, Westchester, NY. *"The People of the State of New York -against- Richard D. DiGuglielmo, Defendant."* Affirmation in Opposition: Indictment No. 96-1403. November 30, 2006.

———. *"The People of the State of New York -against- Richard DiGuglielmo*, Posthearing Brief in Support of Motion to Vacate Pursuant to CPL. 440.10." Indictment No. 96-1403. Mayer, Brown, LLP-Attorneys for Richard D. DiGuglielmo.

Dillon, Michael. "Dobbs Ferry Police Department Supporting Deposition." Dobbs Ferry, NY, Police Department. Case No. 96-00311. Deposition Given: October 7, 1996.

Dobbs Ferry, New York, Police Department. "Transcript of James White." Case No. 96-00311. June 5, 1997

Lubbock Avalanche-Journal. "Cop Killed Man in Brawl over Parking Space," October 24, 1997. http://www.lubbockonline .com/news/102597/LA0691.htm (accessed April 19, 2008).

New York Times. "Ex-Officer Is Sentenced in Parking Lot Killing," December 16, 1997. http://www.nytimes.com/1997/12/16/ny region/ex-officer-is-sentenced-in-parking-lot-killing.html?scp=8&sq =Richard%20D.%20DiGuglielmo&st=cse (accessed July 2, 2008).

O'Donnell, Kevin. "Dobbs Ferry Police Department Supporting Deposition." Dobbs Ferry, NY, Police Department. Case No. 96-00311. Deposition Given: October 3, 1996.

———. "Dobbs Ferry Police Department Supporting Deposition." Dobbs Ferry, NY, Police Department. Case No. 96-00311. Written Deposition Given: October 7, 1996.

———. "Dobbs Ferry Police Department Supporting Deposition." Dobbs Ferry, NY, Police Department. Case No. 96 00311. Deposition Given: October 8, 1996.

Police Department, City of New York. Shooting Incident Report No. 96-77: Firearms Discharge, within the Confines of Dobbs Ferry, New York: Three Shots Fired, Off-Duty Member of the Service, One Civilian D.O.A of Gunshot Wounds: Off Duty-Police Officer Arrested. October 4, 1996.

Richard DiGuglielmo Web Site. "Richard DiGuglielmo: The Facts and the True Story." http://www.richarddiguglielmo.org/gui/content.aspx?page=thetruestory (accessed July 2, 2008).

———. "The Witnesses and Their Stories." http://www.richarddiguglielmo.org/gui/content.aspx?page=mstory (accessed July 2, 2008).

Wekerle, Marianne. "Dobbs Ferry Police Department Supporting Deposition." Dobbs Ferry, NY, Police Department. Case No. 96-00311. Written Deposition: Not Dated.

———. "Dobbs Ferry Police Department Supporting Deposition." Dobbs Ferry, NY, Police Department. Case No. 96-00311. Deposition Given: October 7, 1996.

———. "Dobbs Ferry Police Department Supporting Deposition." Dobbs Ferry, NY, Police Department. Case No. 96-00311. Deposition Given: October 3, 1996.

Williams, Monte. "Ex-Policeman Defends Actions During Off-Duty Fatal Shooting." *New York Times*, April 13, 2001. http://www.nytimes.com/2001/04/13/nyregion/ex-policeman-defends-actions-during-off-duty-fatal-shooting.html?scp=14&sq=Richard%20D.%20DiGuglielmo&st=cse (accessed July 2, 2008).

———. "Jury Awards Damages to Relatives of Man Shot by an Officer." *New York Times*, April 21, 2001. http://www.nytimes.com/2001/04/21/nyregion/jury-awards-damages-to-relatives-of-man-shot-by-an-officer.html?scp =12&sq=Richard%20D.%20DiGuglielmo&st=cse (accessed July 2, 2008).

CHAPTER 13: LOUIS EPPOLITO AND STEPHEN CARACAPPA

Amoruso, D. "Mafia Cops." Gangsters Incorporated. http:// gangstersinc.tripod.com/TheMafiaCops.html (accessed April 19, 2008).

Lawson, Guy, and William Oldham. *The Brotherhoods: The True Story, Two Cops Who Murdered for the Mafia.* New York: Scribner, 2006.

Patterson, L. "Mafia Cops Convicted of Murder." *Las Vegas Now,* April 7, 2006. http://www.lasvegasnow.com/global/story.asp ?s=4737312&clienttype=printable (accessed April 19, 2008).

Radatzky, M., T. Simon, and P. Aronofsky. "Mafia Cop?" *60 Minutes.* May 28, 2006. http://www.cbsnews.com/stories/2006/01/ 05/60minutes/main1180833.shtml (accessed April 19, 2008).

Smith, Greg B. *Mob Cops.* New York: Berkley True Crime, 2006.

Thevenot, Geer C. "Arrests at Piero's: Ex-Detectives Go to Court." *Las Vegas Review-Journal,* March 11, 2005. http://www.review journal.com/lvrj_home/2005/Mar-11-Fri-2005/news/26049284 .html (accessed April 19, 2008).

CHAPTER 14: KEITH WASHINGTON

ABC 7 News. "Keith Washington, P.G. County Sued over Investigation," January 25, 2008. http://cfc.wjla.com/printstory.cfm?id =490832 (accessed November 17, 2008).

Burns, Kenneth P. "Sex, Guns and Kickbacks: This Fall in Prince George's County." *Maryland Politics Today,* August 9, 2007. http://www.marylandpolitics.us/archives/category/keith -washington (accessed November 17, 2008).

Castaneda, Ruben. "Delivery Man Shot by Off-Duty Officer Last Week, Dies." *Washington Post,* February 2, 2007. http://www .washingtonpost.com/wp-dyn/content/article/2007/02/02/ AR2007020200522.html (accessed November 17, 2008).

———. "Ex-Official in PR George's Gets 45 Years in Shooting."

Washington Post, May 28, 2008. http://www.washingtonpost
.com/wp-dyn/content/article/2008/05/27/AR2008052701362
.html (accessed November 17, 2008).

———. "Ex-Official's Call to 911 Is Played in Murder Trial." *Wash-ington Post*, February 16, 2008. http://www.washingtonpost
.com/wp-dyn/content/article/2008/02/15/AR2008021503570
.html (accessed November 17, 2008).

———. "Ex-Official, Jailed in Md., Found with Handcuff Key."
Washington Post, March 5, 2008. http://www.washingtonpost
.com/wp-dyn/content/article/2008/03/04/AR2008030401985
.html (accessed November 17, 2008).

———. "Pr. George's Ex-Official Convicted in Shooting." *Wash-ington Post*, February 26, 2008. http://www.washingtonpost
.com/wp-dyn/content/article/2008/02/25/AR2008022501478
.html (accessed November 17, 2008).

Clint. "Abuse of Authority/Police Brutality: Keith A. Washington, a
Policeman Is Also in Homeland Security, Shoots Two Marlow
Deliverymen Who Were Delivering a Bed to Him! One Dies."
Clint's Blog. February 25, 2007. http://clintjcl.wordpress.com/
2007/02/25/keith-a-washington-is-a-cop-killer/ (accessed
November 17, 2008).

Everett, W. "Keith Washington Convicted of Involuntary
Manslaughter." DCAbloob.com. February 25, 2008. http://www
.dcabloob.com/2008/02/keith-washington-convicted-of.html
(accessed November 17, 2008).

News Channel 8. "Keith Washington Trial to Begin," February 13,
2008. http://www.news8.net/news/stories/0208/495095.html
(accessed November 17, 2008).

Reals, Gary. "Keith Washington Takes the Witness Stand."
WUSA9.com. February 19, 2008. http://www.wusa9.com/print
fullstory.aspx?storyid=68724 (accessed November 17, 2008).

Rich, Eric, and Daniela Deane. "Delivery Man Shot by Off-Duty
Officer Last Week, Dies." *Washington Post*, February 2, 2007.
http://www.washingtonpost.com/wp-dyn/content/article/
2007/02/02/AR2007020200522.html (accessed November 17,
2008).

Rondeaux, Candace. "Pr. George's Official Defends Shooting Two." *Washington Post*, February 24, 2007. http://www.washingtonpost .com/wp-dyn/content/article/2007/02/24/AR2007022301729 .html (accessed November 17, 2008).

Rondeaux, Candace, and Castaneda, Ruben. "Ex-Official Indicted On Murder Charges." *Washington Post*, August 1, 2007. http:// www.washingtonpost.com/wp-dyn/content/article/2007/07/31/ AR2007073101076.html (accessed November 17, 2008).

———. "Prince George's Official Charged in 2nd Gun Case." *Washington Post*, April 7, 2007. http://www.washingtonpost .com/wp-dyn/content/article/2007/04/05/AR200704051698 .html (accessed November 17, 2008).

———. "Ex-Pr. George's Official Indicted." *Washington Post*, June 15, 2007. http://www.washingtonpost.com/wp-dyn/content/article/ 2007/06/14/ AR2007061401323 .html (accessed November 17, 2008).

Segraves, Mark. "Cop Indicted on Murder, Assault Charges." WTOPnews.com. July 31, 2007. http://www.wtop.com/?nid =428&sid=1205849 (accessed November 17, 2008).

Statter, Dave. "New Details from Keith Washington One Day after his Indictment." *WUSA9*. August 2, 2007. http://www .wusa9.com/ printfullstory.aspx?storyid=61383 (accessed November 17, 2008).

Valentine, Daniel. "Washington's Mental Records Barred from Trial." *Business Gazette*, n.d.

Washington Post. "An Officer Indicted," August 2, 2007. http:// www.washingtonpost.com/wp-dyn/content/article/2007/08/01/ AR2007080102162.html (accessed November 17, 2008).

———. "Keith A. Washington Timeline," May 27, 2008. http: //www.washingtonpost.com/wp-dyn/content/article/2008/ 05/27/ AR2008052701999.html (accessed November 17, 2008).

Williams, Clarence, Allan Lengel, and Avis Thomas-Lester. "Pr. George's Official Shot Two, Authorities Say." *Washington Post*, January 25, 2007. http://www.washingtonpost.com/wp-dyn/content/article/ 2007/01/25/AR2007012501076.html (accessed November 17, 2008).

CHAPTER 15: CRAIG PEYER

Cantlupe, Joe, and Lisa Petrillo. *Badge of Betrayal: The Devastating True Story of a Rogue Cop Turned Murderer*. New York: Avon True Crime, 1991.

Davis, Robert L. "State Trooper Charged with Murder after Attempting to Tool the Public!" AuthorsDen. February 23, 2008. http://www.authorsden.com/visit/viewarticle.asp?Author ID=51651&id=37318 (accessed April 19, 2008).

Jones, J. Harry. "Killer Peyer Refused Prosecutors' Offer to Test DNA." *San Diego Union-Tribune*, November 28, 2004. http://www.signonsandiego.com/uniontrib/20041128/news_1n2 8dna.html (accessed June 3, 2008).

Levikow, Paul. "DA Argues against Parole for Convicted Murderer, Former CHP Craig Peyer." Office of the District Attorney, County of San Diego. January 30, 2008. Superior Court Case Number CDC No. D-93018.

Marshall, Scott. "Parole Hearing Today for Ex-CHP Officer Convicted of Murder." *North County Times*, January 30, 2008. http://www.nctimes.com/articles/2008/01/31/news/sandiego/22 _28_541_30_08.prt (accessed April 19, 2008).

Stetz, Michael. "It Has Been 12 Years Since His Daughter Was Murdered, But Sam Knott Still Won't—Can't—Put It All behind Him: He Battles the System and Gets Things Done." *San Diego Union-Tribune*, April 30, 1999. http://www.ticketassassin .com/peyer.html (accessed June 3, 2008).

CHAPTER 16: RICHARD WILLS

Barker, Jeremy. "Richard Wills Timeline." *National Post* (Canada), October 30, 2007. http://network.nationalpost.com/np/blogs/ posted/archive/2007/10/30/richard-wills-timeline.aspx (accessed July 2, 2008).

Blatchford, Christine. "The Remarkable Trial of Richard Wills."

Globe and Mail (Toronto, Canada), October 31, 2007. http://www.theglobeandmail.com/servlet/story/RTGAM.20071 031.wwills31/BNStory/National/?pageRequested=all (accessed July 2, 2008).

Brean, Joseph. "Richard Wills' Strange Request." *National Post* (Canada), October 31, 2007. http://www.nationalpost.com/ story-printer.html?id=331bfc19-bd96-4a47-a8d2-3654ffb3eada (accessed July 2, 2008).

CTV. "Police Name TO. Cop Charged in Woman's Murder." June 17, 2002. http://toronto.ctv.ca/servlet/an/plocal/CTVNews/ 20020617/ctvnews872860/20020617/?hub (accessed July 2, 2008).

Dimanno, Rosie. "Not Even Close to Fair Trial: Wills." TheStar, October 31, 2007. http://www.thestar.com/printArticle/272134 (accessed July 2, 2008).

Hertz, Barry. "Richard Wills Appears Well Behaved after Murder Conviction." *National Post* (Canada), October 31, 2007. http://network.nationalpost.com/np/blogs/toronto/archive/ 2007/10/31/richard-wills-appears-well-behaved-after-murder -conviction.aspx (accessed July 2, 2008).

Kari, Shannon. "Former Police Officer Wills Guilty of Murdering Lover." *National Post* (Canada), October 31, 2007. http://www.canada.com/topics/news/story.html?id=7dad78c9 -8372-470c-8af3-d37133f1b438&k=2959 (accessed July 2, 2008).

———. "Murder Trial of Former Toronto Police Officer Bogged Down." Canada. June 1, 2007. http://www.canada.com/topics/ news/national/story.html?id=f96458fb-ee09-412a-8409-607223 b1c76d&k=15100 (accessed July 2, 2008).

———. "Psychic Reading Part of Investigation Targeting Murder Suspect." *National Post* (Canada), July 25, 2007. http://www.canada.com/topics/news/national/story.html?id=238 e16b2-b1ec-4f38-8933-0bcd212321a0&k=29409 (accessed July 2, 2008).

———. "Richard Wills Found Guilty of First-Degree Murder." *National Post* (Canada), October 31, 2007. http://network.nation

alpost.com/np/blogs/posted/archive/2007/10/31/richard-wills
-found-guilty-of-first-degree-murder.aspx (accessed July 2, 2008).

———. "Theatrics Bog Down Police Officer's Murder Trial."
National Post (Canada), June 15, 2007. http://www.national
post.com/story-printer.html?id=f1e0de0b-ba3e-44c5-97a6-c27
b6471b37b (accessed July 2, 2008).

McMaster, Dr. Jeffrey. "Psychiatric Assessment of Richard Wills."
Whitby Mental Health Center. http://www.scribd.com/doc/
455996/Psychiatric-assessment-of-Richard-Wills (accessed July
2, 2008).

National Post (Canada). "Phone Calls of Richard Wills—MP3."
http://www.imeem.com/nationalpost/music/2PntbhDT/national
-post-richard-wills-trial-phone-messages/ (accessed July 2, 2008).

Pron, Nick. "Jurors Reject Wills' Web of Lies." TheStar, November
1, 2007. http://www.thestar.com/printArticle/272552 (accessed
September 12, 2008).

———. "Officer Left Messages for Mistress Buried in Basement."
Thestar.com, June 19, 2007. http://www.thestar.com/printArticle/
226844 (accessed July 2, 2008).

———. "Wills Defense Cost Taxpayers $1.3M." TheStar, October
31, 2007. http://www.thestar.com/printArticle/272139 (accessed
July 2, 2008).

CHAPTER 17: CHARLES BECKER

Cohen, Stanley. *The Execution of Officer Becker: The Murder of a
Gambler, the Trial of a Cop, and the Birth of Organized Crime.*
New York: Carroll & Graf, 2006.

Gado, Mark. "Killer Cop: Charles Becker." *TruTV* Crime Library.
http://www.trutv.com/library/crime/gangsters_outlaws/cops_oth
ers/becker/1.html (accessed December 12, 2008).

Historyorb.com. "Historical Events for 1912." http://www.historyorb
.com/events/date/1912 (accessed December 12, 2008).

Law Library—American Law and Legal Information. "Charles Becker Trials: 1912–14—Becker Runs Crime Ring from Within Police Department, Tried before New York's Hanging Judge." http://law.jrank.org/pages/2780/Charles-Becker-Trials-1912 -14.html (accessed December 12, 2008).

Slezak, Patty. "Key Figures in Jefferson Market History." http://wotan.liu.edu/~amatsuuchi/timeline/key_figures.html (accessed December 12, 2008).

CHAPTER 18: GERARD SCHAEFER

Mason, Yvonne. *Silent Scream*. LuLu.com, 2008

Murderers Database (United Kingdom). "Gerard Schaefer." http://web.ukonline.co.uk/ruth.buddell/schaefer.htm (accessed December 12, 2008).

Newton, Michael. "Gerard Schaefer." *TruTV* Crime Library. http:// www.trutv.com/library/crime/serial_killers/predators/gerard_sch aefer/1.html (accessed December 12, 2008).

INDEX